A SELECTED EDITION OF W. D. HOWELLS

Volume 27

The Leatherwood God

W. D. HOWELLS

The Leatherwood God

Introduction and Notes to the
Text by Eugene Pattison

Text Established by
David J. Nordloh, with James P. Elliott
and Robert D. Schildgen

INDIANA UNIVERSITY PRESS

Bloomington and London

1976

*Editorial expenses for this volume have been met in part by grants from
the National Endowment for the Humanities administered through the Center
for Editions of American Authors of the Modern Language Association.*

*Copyright © 1975 by Indiana University Press
and the Howells Edition Editorial Board*

*Library of Congress catalog card number: 74-189640
Standard Book Number: 0-253-33285-0*

Manufactured in the United States of America

Acknowledgments

For indispensable support in money and morale the editors of this volume and the Howells Edition Center gladly express their gratitude to John W. Ryan, President, and Lynne L. Merritt, Jr., Vice-President and Dean, Research and Advanced Studies, Indiana University. Gratitude is due as well to Herman B Wells and to the Indiana University Foundation for the generous support provided for the production and printing of this volume. William White Howells and the heirs of W. D. Howells also deserve special acknowledgment for their kind assistance and cooperation.

Professor Pattison is grateful for their help to Professor Charles J. Stoneburner, Denison University, Miss Mary Edith Stoneburner and the late Mrs. Hosea Victor Stoneburner, Salesville, Ohio, Mr. Forrest Thomas, Salesville, Ohio, and Mrs. Gilbert Harley, Quaker City, Ohio. The work on this volume could not have been completed without the assistance of the student staff at the Howells Edition Center, especially Ann Webster, Ann Hofstra and David Kleinman, or the continuing effort of Anthony Shipps of the Indiana University Library and Mrs. Gail Mathews and the staff of the Indiana University Interlibrary Loan Department. Finally, Professor Scott Bennett deserves very special credit for his comprehensive research in the preliminary stages of the textual work on this volume.

Contents

Introduction

AFTER finishing *The Son of Royal Langbrith* in 1904 Howells told
S. Weir Mitchell that he had "one good novel left" to write; "it
involves some tremendous things," he said, "which I can perhaps
help the reader to imagine for me, if I can't do it for him." The
novel was probably *The Leatherwood God*, whose incubation period
was to be one of the longest among Howells' novels. Two years
later he told his brother Joe he considered it "a great scheme,"
and liked to think of making it his "last great novel." During the
final months of work on the novel in 1914 he spoke of it as the fulfillment of plans begun twenty or thirty years earlier, and re-
minded his sister Aurelia that it concerned "that strange episode
in Ohio history which has always fascinated me . . . ."[1] The "episode," published in a volume of the *Ohio Valley Historical Series*
which Howells reviewed in the August 1871 *Atlantic Monthly*, was
Richard H. Taneyhill's "The Leatherwood God. An Account
of the Appearances and Pretensions of Joseph C. Dylks in Eastern
Ohio in 1828."[2] The account told how Dylks, claiming to be
God, had exploited a camp meeting, split a community, and

1. WDH to S. Weir Mitchell, 11 December 1904, MS at the University of Penn-
sylvania; WDH to Joseph A. Howells, 24 February 1907, printed in *Life in Letters
of William Dean Howells*, ed. Mildred Howells (Garden City, N. Y., 1928), II, 235,
cited hereafter as *Life in Letters*. The letter to Aurelia Howells (21 June 1914) is at
Harvard, as are all other manuscript materials unless otherwise noted. Permission
to quote unpublished passages from the letters, diaries and manuscripts of Howells
has been granted by William White Howells for the heirs of the Howells Estate.
Permission to quote from the unpublished materials owned by Harvard has been
granted by the Harvard College Library. Republication of these materials requires
these same permissions.

2. Taneyhill's history is in the *Ohio Valley Historical Series: Miscellanies, No. 7*
(Cincinnati, 1871); Howells' review is in the *Atlantic Monthly*, XXVIII (1871), 255–
256. The "Eastern Ohio" of Taneyhill's title refers to the environs of later Salesville,
about forty miles west of Howells' birthplace at Martin's Ferry, Ohio.

then disappeared. Howells was to follow Taneyhill's narrative so closely in his novel that when the latter was being published in 1916 he asked his publisher to allow him to identify his source and to describe his dependence on it (page 2 of the present edition).

No evidence of a twenty- or thirty-year-old beginning survives outside Howells' own frequent recollections of it; the earliest surviving manuscript dates no earlier than 1900. Yet Howells may have seen the novelistic possibilities of the incident before then, for he had encountered the story at least twice by 1895. Taneyhill's account had been reprinted in 1880, and the incident was narrated briefly in two Ohio histories Howells knew and consulted for his *Stories of Ohio*, where he, in turn, retold the story.[3] The Taneyhill account had been reprinted again in 1906. Howells may have planned his novel any time during these years, but probably late in the period, for when he told Joe in 1912 that he was "trying to take up the story" again, he recalled Joe's having "looked up the ground" for the story "8 or 10 years ago," or between 1902 and 1904.[4] These 1912 recollections of a beginning on the story are mixed with his loneliness for Elinor, who had died two years earlier, and with plans for a reunion with his son, and they suggest that Howells' work on the history was surrounded with family memories and associations. Joe's sudden death during this same period rendered more difficult his work on a novel whose background they had often discussed. He saw through the press his family chronicle, *New Leaf Mills*, but did not resume work on *The Leatherwood God* until early in 1913.

OF EARLY OHIO LIFE

The recollections Howells could associate with Taneyhill's history are reflected in materials surviving from 1862 to 1871. In 1862 Howells had based a poem, "Louis Lebeau's Conversion,"

---

3. Henry Howe, *Historical Collections of Ohio* (Columbus, 1889), I, 730–732; William Henry Venable, *Beginnings of Literary Culture in the Ohio Valley* (Cincinnati, 1891), p. 226; *Stories of Ohio* (New York, 1897), pp. 197–200.
4. 22 June 1912, *Life in Letters*, II, 323–324.

on family talk of frontier camp meetings, and by December 1867 he had written five chapters of a possible early draft of *New Leaf Mills*. In August 1870—a year before his review of Taneyhill's history—he urged his father to read two early volumes of the *Ohio Valley Historical Series*, as a spur to autobiographical writing. From February to May 1871 he had been pressing such considerations, trying to get his father's essay on camp meetings published, making suggestions for his father's memoirs, and discussing their projected June trip over his father's old ground in Eastern Ohio.[5]

Still, in the spring of 1871 Howells had not yet begun to draw other materials together around Taneyhill's history. In his August review, probably written in late spring, Howells called the history "a very curious chapter of superstition," but did not summarize it carefully. He omitted Taneyhill's more sensational details about the worship of Dylks, and the challenge which got him scalped; he ventured no further into speculation than to echo Taneyhill in calling the Leatherwood Creek settlers "unusually intelligent and devout" and in crediting them with "an enlightened and tolerant spirit." Modifying or mistaking details, he romanticized Dylks' appearance, mentioned only *one* of two trials (he would intentionally telescope them in the novel), mislocated Dylks' hiding place, and mistakenly referred to the United Brethren as Moravians.[6] Howells was not giving Taneyhill's history the close scrutiny he later devoted to it.

---

5. "Louis Lebeau's Conversion," *Atlantic Monthly*, X (1862), 534–538. The *New Leaf Mills* manuscript is conjectured from the title of "New Arcady Mills" which Howells gives it in a letter to his sister Annie of 15 December 1867; in 1898 (letters to Aurelia of 17 September and 22 October) he recalled an 1867 visit to the site of *New Leaf Mills*. Howells mentioned the *Ohio Valley Historical Series* volumes and the camp meeting article in a letter of 14 August 1870 to William Cooper Howells; he referred to the memoirs in letters of 8 February and 5 and 12 March 1871; he mentioned the camp meeting article again in letters of 2 April 1871 and 23 April 1871 (*Life in Letters*, I, 164), and he discussed the plans for the trip in letters of 6 and 16 April and 14 and 25 May 1871.

6. For the review, see above, n. 2. Howells had studied the Moravians for "Gnadenhütten" (*Atlantic Monthly*, XXIII [1869], 95–115), for which he had consulted an earlier Moravian historian who had called them "United Brethren." The novel mentions both United Brethren and Moravians (pp. 4, 40 and 53), but not so as to show whether Howells still equated them.

The tone of these early materials is also different from that of *The Leatherwood God*. "Louis Lebeau's Conversion" and Howells' father's camp meeting essay both romanticize camp meeting details of the sort Abel Reverdy would recount (chapter I). The younger Howells' notebook of the June 1871 trip hints at his father's sentimental reminiscences, but its entries are typically objective in the notation of settings and people similar to those used later in *The Leatherwood God*: a dilapidated tavern in Atwater, a "camp-meeting side [site?]" and an "old mill site" near Steubenville, little brick houses, a young man carrying a law book, and a "Slatternly, full breasted woman." Though there are no precise parallels, Howells did use similar details in the novel, having Squire Braile recall the "very passable" tavern which Leatherwood had once had (page 152 in the present edition), making Jim Redfield a law student, and creating a slatternly Sally Reverdy.[7]

However Howells might have hoped to use such material, after returning home he could only assure his father that he had enjoyed the trip, and speculate that someday he would find it "useful to me to have seen it as I did, though at present I don't perceive any literature in the subject."[8] He was not to begin developing such possibilities until the late 1880's and 1890's when he returned to his Ohio experiences to write three autobiographical works, "Year in a Log-Cabin" (1887), *A Boy's Town* (1890), and *The Flight of Pony Baker* (written 1895-1896). In 1895 he finally edited and published his father's memoirs,[9] and in preparing a school reader, *Stories of Ohio* (1897), he found an opportunity to indulge his earliest literary passion—the reading of history.

In *Stories of Ohio* Howells was much more careful with Taney-

---

7. William Cooper Howells, "Camp Meetings in the West Fifty Years Ago," *Lippincott's Magazine*, X (1872), 203–212; notebook for Italy, 1864, and Boston to Quebec, 1870, with entries for the Ohio trip dated 3–7 June 1871. Howells gave parallel descriptions of the trip in letters to Elinor M. Howells, 4–5 and 7 June 1871.

8. WDH to William Cooper Howells, 25 June 1871.

9. William Cooper Howells, *Recollections of Life in Ohio, 1813–1840* (Cincinnati, 1895).

hill's history than he had been in 1871. Disciplining the material to new purposes, he recounts it with understanding for fanaticism and foolishness, but certain nuances of his narrative imply his disapproval of the imposture. Its first two sentences give poverty and ignorance as the causes of the "religious excitement" expressed in camp meetings and superstitions. "The wildest of these perhaps was the Leatherwood God," he continues, calling Dylks "this fanatic or impostor, who was indeed both one and the other . . . ." Taking from Henry Howe's *Historical Collections of Ohio* a reference to the "soft and pliable" leatherwood bark,[10] Howells compares the texture of the Leatherwood faith to it, and slightly decreases Taneyhill's stress on the intelligence and tolerant spirit of the Leatherwood settlers. He describes Dylks more realistically than he had in 1871, and other inaccuracies of the 1871 review are removed. But the account concludes with mild irony: two of the well-to-do converts, Howells wrote, "lived and died in the full faith that Joseph C. Dylks was God Almighty, though he never did anything to prove it but snort like a startled horse, wear long hair on foot and halo on horseback, and fail in everything else he attempted." This and the concluding reference to the return of a "fat and sleek" Dylksite preacher are not far from the attitude of Squire Braile. However, Howells was not prepared to give his school readers of 1897 the full irony he would incorporate into the novel of 1916.

His future concern, already evident here, was to discover the meaning and significance of the past in order to instruct the present. He admitted in *Stories of Ohio* that a "teasing sense of . . . obscurity" surrounded the history of early white settlements, but insisted that their story, as "the beginning of a mighty history," could not be separated from "the life of the whole race." Even their past mistakes could be valuable, for he concluded not only about the Leatherwood episode but also about a Mormon bank fraud and a Women's Temperance Crusade as well that

It is not ill for them [the people of Ohio] that they should now

---

10. Howe, I, 732.

and then have been mistaken. This has helped to keep them modest in the midst of their prosperity, and their eminence in saving and governing the union of these states. Such as they are, they seem to me, historically, the first of the Americans.[11]

This immersion in Ohio's past had led Howells to re-explore the Taneyhill narrative in conjunction with other historical material, as he had not done in 1871; it also strengthened his conviction that the midwestern past was the key to understanding the American character.

Perhaps this is why Howells became ambitious to turn Ohio incidents into fiction. Just before finishing *Stories of Ohio* he proposed an "Ohio novel" (probably *The Kentons*) to Henry Mills Alden. In 1902 he considered writing a book about the survival of primitive American traits along the Ohio River and was also tempted to write a poetical reminiscence of early life in Jefferson after the style of George Crabbe. Except for *The Kentons* and an essay, "Floating Down the River on the O-hi-o," none of these plans were carried out.[12] But all the while his nostalgia for Ohio scenes and history continued and finally issued in *New Leaf Mills*, a chronicle of his family's life at Eureka Mills in 1850. This nostalgia was again enlivened in 1906 by a poem by W. H. Venable which drew Howells' mind to "the vanished Ohio of [his] Miami-haunted and haunting boyhood."[13]

Howells recognized, even after finishing *The Leatherwood God*, that historical fiction, with its opportunities for romance, was an anomaly for him, for he wrote Frederick A. Duneka of Harper and Brothers that the novel was "historical, oddly enough." But before completing it Howells had immersed himself in reading ancient histories and had confirmed his decision to write *The Leatherwood God* by developing a rationale for writing fiction about

---

11. Pp. 26, 287.

12. Alden to WDH, 28 April 1897. WDH to Charles Eliot Norton, 19 March 1902 (*Life in Letters*, II, 153–154). WDH to Aurelia Howells, 20 July, 17 and 23 August and 7 September 1902. "Floating Down the River on the O-hi-o," "Editor's Easy Chair," *Harper's Monthly*, CV (June 1902), 146–151.

13. WDH to W. H. Venable, 6 December 1906, MS at Ohio Historical Society.

regional history. He urged in the "Easy Chair" of March 1912 that "the parochial" in novels was preferable to the national or universal, and by June he had located his earlier beginning of *The Leatherwood God* and now saw the story so clearly that he felt sure it would not be difficult to write.[14]

FROM HISTORY TO FICTION

This earlier beginning is probably represented in the surviving manuscripts only by the thirty leaves of the American Academy manuscript which were prepared on paper which Howells used around 1900 (see A Note on the Manuscript and Typescripts, page 187). The remainder of the earliest extant manuscript draft, which was apparently being written at the same time that the full typescript prepared from it was also being prepared, offers no evidence of the extent to which it is either a recopying, a recopying with revision, or a stage of new writing. In a letter of 20 December 1914 Howells asked Duneka, who had some manuscript version of *The Leatherwood God* in the Harper office, to return it to him because it was his only copy;[15] thus the recopying or rewriting of the text and the virtually simultaneous typing from it probably took place after that time. His letters do not report the exact progress of the work on *The Leatherwood God*, and it is impossible to trace the composition very precisely.

Still, the periods of work on *The Leatherwood God* from 1912 to 1914 are quite clearly defined. Howells had told his brother Joe in June 1912 that he planned to resume work on the novel, but after Joe's death on 10 August Howells probably did not return to it for some months. On 5 February 1913, he told Hamlin Garland that he was at work on the book,[16] but he was slowing down by the 23rd of that same month when he wrote his sister Aurelia,

---

14. WDH to Duneka, 23 September 1914, MS in George Arms' collection. The historians included Herodotus, Plutarch, Tacitus and Livy. WDH to T. S. Perry, 23 September 1914, MS at Colby College. "Editor's Easy Chair," *Harper's Monthly*, CXXIV (1912), 636. WDH to Joseph A. Howells, 22 June 1912, *Life in Letters*, II, 324.

15. MS in John Carter Brown Library, Brown University.

16. MS at University of Southern California.

taking stock of *New Leaf Mills* and finding it thin, and saying that he worked only feebly on *The Leatherwood God*.[17]

Letters to his daughter Mildred in April and May 1913 indicate that Howells found *The Leatherwood God* easier to develop as he began to receive praise for *New Leaf Mills*. He wrote on 14 April: "I am curiously interested again in The Leatherwood God [sic]; it grows clearer and greater in my mind . . . ." Five days later he read to Thomas Sargeant Perry what he had finished and then on 20 April wrote to Mildred: "He thinks it the broadest and strongest thing I've done yet, which is pretty well for 76." Another good notice of *New Leaf Mills* was followed by another two-week stint of work reported in letters of 29 and 30 April. Yet after "hammering away" at it on 1 May and reporting further progress to Perry a week later,[18] he was again slowing down by the 15th, when he wrote to Mildred, "My brain seems to have struck, but I hope to arbitrate with it."

A year passed before Howells returned to the novel. He sailed to England for July and August, and the spiritualist satire *The Seen and Unseen at Stratford-on-Avon*, which the trip inspired, occupied him until the end of the year. In the first half of 1914 he worked on an essay for *Harper's Monthly* titled "In an Old-Time State Capital," later reworked for *Years of My Youth*. By 21 June he was telling Aurelia that "after a long season of autobiography" he had resumed *The Leatherwood God*, but again he was having difficulty with it: "the dreadfulness and the mystery of the imposture rather distress me and I wish I had some cheerfuller theme." By 23 September he was able to tell Duneka[19] and Perry that he had completed the novel, but a month later (19 October) he was asking Perry for the names of religious impostors to use in the last chapter.[20]

A major problem at all stages of composition, clearly shown

---

17. On completion and reception of *New Leaf Mills* see *Life in Letters*, II, 259, 290, 297–299 and 324 and WDH to Aurelia Howells, 15 August 1911 and 23 February 1913.

18. MS at Colby College.

19. MS in George Arms' collection.

20. MSS at Colby College.

in surviving manuscripts, was how to be faithful to Taneyhill's historical data while transmuting it into fiction. All through the novel, Howells was summarizing, paraphrasing and quoting Taneyhill. The revision of the typescript prepared from the manuscript employed the history for major structures and details in eleven chapters; Howells' total dependence on Taneyhill ran to twenty-six of Taneyhill's thirty sections, and he often paraphrased or transcribed with only slight alterations. He added details from Taneyhill at least three times in the manuscript, and once or twice in the typescript. In the manuscript, for example, he inserted rumors about Dylks' motives and the report of Reverend Davis' conversion (Taneyhill, pages 29-32; present edition, page 62), and in revising the typescript he inserted a conversation about what the Little Flock should call Dylks (pages 56-57). Only once does Howells appear to have deleted historical details: a gap in the typed pagination near the end of chapter XIV suggests that twenty-eight pages of typescript were discarded; if they followed Taneyhill's history, they would have told of the religious strife following Dylks' escape.[21]

Nevertheless, Howells rendered the historian's reconstructions more credible as fiction.[22] In so doing, he used at least three strategies. One made the novel more complex by creating Squire Braile and Abel Reverdy as commentators.[23] Their roles are es-

---

21. Taneyhill, pp. 38–40. The deletion is especially obvious in the typescript. There, p. 142 is renumbered from a typed 170, and bears a typed chapter heading not in any published version. TS p. 142 reports Braile's presence, which is inconsistent with TS p. 141 (present edition, pp. 105, 104), and his rebuke of the brawlers could apply to any fight.

A copy of Taneyhill which Mildred Howells said her father "used to verify facts in his novel of 'The Leatherwood God'" is at Harvard; it is almost completely unmarked.

22. See George F. Kummer, "Introduction," Richard H. Taneyhill, *The Leatherwood God* (Gainesville, 1965), p. xiii; Eugene H. Pattison, *William Dean Howells' The Leatherwood God: Genesis, Artistry, and Reception* (unpublished dissertation, University of Michigan [Ann Arbor: University Microfilms], 1963), chapter I; and Haskell S. Springer, "*The Leatherwood God:* From Narrative to Novel," *Ohio History,* LXXIV (1965), 191–202.

23. Squire Braile was suggested by the historical justice of the peace, James Frame, the son of a Methodist, whom Howells made into a skeptic. Before settling on "Matthew Braile," Howells had called him "Michael Brill" (the name of a Dylks convert), "Grame" and "Graile." Abel Reverdy is Howells' own creation entirely.

tablished early in the first chapter, and later Abel reports almost *verbatim* Taneyhill's account of Dylks' battle with Satan (pages 51-52). But in the novel, Howells changed the historian's careful documentation into a chain of hearsay. Taneyhill had introduced the incident by saying:

> The following account of this clerical tour was placed in my hands by a gentleman whose father received the statements embodied in it from McCormick himself, which he reduced to writing at the time. The writer was one of Dylks' disciples, and placed implicit faith in what was told him by Mr. McCormick. Coming as it does from a genuine believer, who stood high in the Dylks' brotherhood, through an honorable source, I do not hesitate to pronounce it official.[24]

In Howells' hands this became Abel's report of what " 'Brother Enraghty told, and Sally she got it putty straight from the wife of the man that he told it to' " (page 50). Howells also introduces another commentator in chapter XXIII, where a fictional visitor, T. J. Mandeville, asks Braile about the whole story.

By a second fictional strategy Howells reduced the mystery of Dylks' actions and his hypnotic hold over Leatherwood, giving plausible explanations and de-emphasizing the intelligence of the Leatherwood settlers. Two examples will illustrate. An early sentence in the prologue, cancelled in part in the manuscript and then completely in the typescript, credited the community not only with "toleration," but with "a common intelligence far beyond that of other pioneer communities" (MS, page 3; TS, page 2). In the typescript of chapter II Howells cancelled a passage, already reduced in the manuscript, which reported the preacher's Methodist fervor inhibited by his "Presbyterian birth and breeding" (MS, second pagination series, page 28). In the final version the preacher's revivalistic warmth was simply overwhelmed by Dylks' hypnotic presence (TS, page 24). Keeping within the general context of Taneyhill's history, but leaning on

---

24. Taneyhill, pp. 20–21.

his own knowledge of frontier revivalism, Howells the realist was beginning to remove the historical mystery.

Using a third strategy Howells transformed the history by inventing fictional subplots which give dramatic perspectives on Dylks' "appearance and pretensions." It is impossible to determine when Howells formulated these subplots, but it may be that writing *New Leaf Mills* helped him create one of them. Several details in the relationship between Jane Gillespie and Dylks find their parallel in the affair between handsomely seductive Captain Bickler and the willful Rosy Hefmyer of *New Leaf Mills*.[25] And one cancelled manuscript passage in chapter VII suggests how consciously Howells was using Jane's story as a dramatic extension of Leatherwood's worship of Dylks: after saying that Jane did not seem to hear her Aunt Nancy (page 46), the manuscript originally read, "as if . . . the magic which was to seal the senses of the people of Leatherwood against light and knowledge were already working in her" (MS, second pagination series, page 107).

No documents survive to enable us to discover the source of the character of Nancy Billings,[26] but several manuscript revi-

---

25. That a common source may lie behind Rosy Hefmyer and Jane Gillespie is suggested by the appearance in the manuscript of one reference to Jane as "Ann" (MS, second pagination series, p. 109, corrected in TS, p. 63). Howells said that the real-life prototype of Rosy was named Ann Stepmeyer (*Life in Letters*, II, 298).

26. Several sources may be alleged. Haskell S. Springer ("*The Leatherwood God*," p. 199, n. 13, and pp. 194–196) points to parallel elements in Shaker history, and argues that Mormonism's plural marriages may have suggested Dylks' sexual *mana*. Second, Howells could have recalled cases of desertion and bigamy from Henry Howe's *Historical Collections of Ohio* (I, 288). Howe noted that men often disappeared to escape creditors in the early 1800's. One such man, an Easterner, was seen years later in Marietta, Ohio. Another, missing from 1829 to 1834, heard that his "widow" had remarried, and returned to Athens, Ohio, to let her choose between husbands. She took him back, and her "second husband" left quietly. Third, Howells knew the reputation of his home county of Ashtabula for criminal bigamy (see Annie Howells Fréchette, "A Banner Divorce County," *Century Magazine*, n.s. XXVII [1900], 636–640, and Howells' comment on the article in a 27 August 1899 letter to Aurelia Howells). Finally, Howells alluded to a man who mismanaged his father's Virginia farm, and somehow mistreated his sister Victoria, in terms similar to those with which he described Dylks (relevant letters are those from WDH to William Cooper Howells, 9 August 1888, and to Aurelia Howells, 7 January 1889, 2 July 1905 and 25 May 1906).

sions suggest that Howells wanted her both to reflect Jane's infatuation and to be a tormented wife. At first Howells made Nancy as intense and fierce as Jane but later struck several short passages in order to render her more stable. Originally he had her want to kill Dylks, but he cancelled this and even refused to let her turn her hatred of Dylks toward Jane (MS, second pagination series, page 67; second pagination series, page 108). Howells began a passage with Nancy saying bitterly, "After the plow has gone over you, I reckon you don't mind the harrow much" (fourth pagination series, page 88); but he cancelled this in the typescript, so that she says "It's like as if my soul was dead" (TS, page 83) with a finality that goes beyond bitterness. And in chapter IX, where Dylks visits Nancy, Howells finally decided against her threatening Dylks with a hot iron (TS, page 90). In the final version Nancy, in contrast to Jane, becomes a woman with enough self-control to counsel her niece, although in vain: for in the typescript Howells changes a plea in favor of the weak suitor Hughey Blake into a final warning against Jim Redfield (page 135).

Howells had written Duneka that the novel had "no 'love interest' of the merchantable sort,"[27] and his avoidance of such material in the manuscript and typescript is quite clear both in his treatment of Nancy, who he later told Garland was the chief figure, and in his working toward a subtle linkage between Jim Redfield, the only man strong enough to tame Jane, and the heroes of early Western history. The source for Redfield was the historical James Foreacre, a much older man. Howells credited Redfield with several acts of opposition to Dylks ascribed to historical persons, but, refusing to romanticize him, he cancelled three passages which in varying ways allied Redfield with "the breed of Boones, and Kentons and Poes, who had made the region a battleground of the white men and red men for fifty years . . ." (TS, pages 120-121) and left him a more realistically drawn young community leader. The "love interest" may at one

---

27. WDH to Duneka, 23 September 1914, MS in George Arms' collection.

stage have been developed more fully in deleted typescript pages which followed Jim's first shy words to Jane at the end of chapter XVIII.[28]

Still not entirely satisfied with his plot, Howells added before the novel was serialized a page of dialogue between the Brailes to report the outcome of the Redfield marriage, and then later, before the book was published, he further touched up passages showing Jane's maternal instinct (pages 158-159). Howells' attention to details was evident in these few last revisions, but the overall structure and tone remained that of the corrected typescript.

PUBLICATION AND RECEPTION

Although in July 1915 Howells expected *The Leatherwood God* to appear the following spring, its publication was delayed by a reorganization of Harper and Brothers. In May 1915 Colonel Harvey, the colorful president of Harper and Brothers, retired under the pressure of the publishing firm's insolvency, and Duneka feared that he and Howells might be released by the end of the year. In late October, anticipating Harper and Brothers' budget cuts, Howells made new arrangements with them limiting his work to the "Easy Chair." Under these arrangements, Harper and Brothers were to have options on any new material, but Duneka conceded rights to *The Leatherwood God* on the grounds that it had been conceived before Howells' agreement of 1900 with Harper and Brothers. On 12 November Duneka reiterated his understanding concerning the serial rights, but added that Harper and Brothers wanted sole rights to any new books.[29]

Thus when the Century Company began negotiating for rights to *The Leatherwood God*, it became necessary to clarify the arrangements with Harper. On 6 December 1915 Douglas Z. Doty of the Century Company offered $5,000 for serialization, and de-

---

28. The typescript pages originally numbered 208–240, between renumbered pages 180 and 181, are lacking; see A Note on the Manuscript and Typescripts, p. 188.

29. WDH to W. A. Gill, 27 July 1915, MS at Bristol Public Libraries; Duneka to WDH, 10 May 1915; WDH to Mildred Howells, 2 November 1915; Duneka to WDH, 12 November 1915.

manded book rights at a 20% royalty. Howells immediately wrote Duneka suggesting that it would be to their common advantage if another company printed one of his books; the "Centurions" could even give Harpers free advertising by listing Howells as author of several novels published by them. Duneka replied (8 December 1915) that he and his Harper associates were opposed to the *Century Magazine* serialization, and asked for a week to sell the serial rights elsewhere. In a letter the following day Howells firmly pressed Duneka for concessions to the Century Company, repeating his argument of "common advantage," and on 11 December he agreed to Doty's terms. The contract signed on 14 December conceded collected-set rights, which Duneka promptly accepted for the Harpers, though Doty insisted that collected-set publication be delayed for a year after the Century book appeared.[30]

By 21 March 1916 Howells had approved Henry Raleigh's illustrations, and shortly after the first serial installment appeared in the April *Century Magazine*, Doty was able to offer a British serialization in *Cornhill Magazine*. But Curtis Brown, a London literary agent, finally arranged to have the novel instead published in England by Herbert Jenkins, and by October he was also arranging for publication in Paris by Louis Conard. The Century Company's edition was probably on sale during the last week in October and it and the Jenkins edition were deposited for copyright in the first week of November. At the same time, Brown sought French, Dutch, and Scandinavian translation rights, and by January he was trying to secure French rights for dramatization and filming. Howells had told Garland six months earlier that he would accept the same terms for American filming that Garland received,[31] but no record of filming or translation has been located.

30. WDH to Duneka, 7 December 1915, MS at Brown University; W. W. Ellsworth (Century Company) to WDH, 11 December 1915; Duneka to WDH, 16 December 1915; Doty to WDH, 17 December 1915.

31. Doty to WDH, 30 March and 17 April 1916; Curtis Brown to WDH, 21 August, 10 and 23 October, 3 November 1916, 13 and 19 January 1917; WDH to Hamlin Garland, 17 July 1916, MS at the University of Southern California.

Howells' profit from the novel derived solely from its book and serial publications. By 1 January 1917 the Century Company had issued two printings totalling 10,000 copies and had sold 6,495 copies. By 31 March the publisher reported American sales of 7,076 and Canadian sales of 1,039; Howells' royalty was $2,041.03. A year later Howells received modest payment for the English rights, and on 21 November 1919 Brown reported that Jenkins planned a cheap edition of the novel.[32]

The keen negotiations for the novel and the several overtures for film or translation rights attest to *The Leatherwood God's* initial success. Howells welcomed Garland's response, one of the first, and felt gratified that his cousin Mira Lloyd Dock had discovered "a sense of our own kind [of] backwoods ancestry in it"; he encouraged her to praise it "month by month." The New York *Times Book Review* began to follow the serialization in April, and Doty reported Hildegard Hawthorne's comment that it was "as young and vital as though he [Howells] counted but forty years, and as full of mellow wisdom as if he were a hundred." By 11 June Howells was able to write Aurelia Howells that it had "nothing but liking as yet, and if the country prospers, the book ought to sell."[33]

A sense of declining powers had often distressed him over the twelve years in which he planned and wrote *The Leatherwood God*, and in October 1916 when it was finally to be published as a book he was still anxious about its success. But the novel gained warm initial acceptance. The New York *Times Book Review* discussed it first with *The Mysterious Stranger*, and insisted on the "essential contemporaneousness" of both books. Religion was a touchy subject in 1916, and the reviewer expected the first installment to arouse curiosity. As the serial unfolded he continued to notice the story's strangeness, which he observed prompted the author to

---

32. Doty to WDH, 9 January 1917; Century Company royalty statement, 30 April 1917; WDH to Curtis Brown, 5 May 1918, MS in The Barrett Collection, University of Virginia; Curtis Brown to WDH, 21 November 1919.

33. *Life in Letters*, II, 356; WDH to Mira Lloyd Dock, 16 April 1916, MS at Library of Congress; Doty to WDH, 2 June 1916; *Life in Letters*, II, 364.

acknowledge its historical source. His final review stated the two themes that would dominate in later reviews: it recognized the "dangers of offense" in the story, but persisted in appreciating the novel's additions to Howells' "gallery of realistic portraits."[34]

For another three months reviewers praised the realistic portrayals of frontier life, though a few reviewers qualified their recognition by insisting that the novel was a romance. *Publishers' Weekly* called it "a radical departure from Mr. Howells's accustomed manner," and the Boston *Evening Transcript* claimed that Howells had retreated from his attacks on historical romance with what it called the "vigorous romanticism" of the novel. But the reviewer appreciated the novel's style, dialect writing, and portrayal "of certain moments in the lives of the hardy settlers whose pioneer enthusiasm helped to found the republic . . . ."[35]

Discussion of the novel's religious issues was more persistent. The *Times Literary Supplement* took this up on 16 November, first classifying all religious impostors and then identifying Dylks' type as a mixture of the deliberate and the self-deceiving. The review went on to praise the novel's style and artistry, but concluded with the suggestion that it might have been more effective if Dylks had told his own tale. The Springfield *Republican* stressed the novel's social psychology of religion, laying emphasis on the isolation of Leatherwood and the "autohypnotism that brings Dylks to the border of a belief in his own claims." H. W. Boynton echoed this in two reviews, first simply praising the novel and noting the "universal interest" of the episode, and later calling Dylks "an amazing portent" of such impostors as Cagliostro, Joseph Smith, Alexander Dowie, and Mary Baker Eddy. Another reviewer, in the *Independent*, concluded—

> Those who have watched with sorrowful wonder the growth and progress of one sentimental pseudo-religion or cult after

---

34. New York *Times Book Review*, 30 April 1916, p. 184; 28 May 1916, p. 224; 29 October 1916, pp. 453, 460.

35. Frederick Taber Cooper, "The Story of a False Prophet," *Publishers' Weekly*, XC (1916), 1403; E. F. K., "Mr. Howells's Vigorous Romanticism," Boston *Evening Transcript*, 1 November 1916, section 2, p. 8.

another in this country of ours, the miraculous success of the faking leadership that promises to work the miracles of Jehovah and never does—those men and women, I think, will find most in this book.

Still, few American reviewers had grasped Howells' religious intent by the end of the year. *Catholic World* recognized the revivalistic excesses and the impostor's power, but considered Howells' theme "unworthy of his pen," and it remained for a British periodical, *The Athenæum*, to note briefly that Howells probably expected the reader to appreciate "the breadth of real reverence for the God ideal" behind Squire Braile's "rather cynical philosophy." It must have been reviews such as this that prompted Howells to write his sister Annie that "the English have received it intelligently, and the American critics, though kind, most ignorantly."[36]

With a few notable exceptions, the critics continued to be kind and added to the praise of the realistic characterization a new appreciation of the "Americanism" of setting and atmosphere. *The Nation* (London) found it full of "the breadth and clarity of this ripened American spirit, one both tolerant and shrewd, large in its human horizon, yet keen in his swift dissection of fraud and frailty." One would find "more striking evidence" of these resources in the novel, the London *Spectator* said, than in *Years of My Youth*.[37]

While some reviewers called its humor "Rabelaisian" and ranked Dylks with Silas Lapham and Dr. Boynton as tragic figures, the preference was generally for Howells' other novels; *The Leatherwood God* was rarely accorded first rank. No doubt much of the critics' praise was tribute to Howells' reputation, but in January 1917 H. L. Mencken dispensed with professional cour-

36. *Times Literary Supplement*, 16 November 1916, p. 548; Springfield *Republican*, 20 November 1916, p. 6; H. W. Boynton, "Some Outstanding Novels of the Year," *Nation*, CIII (1916), 507; "Some Stories of the Month," *Bookman*, XLIV (1917), 504; *Independent*, LXXXVIII (1916), 550; *Catholic World*, CIV (1916), 397; *Athenæum*, No. 4612 (1916), 596; *Life in Letters*, II, 367.

37. *Review of Reviews*, LIV (1916), 678; *Nation* [London], XX (1916), 424–425; *Spectator*, CXVIII (1917), 209–210.

tesy. He thought *The Leatherwood God*, like Howells' other novels, was shallow in ideas, feelings and the tragic sense; he called it "little more than a stale anecdote" lacking in the religious psychology of either self-deception or credulity. The novel failed to provide what Mencken required of it: "a revealing look into the heads of . . . the saleratus-sodden, hell-crazy, half-witted Methodists and Baptists of a remote Ohio settlement of seventy or eighty years ago."[38]

There was more insight in a March 1917 *Atlantic Monthly* article by Helen and Wilson Follett:

> It shall not be said here that he intended this story as a sly and subtle *exposé* of all religion through direct physical revelation: all that the evidence warrants is the assertion that he *may* so have intended it, and that if so he could not have done much more to sharpen its point. Clearly it expresses his contempt of the faith that demands a sign. And in Squire Matthew Braile, the shrewd and humorous 'infidel' of Leatherwood, we have not only a striking individual of one of Mr. Howells's most sympathetic types, but also the intellectual point of view of the book. . . . In all this quizzical irony did Mr. Howells mean to say, for hearing ears only, that Christianity is to him, not the water and the wine, the loaves and fishes, the empty tomb, the harps and crowns, but a rule of life which can neither be given nor taken away by any of these, and which is real whatever becomes of them?[39]

The novel would not again receive such perceptive analysis for some time. While a few later reviewers would praise the novel, its popularity was to decline with that of its author. In 1925 Ernest Boyd, reviewing Harvey's study of Howells, recalled how much "the venerable novelist" had been patronized when his

---

38. *North American Review*, CCIV (1916), 938–939; *Bookman*, XLIV (1917), 504; Arthur H. Quinn, "The Thirst for Salvation," *Dial*, LXI (1916), 534–535; C. E. Lawrence, *Living Age*, n.s. CCXCIV (1917), 173–177; New York *Herald*, 31 December 1916, Magazine Section, p. 4; H. L. Mencken, "Suffering Among Books," *Smart Set*, LI (1917), 267.

39. Helen and Wilson Follett, "Contemporary Novelists: William Dean Howells," *Atlantic Monthly*, CXIX (1917), 369–370.

last few books, despite the lengthy reviews they received, caused very little excitement. By that time Howells' reputation was in eclipse, and it was not until Robert B. Sinclair's short article in 1945 that his two Ohio novels received more than passing notice.[40] *The Leatherwood God*, which Howells intended to be his "last great novel," had become instead one of his unknown novels.

E.H.P.

---

40. Ernest Boyd, "Readers and Writers," *Independent*, CXIV (1925), 20; Robert B. Sinclair, "Howells in the Ohio Valley: An Example for a Generation of Novelists," *Saturday Review of Literature*, XXVIII (6 January 1945), 22–23.

Howells in 1916

The Leatherwood God

PUBLISHER'S NOTE

THE AUTHOR thinks it well to apprise the reader that the historical outline of this story is largely taken from the admirable narrative of Judge Taneyhill in the *Ohio Valley Series*, Robert Clarke Co., Cincinnati. The details are often invented, and the characters are all invented as to their psychological evolution, though some are based upon those of real persons easily identifiable in that narrative. The drama is that of the actual events in its main development; but the vital incidents, or the vital uses of them, are the author's. At times he has enlarged them; at times he has paraphrased the accounts of the witnesses; in one instance he has frankly reproduced the words of the imposter as reported by one who heard Dylks's last address in the Temple at Leatherwood and as given in the Taneyhill narrative. Otherwise the story is effectively fiction.

ALREADY in the third decade of the nineteenth century, the settlers in the valley of Leatherwood Creek had opened the primeval forest to their fields of corn and tobacco on the fertile slopes and rich bottomlands. The stream had its name from the bush growing on its banks, which with its tough and pliable bark served many uses of leather among the pioneers. They made parts of their harness with it, and the thongs which lifted their door-latches, or tied their shoes, or held their working clothes together. The name passed to the settlement, and then it passed to the man who came and went there in mystery and obloquy, and remained lastingly famed in the annals of the region as the Leatherwood God.

At the time he appeared the community had become a centre of influence spiritual as well as material, after a manner unknown to later conditions. It was still housed, for the most part, in the log cabins which the farmers built when they ceased to be pioneers, but in the older clearings, and along the creek a good many frame dwellings stood, and even some of brick. The population, woven of the varied strains from the north, east and south which have mixed to form the Middle Western people, enjoyed an ease of circumstance not so great as to tempt their thoughts from the other world and fix them on this. In their remoteness from the political centres of the young Republic, they seldom spoke of the civic questions stirring the towns of the East; the commercial and industrial problems which vex modern society were unknown to them. Religion was their chief interest and the

3

seriousness which they had inherited from their Presbyterian, Methodist, Lutheran and Moravian ancestry was expressed in their orderly and diligent lives; but in the general prosperity the stringency of their several creeds had so far relaxed that their distinctive public rite had come to express a mutual toleration. The different sects had their different services; their ceremonials of public baptism, their revivals, their camp-meetings; but they gathered as one Christian people under the roof of the log-built edifice, thrice the size of their largest dwelling, which they called the Temple.

I

A STORM of the afternoon before had cleared the Mid-August air. The early sun was hot, but the wind had carried away the sultry mists, and infused a fresh life in the day. Where Matthew Braile sat smoking his corncob pipe in the covered porchway between the rooms of his double log cabin he insensibly shared the common exhilaration, and waited comfortably for the breakfast of bacon and coffee which his wife was getting within. As he smoked on he inhaled with the odors from her cooking the dense rich smell of the ripening corn that stirred in the morning breeze on three sides of the cabin, and the fumes of the yellow tobacco which he had grown, and cured, and was now burning. His serenity was a somewhat hawklike repose, but the light that came into his narrowed eyes was of amused liking as a man on a clay-bank horse rode up before the cabin, in the space where alone it was not hidden by the ranks of the tall corn. The man sat astride a sack with a grist of corn in one end balanced by a large stone in the other, and he made as if he were going on to the mill without stopping; but he yielded apparently to a temptation from within, since none had come from without. "Whoa!" he shouted at the claybank, which the slightest whisper would have stayed; and then he called to the old man on the porch, "Fine mornun', Squire!"

Braile took out his pipe, and spat over the edge of the porch, before he called back, "Won't you light and have some breakfast?"

"Well, no, thank you, Squire," the man said, and at the same time he roused the claybank from an instant repose, and pushed her to the cabin steps. "I'm just on my way down to Brother Hingston's mill, and I reckon Sally don't want me to have any breakfast till I bring back the meal for her to git it with; anyway that's what she said when I left." Braile answered nothing, and the rider of the claybank added, with a certain uneasiness as if for the effect of what he was going to say, "I was up putty late last night, and I reckon I overslep'." Then, as Braile remained silent, he went on briskly, "I was wonderin' if you hearn about the curious doin's last night at the camp-meetun'."

Braile said without ceasing to smoke, "You're the first one I've seen this morning, except my wife. She wasn't at the camp-meeting." His aquiline profile, which met close at the lips from the loss of his teeth, compressed itself further in leaving the whole burden of the affair to the man on the claybank, and his narrowed eyes were a line of mocking under the thick gray brows that stuck ·out like feathers above them.

"Well, sir, it was great doun's," the other said, wincing a little under the old man's indifference.

Braile relented so far as to ask, "Who was at the bellows?"

The other answered with a certain inward deprecation of the grin that spread over his face, and the responsive levity of his phrase, "There was a change of hands, but the one that kep' the fire goun' the hardes' and the hottes' was Elder Grove."

Braile made "Hoonch!" in the scornful guttural which no English spelling can represent.

"Yes, sir," the man on the claybank went on, carried forward by his own interest, but helpless to deny himself the guilty pleasure of falling in with Braile's humor, "he had 'em goin' lively, about midnight, now I tell you: whoopun' and yellun', and rippun' and stavun', and fallun' down with the jerks, and pullun' and haulun' at the sinners, to git 'em up to the mourners' bench, and hurrahun' over 'em, as fast as they was knocked down and drug out. I never seen the beat of it in all *my* born days."

"You don't make out anything very strange, Abel Reverdy," Braile said, putting his pipe back into his mouth and beginning to smoke it again into a lost activity.

"Well, I hain't come to it yit," Reverdy apologized. "I reckon there never was a bigger meetun' in Leatherwood Bottom, anywhere. Folks there from twenty mile round, just slathers; I reckon there was a thousand if there was one."

"Hoonck!" Braile would not trouble to take out his pipe in making the sound now; the smoke got into his lungs, and he coughed.

Reverdy gained courage to go on, but he went on in the same strain, whether in spite of himself or not. "There was as many as four exhorters keepun' her up at once to diff'ent tunes, and prayun' and singun' everywhere, so you couldn't hear yourself think. Every exhorter had a mourners' bench in front of him, and I counted as many as eighty mourners on 'em at one time. The most of 'em was settun' under Elder Grove, and he was poundun' the kingdom into 'em good and strong. When the Spirit took him he roared so that he had the Hounds just flaxed out; you couldn't ketch a yelp from 'em."

"Many Hounds?" Braile asked in a sort of cold sympathy with the riotous outlaws known to the religious by that name.

"Mought been 'fore I got there. But by that time I reckon they was most of 'em on the mourners' benches. They ought to tar and feather some of them fellers, or ride 'em on a rail anyway, comun' round, and makun' trouble on the edge of camp-meetun's. I didn't hear but one toot from their horns, last night, and either because the elder had shamed 'em back into the shadder of the woods, or brought 'em forwards into the light, there wasn't a Hound, not to *call* a Hound, anywheres. I tell you it was a sight, Squire; you ought to 'a' been there yourself." Reverdy grinned at his notion. "They had eight camp-fires goun' instead o' four, on top of the highest stageun's yit, so the whole place was lit up as bright as day; and when the elder stopped short and sudden, and the other exhorters held back their tommyhawks, and all the saints and sinners left off their groanun' and jerkun' to see what was comun', now it was a great sight, I tell you, Squire. The elder he put up his hand and says he, 'Let us pray!' and the blaze from all them stageun's seemed to turn itself right onto him, and the smoke and the leaves hung like a big red cloud over him and everybody had their eyes fastened tight on his face, like they couldn't turn 'em anywhere else if they tried. But he didn't begin prayun' straight off. He seemed to stop, and then says he, 'What shall we pray for?' and just then there come a kind of a snort, and a big voice shouted out, 'Salvation!' and then there come another snort,—*Hooff!*—like there was a scared horse got loose right in there among the people; and some of 'em jumped up from their seats, and tumbled over the benches, and some of 'em bounced off, and fell into fits, and the women screeched and fainted, thick as flies. It give me about the worst feelun' I ever had in my life: went through me like a axe, and others said the same; some of 'em said it was like beun' scared in the dark, or more like when you think you're just goun' to die."

Abel Reverdy stopped for the effect on Braile, who had been smoking tranquilly throughout, and who now asked quietly, "And what was it?"

"What was it? A man! A stranger that nobody seen before, and nobody suspicioned was there till they hearn him give that kind of a snort, and they seen him standun' right in front of the mourners' bench under Elder Grove's pulpit. He was in his bare head, and he had a suit of long, glossy, jet-black hair hengun' down back of his ears clean to his shoulders. He was kind of pale like, and sad-lookun', and he had a Roman nose some like yourn, and eyes like two coals, just black fire, kind of. He was putty thickset, round the shoulders, but he slimmed down towards his legs, and he stood about six feet high. But the thing of it," Reverdy urged, seeing that Braile remained outwardly unmoved, "was the way he was dressed. I s'pose the rest beun' all in brown jeans, and linsey-woolsey, made us notice it more. He was dressed in the slickest kind of black broad-cloth, with a long frock-coat, and a white cravat. He had on a ruffled shirt, and a tall beaver hat, the color of the fur, and a pair of these here high boots, with his breeches strapped down under 'em."

Braile limbered himself from his splint-bottom chair, and

came forward to the edge of the porch, as if to be sure of spitting quite under the claybank's body. Not until he had folded himself down into his seat again and tilted it back did he ask, "Goin' to order a suit?"

"Oh, well!" said Reverdy, with a mingling of disappointed hope, hurt vanity, and involuntary pleasure. If he had been deeply moved by the incident which he had tried to make Braile see with his own sense of its impressiveness, it could not have been wholly with the hope of impressing Braile that he had stopped to tell it. His notion might have been that Braile would ridicule it, and so help him throw off the lingering hold which it had upon him. His pain and his pleasure both came from Braile's leaving the incident alone and turning the ridicule upon him. That was cruel, and yet funny, Reverdy had inwardly to own, as it touched the remoteness from a full suit of black broadcloth represented by his hickory shirt and his butternut trousers held up by a single suspender passing over his shoulder and fastened before and behind with wooden pegs. His straw hat, which he had braided himself, and his wife had sewed into shape the summer before, was ragged round the brim, and a tuft of his yellow hair escaped through a break in the crown. It was as far from a tall hat of fur-colored beaver as his bare feet were from a pair of high boots such as the stranger at the camp-meeting had worn, though his ankles were richly shaded in three colors from the road, the field and the barnyard. He liked the joke so much that the hurt of it could hardly keep him from laughing as he thumped his mare's ribs with his naked heels and bade her get up.

She fetched a deep sigh, but she did not move.

"Better light," Braile said, "you wouldn't get that corn ground in time for breakfast, now."

"I reckon," Reverdy said aloud, but to himself, rather than Braile, and with his mind on his wife in the log cabin where he had left her in high rebellion which she promised him nothing but a bag of cornmeal could reduce, "she don't need to wait for me, exactly. She could grate herself some o' the new corn, and she's got some bacon, anyway."

"Better light," Braile said again.

The sound of frying within, which had risen above their voices, had ceased, and after a few quick movements of feet over the puncheon floor, with some clicking of knives and dishes, the feet came to the door opening on the porch and a handsome elderly woman looked out.

She was neatly dressed in a home-woven linsey-woolsey gown, with a blue check apron reaching to its hem in front, and a white cloth passed round her neck and crossed over her breast; she had a cap on her iron gray hair.

Braile did not visibly note her presence in saying, "The woman will want to hear about it."

"Hear about what?" his wife asked, and then she said to Reverdy, "Good morning, Abel. Won't you light and have breakfast with us? It's just ready. I reckon Sally will excuse you."

"Well, she will if *you* say so, Mrs. Braile." Reverdy made one action of throwing his leg over the claybank's back to the ground, and slipping the bridle over the smooth peg left from the limb of the young tree-trunk which formed one of the posts of the porch. "My!" he said, as he followed his hostess indoors, "you do have things nice. I never come here without wantun' to have my old shanty whitewashed inside like yourn is, and the logs plastered outside; the mud and moss of that chinkin' and daubin' keeps fallun' out, and lettun' all the kinds of weather there is in on us, and Sally she's at me about it, too; she's worse'n I am, if anything. I reckon if she had her say we'd have a two-room cabin, too, and a loft over both parts, like you have, Mis' Braile, or a frame house, even. But I don't believe anybody but you could keep this floor so clean. Them knots in the puncheons just shine! And that chimbly-piece with that plaster of Paris Samuel prayin' on it, well if Sally's as't me for a Samuel once I reckon she has a hunderd times; and that clock! It's a pictur'." He looked about the interior as he took the seat offered him at the table, and praised the details of the furnishing with a reference to the effect of each at home. In this he satisfied that obscure fealty of the husband who feels that such a connection of the absent wife with some actual experience of his is equivalent to their joint presence. It was not so much to praise Mrs. Braile's belongings to her as to propitiate the idea of Mrs. Reverdy that he continued his flatteries. In the meantime Braile, who came in behind him, stood easing himself from one foot to the other, with an ironical eye slanted at Reverdy from under his shaggy brows; he dropped his head now, and began walking up and down the room while he listened in a sort of sarcastic patience.

"Ain't you goin' to have anything to eat, Mr. Braile?" his wife demanded, with plaintive severity.

Braile pulled at his cob-pipe which muttered responsively, "Not as long as I've got anything to smoke. Gets up," he explained to Reverdy, "and jerks it out of my mouth, when we haven't got company."

"I reckon Abel knows how much to believe of that," Mrs. Braile commented, and Reverdy gave the pleased chuckle of a social inferior raised above his level by amiable condescension. But as if he thought it safest to refuse any share in this intimacy, he ended his adulations with the opinion, "I should say that if these here two rooms was th'owed together they'd make half as much as the Temple."

Braile stopped in his walk and bent his frown on Reverdy, but not in anger. "This *is* the Temple: Temple of Justice—Justice of the Peace. Do you people think there's only one kind of temple in Leatherwood?"

Reverdy gave his chuckle again. "Well, Squire, I ought to know, anyway, all the log-rollin' I done for you last 'lection time. I didn't hardly believe you'd git in, because they said you was a infidel."

"Well, you couldn't deny it, could you?" Braile asked, with increasing friendliness in his frown.

"No, I couldn't deny it, Squire. But the way I told 'em to look at it was, Mis' Braile was Christian enough for the whole family. Said *you* knowed more law and *she* knowed more gospel than all the rest of Leatherwood put together."

"And that was what elected the family, was it?" Braile asked.

"Well, I hope Mrs. Braile won't refuse to serve," he said, and he began his walk again. "Tell her about that horse that broke into the meetin' last night, and tried to play man."

Reverdy laughed, shaking his head over his plate of bacon and reaching for the corn-pone which Mrs. Braile passed him. "You do beat all, Squire, the way you take the shine off of religious experience. Why," he addressed himself to Mrs. Braile, "it wasn't much, as fur as anybody could make out. It was just the queerness of the whole thing." Reverdy went over the facts again, beginning with deprecation for the squire but gathering respect for them in the interest they seemed to have for Mrs. Braile.

She listened silently, and then she asked, "And what became of him?"

"Well that's where you got me, Mrs. Braile. Don't anybody know what become of him. Just kind of went out like a fire, when the Power was workun' the hardest, and wasn't there next time you looked where he been. Kind o' th'owed cold water on the meetun' and folks begun goun' home, and breakun' up and turnun' in; well it was pretty nigh sun-up, anyway by that time. I don' know! Made *me* feel all-overish. Seemed like I'd been dreamun' and that man was a Vision." Reverdy had lifted an enraptured face, but at sight of Braile pausing in sarcastic pleasure, he dropped his head with a snicker. "I know the squire'll laugh. But that's the way it was."

"He'll laugh the other side of his mouth, some day, if he keeps on," Mrs. Braile said with apparent reproof and latent pride. "Was Sally at the meetin' with you?"

"Well, no, she wasn't," Reverdy began, and Braile asked:

"And did you wake her up and tell her about it?"

"Well, no, I didn't, squire, that's a fact. She woke *me* up. I just crep' in quiet and felt out the soft side of a puncheon for a nap, and the firs' thing I know was Sally havin' me by the shoulder, and wantun' to know about gittun' that corn groun' for breakfas'. My! I don't know what she'll say, when I *do* git back." Reverdy laughed a fearful pleasure, but his gayety was clouded by a shadow projected from the cabin door.

"Well, I mought 'a' knowed it!" a voice at once fond and threatening called to Reverdy's quailing figure. The owner of the voice was a young woman unkempt as to the pale hair which escaped from the knot at her neck, and stuck out there and dangled about her face in spite of the lax attempts made to gather it under the control of the high horn comb holding its main strands together. The lankness of her long figure showed in the calico wrapper which seemed her sole garment; and her large features were respectively lank in their way, nose and chin and high cheek bones; her eyes wabbled in their sockets with the sort of inquiring laughter that spread her wide, loose mouth. She was barefooted, like Reverdy, on whom her eyes rested with a sort of burlesque menace, so that she could not turn them to Mrs. Braile in the attention which manners required of her, even when she added, "I just 'spicioned that he'd 'a' turned in here, soon's I smelt your breakfas', Mrs. Braile; and the dear knows whether I blame him so much, nuther."

"Then you'd better draw up too, Sally," Mrs. Braile said, without troubling herself to rise from her own chair in glancing toward another for Mrs. Reverdy.

"Oh, no, I couldn't, Mrs. Braile. I on'y just meant how nice it smelt. I got me something at home before I left, and I ain't a bit hungry."

"Well, then, you eat breakfast for *me—I'm* hungry," the Squire said. "Sit down! You couldn't get Abel away now, if you went on an hour. Don't separate families!"

"Well, just as you say, Squire," Mrs. Reverdy snickered, and she submitted to pull up the chair which Mrs. Braile's glance had suggested. "It beats all what a excitement there is in this town about the goin's on at the camp-meetin', last night. If I've heard it from one I've heard it from a dozen. I s'pose Abel's tol' you?" she addressed herself impartially to Mrs. Braile across the table and to the squire tilted against the wall in his chair, and smoking behind his wife.

"Not a word," the squire said, and his wife did not trouble herself to protest; Reverdy opened his mouth in a soundless laugh at the squire's humor, and then filled it with bacon and cornpone, and ducked his head in silence over his plate. "What goings on?"

"Why that man that come in while Elder Grove was snatchun' the brands from the burnin', and snorted like a horse— But I *know* Abel's tol' you! It's just like one of your jokes, Squire Braile; ain't it Mrs. Braile?" Sally referred herself to one and the other.

"You won't get either of us to say, Sally," Mrs. Braile let the squire answer for both. "You'd better go on. I couldn't hear too often about a man that snorted like a horse, if Abel *did* tell. What did the horses hitched back of the tents think about it? Any of 'em try to shout like a man?"

"Well, you may laugh, Squire Braile," Sally said with a toss of her head for the dignity she failed of. She slumped forward with a laugh, and when she lifted her head she said through the victual that filled her mouth, "I dunno what the horses thought, but the folks believe it was a apostle, or somepin."

"Who said so? Abel?"

"Oh, pshaw! D'you suppose I b'lieve anything Abel Reverdy says?" and this gave Reverdy a joy which she shared with him; he tried to impart it to Mrs. Braile impassively pouring him a third cup of coffee. "I jus' met Mis' Leonard comun' up the cross-road, and she tol' me she saw our claybank hitched here, and I 'spicioned Abel wasn't fur off, and that's why I stopped."

The husband and wife looked across the table in feigned fear and threat that gave them pleasure beyond speech.

"She didn't say it was your claybank that snorted?" the Squire gravely inquired.

"Squire Braile, you surely will kill me," and the husband joined the wife in a shout of laughter. "Now I can't hardly get back to what she *did* say. But I can tell you it wasn't anything to laugh at. Plenty of 'em keeled over where they sot, and a lot bounced up and down like it was a earthquake and pretty near all the women screamed. But he stood there, straight as a ramrod, and never moved a eye-winker. She said his face was somepin awful: just so solemn and still! He never spoke after that one word 'Salvation,' but every once in a while he snorted. Nobody seen him come in, or ever seen him before till he first snorted, and then they didn't see anybody else. The preacher he preached along, and tried to act like as if nothun' had happened, but it was no use; nobody didn't hardly pay no attention to him 'ceptun' the stranger himself; he never took his eyes off Elder Grove; some thought he was tryin' to charm him, like a snake does a bird; but it didn't faze the elder."

"Elder too old a bird," the Squire suggested.

"Yes, I reckon he mought been," Sally innocently assented.

"And when he gave the benediction, the snorter disappeared in a flash, with a strong smell of brimstone, I suppose."

"Why, that was the thing of it, Squire. He just staid, and shuck hands with everybody, pleasant as a basket of chips; and he went home with David Gillespie. He was just as polite to the poorest person there, but it was the big bugs that tuck the most to him."

"Well," the squire summed up, "I don't see but what your reports agree, and I reckon there must be *some* truth in 'em. Who's that up there at the pike crossing?" He did not trouble himself to do more than frown heavily in the attempt to make out the passer. Mrs. Reverdy jumped from her chair and ran out to look.

"Well, as sure as I'm alive, if it ain't that Gillespie girl! I bet she'll know all about it. I'll just ketch up with her, and get the news out of her, if there is any. Say, say, Jane," she called to the girl, as she ran up the road with the cow-like gait which her swirling skirt gave her. The girl stopped for her; then in apparent haste she moved on again, and Sally moved with her out of sight; her voice still made itself heard in uncouth cries and laughter.

Braile called into the kitchen where Reverdy had remained in the enjoyment of Mrs. Braile's patient hospitality, "Here's your chance, Abel!"

"Chance?" Reverdy questioned back with a full mouth.

"To get that corn of yours ground, and beat Sally home."

"Well, Squire," Reverdy said, "I reckon you're right." He

came out into the open space where Braile sat. "Well, I won't fergit *this* breakfast very soon." He offered his gratitude to Mrs. Braile over his shoulder, as he passed through the door.

"You're welcome, Abel," she answered kindly, and when he had made his manners to the impassive Squire and mounted his claybank and thumped the horse into motion with his naked heels, she came out into the porch and said to her husband, "I don't know as I liked your hinting him out of the house that way."

Braile did not take the point up, but remained thoughtfully smiling in the direction his guest had taken. "The idea is that most people marry their opposites," he remarked, "and that gives the children the advantage of inheriting their folly from two kinds of fools. But Abel and Sally are a perfect pair, mental and moral twins; the only thing they don't agree in is their account of what became of that snorting exhorter. But the difference there isn't important. If an all-wise Providence has kept them from transmitting a double dose of the same brand of folly to posterity, that's one thing in favor of Providence." He took up his wife's point now. "If I hadn't hinted him away, he'd have stayed to dinner; *you* wouldn't hinted him away if he'd stayed to supper."

"Well, are you going to have some breakfast?" his wife asked. "I'll get you some fresh coffee."

"Well, I *would* like a little—with the bead on—Martha, that's a fact. Have I got time for another pipe?"

"No, I don't reckon you have," his wife said, and she passed into the kitchen again, where she continued to make such short replies as Braile's discourse required of her.

He knocked his pipe out on the edge of his still uptilted chair, as he talked. "One fool like Abel I can stand, and I was just going to come in when Sally come in sight; and then I knew that two fools like Abel would make me sick. So I waited till the Creator of heaven and earth could get a minute off and help me out. But He seemed pretty busy with the solar system this morning, and I had about given up when He sent that Gillespie girl in sight. I knew that would fetch Sally; but it was an inspiration of my own to suggest Abel's chance to him; I don't want to put *that* on your Maker, Martha."

"It was your inspiration to get him to stay in the first place," Mrs. Braile said within.

"No, Martha; that was my unfailing obedience to the sacred laws of hospitality; I *didn't* expect to fall under their condemnation a second time, though." Mrs. Braile did not answer, and by the familiar scent from within, Braile knew that his coffee must be nearly ready. As he dropped his chair forward, he heard a sound of frying, and "Pshaw, Martha!" he called. "You're not getting me some fresh bacon?"

"Did you suppose there'd be some left?" she demanded, while she stepped to and fro at her labors. Her steps ceased and she called, "Well, come in now, Matthew, if you don't want *every*-thing to get cold—like the pone is."

Braile obeyed, saying, "Oh, I can stand cold *pone*," and at sight of the table with the coffee and bacon renewed upon it, he mocked tenderly, "Now just to reward you, Martha, I've got half a mind to go with you to the next meeting in the Temple."

"I don't know as I'm goin' myself," she said, pouring the coffee.

"I wish you would, just to please me," he teased.

II

No one could say quite how it happened that the stranger went home from the camp-meeting with old David Gillespie and his girl. Many had come forward with hospitable offers, and the stranger had been affable with all; but he had slipped through the hands he shook and had parried the invitations made him. Gillespie had not seemed to invite him, and his shy daughter had shrunk aside when the chief citizens urged their claims; yet the stranger went with them to their outlying farm, and spent all the next day there alone in the tall woods that shut its corn fields in.

Sally Reverdy had failed to get any light from the Gillespie girl when she ran out from Squire Braile's cabin. The girl seemed still under the spell that was said to have fallen upon many at the meeting, and it appeared to Sally that she did not want to talk; at any rate she did not talk to any satisfactory end. A squirrel hunter believed he had caught a glimpse of the stranger in the chestnut woods behind the Gillespie spring-house, but he was not a man whose oath was acceptable in the community and his belief was not generally shared. It was thought that the stranger would re-appear at the last night of the camp-meeting, but the Gillespies came without him, and reported that they had expected he would come by himself.

The camp-meeting broke up after the Sunday morning service and most of the worshippers, sated with their devotional experience, went home, praising the Power in song as they drove away in the wagons laden with their camp furniture, and their children strewn over the bedding. But for others the fire of the revival burned through the hot, long August Sabbath day, and a fervent congregation crowded the Temple where the impulse of the week past held over to the night unabated. The spacious log-built house was packed from wall to wall; the men stood dense; the seats were filled with women; only a narrowed space was left below the pulpit for those who might wish to rise and confess Christ before the congregation. The people waited in a silence broken by their deep breathing, their devout whispering, the scraping of their feet; now and then a babe, whose mother could not leave it at home, wailed pitifully or spitefully till it was coaxed or scolded still; now and then some one coughed. The air was thick; a bat scandalized the assemblage by flying in at the open door, and wavering round the tallow candles on the pulpit; one of the men beat it down with his hat, and then picked it up and crowded his way down the aisle, out into the night with it. When he came back it was as if he had found the stranger whom they were all consciously expecting, and had brought him in, together with David Gillespie and his girl. She was tall and straight, like her father, and her hair was red, like his; her eyes were fiercely blue, and the look in them was both wilful and dreamy.

The stranger smiled and took the hands stretched to him in passing by several of the different sectaries who used the Temple. Gillespie seemed not to notice or to care for the greetings to his guest, and his girl wore her wonted look of vague aloofness.

Matthew Braile had been given a seat at the front, perhaps in deference to his age and dignity; perhaps in confusion at his presence. He glanced up at the stranger with a keen glint through his branching eyebrows, and made a guttural sound; his wife pushed him; and he said, "What?" and "Oh!" quite audibly; and she pushed him again, for answer.

The Gillespies sat down with the stranger on the foremost bench. He wore the black broadcloth coat of the Friday night before; his long hair was combed back from his forehead and fell down his shoulders almost to his middle; the glances of his black eyes roved round the room, but were devoutly lowered at the prayer which opened the service. It was a Methodist who preached, but somehow to-night he had not the fervor of his sect; his sermon was cold, and addressed itself to the faith rather than the hope of his hearers. He spoke as from the hold of an oppressive spell; at times he was perplexed, and lost his place in his exhortation. In the close heat some drowsed, and the preacher was distracted by snoring from a corner near the door. He lifted his voice as if to rouse the sleeper, or to drown his noise; but he could not. He came to the blessing at last, and the torpid congregation stirred to go out in disappointment. Suddenly the loud snort that had dismayed the camp-meeting sounded through the heavy air, and then there came the thrilling shout of "Salvation!"

The people did not need to look where the stranger had been sitting; he had done what they hoped, what they expected, and he was now towering over those near him, with his head thrown back, and his hair tossed like a mane on his shoulders. The people stopped; some who had gone out crowded in again; no one knew quite what to do. The minister halted on the pulpit stairs; he had done his part for the night, and he did not apparently resent the action of the man who now took it on him to speak.

A tall, stout man among those who had lingered, spoke from the aisle. He was the owner of the largest farm in the neighborhood and he had one of the mills on the creek. In his quality of miller everybody knew him, and he had the authority of a public character. Now he said:

"We want to hear something more than a snort and a shout from our brother here. We heard *them* Friday night, and we've been talkin' about it ever since."

The appeal was half joking, half entreating. The minister was still hesitating on the pulpit stairs, and he looked at the stranger. "Will you come up, Brother"—

"Call me Dylks—for the present," the stranger answered with a full voice.

"Brother Dylks," the minister repeated, and he came down, and gave him the right hand of fellowship.

The Gillespies looked on with their different indifference. Dylks turned to them: "Shall I speak?"

"Speak!" the girl said, but her father said nothing.

Dylks ran quickly up the pulpit steps: "We will join in prayer!" he called out and he held the congregation, now returned to their places, in the spell of a quick short supplication. He ended with the Lord's Prayer; then he said, "Let us sing," and line after line he gave out the hymn,

> "Plunged in a gulf of dark despair
> We wretched sinners lay."

He expounded each stanza, as to the religious sense and the poetic meaning, before he led the singing. He gave out a passage of scripture, as a sort of text, but he did not keep to it; he followed with other passages, and his discourse was a rehearsal of these rather than a sermon. His memory in them was unerring; women who knew their Bibles by heart, sighed their satisfaction in his perfectness; they did not care for the relevance or irrelevance of the passages; all was scripture, all was the one inseparable Word of God, dreadful, blissful, divine, promising heaven, threatening hell. Groans began to go up from the people held in the strong witchery of the man's voice. They did not know whether he spoke long or not. Before they knew, he was as if sweeping them to their feet with a repetition of his opening hymn, and they were singing with him:

> "Plunged in a gulf of dark despair
> We wretched sinners lay."

It ended, and he gave his wild brutish snort, and then his heart-shaking cry of "Salvation!"

Some of the chief men remained to speak with him, to contend for him as their guest; but old Gillespie did not contend with them. "You can have him," he said to the miller, Peter Hingston, "if he wants to go with you." He was almost rude, and his daughter was not opener with the women who crowded about her trying to make her say something that would feed their hunger to know more. She remained hard and cold, almost dumb; it seemed to them that she was not worthy to have had him under her father's roof. As for her father they had no patience with him for not putting in a word to claim the stranger while the others were pressing him to come home with them. In spite of the indifference of Gillespie and his girl Dylks elected to remain with them, and he went away into the night between them.

When Matthew Braile made his escape with his wife from the crowd, and began to walk home through the dim, hot night, he said, "Is Jane Gillespie any particular hand at fried chicken?"

"Now, you stop, Matthew," his wife said.

"Because that would account for it. I reckon it was fried chicken the ravens brought to Elijah. All men of God are fond of fried chicken."

His wife would not dispute directly with his perversity; she knew that in this mood of his it would be useless trying to make him partake the wonder she felt with her neighbors that the stranger had chosen David Gillespie again for his host out of the many leading men who had pressed their hospitality upon him, and that he should have preferred his apathy to their eagerness.

"I wish he had worn his yellow beaver hat in the pulpit," Braile went on. "It must have been a disappointment to Abel Reverdy, but perhaps he consoled himself with a full sight of the fellow's long hair. He ought to part it in the middle, like Thomas Jefferson, and do it up in a knot like a woman. Well, we can't have everything even in a man of God; but maybe he isn't *really* a man of God. That would account for a good many things. But I think he shows taste in preferring old Gillespie to Peter Hingston; next to Abel Reverdy he's the biggest fool in Leatherwood. Maybe the prophet knew by instinct that there would be better fried chicken at Gillespie's."

His wife disdained to make a direct answer. "You may be sure they give him of their best, whatever it is. And the Gillespies may be poor, but when it comes to respectability and good works they've got a right to hold their heads up with the best in *this* settlement. That girl has done all the work of the house since her mother died when she wasn't a little thing half grown; and old David has slaved off his mortgage by himself till his farm's free and clear; and he don't owe anybody a cent."

"Oh, I don't say anything against the Gillespies; all I say is that Brother Dylks knows which side his bread is buttered on; inspired, probably."

"What makes you so bitter, to-night, Matthew?" his wife halted him a little, with her question.

"Well, the Temple always leaves a bad taste in my mouth: I hate to see brethren agreeing together in unity. You oughtn't to have taken me, Martha"—

"I'll never take you again!" she said.

"And that man's a rascal, if ever there was one. Real men of God don't wear their hair down to their waists and come snorting and shouting in black broadcloth to a settlement like this for the good of folks' souls."

"You've got no right to say that, Matthew. And if you go round talking that way you'll make yourself more unpopular than you are already."

"Oh, I'll be careful, Martha. I'll just think it, and perhaps put two or three of the leading intellects like Abel and Sally on their guard. But come, Martha, you know as well as I do he's a rascal. Don't you believe it?"

"I believe in giving everybody a chance. Don't your own law-books say a man's innocent till he's proved guilty?"

"Something like that. And I'm not trying Brother Dylks in open court at present. I'll give him the benefit of the doubt if he's ever brought before my judgment seat. But you've got to allow, Martha, that the long hair and the black broadcloth and the snort and shout are against him."

"I don't believe in them any more than you do," she owned. "But don't you persecute him because he's religious, Matthew."

"Oh, I don't object to him because he's religious, though I think there's more religion in Leatherwood already than any ten towns would know what to do with. He's got to do much worse than preach his brand of religion before I'd want to trouble him."

They were at the hewn log which formed the step to the porch between the rooms of their cabin. A lank hound rose from the floor, and pulled himself back from his forthplanted paws, and whimpered welcome to them; a captive coon rattled his chain from his corner under the porch roof.

"Why don't you let that poor thing go, Matthew?" Mrs. Braile asked.

"Well, I will, some day. But the little chap that brought it to me was like our"—

He stopped; both were thinking the same thing and knew they were. "I saw the likeness from the first, too," the wife said.

III

THE GILLESPIES arrived at their simpler log cabin half an hour later than the Brailes at theirs. It was on the border of the settlement, and beyond it for a mile there was nothing but woods, walnut and chestnut and hickory, not growing thickly as the primeval forest grew to the northward along the lake, but standing openly about in the pleasant park-like freedom of the woodspastures of that gentler latitude. Beyond the wide stretch of trees and meadowlands, the corn fields and tobacco patches opened to the sky again. On their farther border stood a new log cabin, defined by its fresh barked logs in the hovering dark.

Gillespie pulled the leatherwood latchstring which lifted the catch of his door, and pushed it open. "Go in, Jane," he said to his daughter, and the girl vanished slimly through, with a glance over her shoulder at Dylks where he stood aloof by a few steps from her father.

Gillespie turned to his guest. "Did you see her?" he asked.

"Yes, I walked over to her house this morning."

"Did any one see *you?*"

"No. Her man was away."

Gillespie turned with an effect of helplessness, and looked down at the woodpile where he stood. "I don't know," he said, "what keeps me from splitting your head open with that axe."

"I do," Dylks said.

"Man!" the old man threatened, "don't go too far."

"It wasn't the fear of God which you pretend is in your heart, but the fear of man." Dylks added with a vulgar drop from the solemnity of his words, "You would hang for it. I haven't put myself in your power without counting all the risks to both of us."

Gillespie waved his answer off with an impatient hand.

"Did she know you?"

"Why not? It hasn't been so long. I haven't changed so much— I wear my hair differently and I dress better since I've been in Philadelphia. She knew me in a minute as well as I knew her. I didn't ask for her present husband; I thought one at a time was enough."

"What are you going to do?"

"Nothing—first. I might have told her she had been in a hurry. But if she don't bother me I won't her. We got as far as that. And I reckon she won't, but I thought we'd better have a clear understanding, and she knows now it's bigamy in her case, and bigamy's a penitentiary offence. I made that clear. And now see here, David: I'm going to stay here in this settlement, and I don't want any trouble from you, no matter what you think of my doings, past, present or future. I don't want you to say anything or *look* anything. Don't you let on, even to that girl of yours, that you ever saw me before in your life. If you do, you'll wish you *had* split my head open with that axe. But I'm not afraid; I've got you safe, and I've got your sister safe."

Gillespie groaned. Then he said desperately, "Listen here, Joseph Dylks! I know what you're after here because you always was: other people's money. I've got some money; I've got three hundred dollars saved up since I paid off the mortgage. If you'll take it and go"—

"Three hundred dollars! No, no! Keep your money, old man. I don't rob the poor." Dylks lifted himself, and said with that air of mysterious mastery which afterwards won so many to his obedience, "I work my work. Let no man gainsay me or hinder me." He walked to and fro in the starlight, swelling, with his head up and his mane of black hair cloudily flying from his shoulders as he turned. "I come from God."

Gillespie looked at him as he paced back and forth. "If I didn't know you for the common scoundrel that married my sister against my will, and lived on her money till it was gone, and then left her and let her believe he was dead, I might believe you *did* come from God—or the Devil, you—you turkey cock, you—stallion! But you can't prance *me* down, or snort me down. I don't agree to anything. I don't say I won't tell who you are when it suits me. I won't promise to keep it from this one or that one or any one. I'll let you go just so far, and then"—

"All right, David! I'll trust you, as I trust your sister. Between you I'm safe. And now, you lay low! That's my advice." He dropped from his mystery and his mastery to a level of colloquial teasing. "I'm going to rest under your humble roof tonight, and tomorrow I'm going to the mansion of Peter Hingston. His gates will be set wide for me, and all the double log-cabin palaces and frame houses of this royal city of Leatherwood will hunger for my presence. You could always hold your tongue, David, and you can easily leave all the whys and wherefores to me. I won't go from your hospitality with an ungrateful tongue; I will proclaim before the assembled multitudes in your Temple that I left you secure in the faith, and that I turned to others because they needed me more. I am not come to call the righteous but sinners to repentance; they will understand that. So good night, David, and good morning: I shall be gone before even you are up."

Gillespie made no answer as he followed his guest indoors. Long before he slept he heard the man's powerful breathing like that of some strong animal in its sleep: an ox lying in the field or a horse standing in its stall. At times it broke chokingly and then he snorted it smooth and regular again. At daybreak Gillespie thought of rising, but he drowsed, and he was asleep when his daughter came to the foot of the ladder which climbed to his chamber in the cabin loft, and called to him that his breakfast was ready.

IV

THE FIGURE of a woman who held her hooded shawl under her chin, stole with steps often checked through the limp, dew-laden grass of the woods pasture and slipped on the rotting logs. But she caught herself from tumbling, and safely gained the border of Gillespie's cornfield. Then she sat down trembling on the stone doorstep of the spring-house, and waited rather than rested in the shelter of the chestnut boughs that overhung the roof. She was aware of the spring gurgling under the stone on its way into the sunshine, from the crocks of cream-covered milk and of butter in the cool dark of the hut; she sensed the thick August heat of the sun already smiting its honeyed odors from the corn; she heard the scamper of the squirrels preying upon the ripening ears, and whisking in and out of the woods or dropping into the field from the tips of the boughs overhanging the nearer rows; but it all came blurred to her consciousness.

She was recognizably Gillespie's sister, but her eyes and hair were black. She was wondering how she could get to speak with him when Jane was not by. He would send the girl away at any sign from her, but she could not have that; the thing must be kept from the girl but not seem to be kept. She let her arms rest on her knees and her helpless hands hang from them; her head was bowed, and her whole body drooped under the burden of her heart as if it physically dragged her down. Jane would be coming soon with the morning's milk to pour into the crocks; she heard a step; the girl was coming; but she must rest a moment.

"What are you doing here, Nancy?" her brother's voice asked.

"Oh, is it you David? Oh, blessed be the name of the Lord! Maybe He's going to be good to me, after all. David, is he gone?"

"He's gone, Nancy."

"In anger?"

"He's gone; I don't care whether he's gone in anger or not."

"Did he tell you he saw me?"

"Yes."

"And did you promise him not to tell on him? To Jane? To any one?"

"No." Gillespie stood holding a bucket of milk in his hand; she sat gathering her shawl under her chin as if she were still coming through the sun-cleft shadows of the woods pasture.

"Oh, David!"

"What do you want me to do, Nancy?"

"I don't know, I don't know. I haven't slept all night."

"You mustn't give way like this. Don't you see any duty for you in the matter?"

"Duty? Oh David!" Her heart forboded the impossible demand upon it.

Gillespie set his bucket of milk down beside the spring. "Nancy," he said, "a woman cannot have two husbands. It's a crime against the State. It's a sin against God."

"But I haven't *got* two husbands! What do you mean, David? Didn't I believe he was dead? Didn't you? Oh, David, what— Do you think I've done wrong? You *let* me do it!"

"I don't think you've done wrong; but look out you don't do it. You *are* doing it, now. I can't let you do it. I can't let you live in sin!"

"In sin? Me?"

"You. Every minute you live now with Laban you live in sin. Your first husband, that was dead, is alive. He can't claim you unless you allow it; but neither can your second husband, now. If you live on with Laban a day longer—an hour—a minute— you live in deadly sin. I thought of it all night but I had not thought it out till this minute when I first saw you sitting there and I knew how miserable you were, and my heart seemed to bleed at the sight of you."

"You may well say that, David," the woman answered with a certain pride in the vastness of her calamity. "If it was another woman I couldn't bear to think of it. *Why* does He do it? *Why* does He set such traps for us?"

"Nancy!" her brother called sternly.

"Oh, it's easy enough for you! But if Rachel was here, she'd see it different."

"Woman!" her brother said, "don't try to hide behind the dead in your sin."

"It's *no* sin! I was as innocent as the babe unborn when I married Laban—as innocent as he was, poor boy, when he would *have* me; and we all thought *he* was dead. Oh, *why* couldn't he have been dead?"

"This is murder you have in your heart now, Nancy," the old man said, with who knows what awful pleasure in his casuistry, so pitilessly unerring. "If the life of that wicked man could buy you safety in your sin you could wish it taken."

"Oh, oh, oh! What shall I do, what shall I do!" She wailed out the words with her head fallen forward on her knees, and her loose hair dripping over them.

"Do? Go home, and bring your little one, and come to me. I will deal with Laban when he gets back tonight."

She started erect. "And let him think I've left him? And the neighbors, let them think we've quarreled, and I couldn't live with him?"

"It won't matter what the world thinks," Gillespie said, and he spoke of the small backwoods settlement as if it were some great centre of opinion such as in large communities dispenses fame and infamy, and makes its judgments supremely dreaded. "Besides," he faltered, "if no one is knowing but ourselves to his coming back, it can seem as if *he* left *you*."

"And I live such a lie as that? Is this *you*, David?"

It was she who rose highest now, as literally she did, in standing on the stone where she had crouched above the level of his footing.

"I—I say it to spare you, Nancy. I don't wish it. But I wish to make it easy—or a little bit easier—something you can bear better."

"Oh, I know, David, I know! You would save me if you could. But maybe—maybe, it ain't what we think it is. Maybe he was outlawed by staying away so long."

Neither of them named Dylks, but each knew whom the other meant, throughout their talk.

"A lawyer might let you think so till he got all your money."

"Matthew Braile wouldn't."

"That infidel?"

She drooped again. "Oh well, I must do it, I must do it! I'll go and get ready and I'll come to you. What will Jane think?"

"I'll take care of what Jane thinks. When do you expect Laban back?"

"Not before sundown. I'll not come till I see him."

"We'll be ready for you."

He moved now to open the springhouse door; she turned, and was lost to him in the lights and shadows of the woods-pasture. On its further border her cabin stood, and from it came the sound of a pitiful wail; at the back door a little child stood, staying itself by the slats let into grooves in the jambs. She had left it in its low cradle asleep, and it must have waked and clambered out and crept to the barrier and been crying for her there; its small face was soaked with tears.

She ran forward with long leaps out of the cornfield and caught it to her neck and mumbled its wet cheeks with hungry kisses. "Oh, my honey, my honey! Did it think its mother had left"—

She stopped at the word with a pang, and began to go about the rude place that was the simple home, where after years of hell she had found an earthly heaven. Often she stopped, and wondered at herself; it seemed impossible she could be thinking it, be doing it, but she was thinking and doing it, and at sundown she knew by the eager shadow of a man in the doorway, pausing to listen if the baby were awake, all had been thought and done.

V

THE EMOTIONAL frenzies, recurring through the day, were past, and she could speak steadily to the man, in the absence of greeting which often emphasises the self-forgetfulness of love as well as marks the formlessness of common life: "Your supper's waiting for you, Laban; I've had mine; you must be hungry. It's out in the shed; it's cooler there. Go round; baby's asleep."

The man obeyed, and she heard him drop the bucket into the well, and lift it by the groaning sweep, and pour the water into the basin, and then splash himself, face and head, with murmurs of comfort, presently muffled in the towel. Her hearing followed him through his supper, and she knew he was obediently eating it, and patiently waiting for her to account for whatever was unwonted in her greeting. She loved him most of all for his boy-like submission to her will and every caprice of it, but now she hardly knew how to deny his tacit question as he ventured in from the shed.

"Don't come near me, Laban," she said with a stony quiet. "Don't touch me. I ain't your wife, any more."

He could not speak at first; then it was like him to ask, "Why —why— What have I done, Nancy?"

"*You*, you poor soul?" she answered. "Nothing but good, all your days! He's come back."

He knew whom she meant, but he had to ask, "Joseph Dylks? Why I thought he was"—

"Don't say it! It's murder! I don't want you to have his blood on you *too*. Oh, if he was *only* dead! Yes, yes! I have a right to wish it! Oh, God be merciful to me a sinner!"

"When—when—how did you know it, Nancy?"

"Yesterday morning or day before—just after you left. I reckon he was waiting for you to go. I'm glad you went first." The man looked up at the rifle resting on the pegs above the fireplace. "Laban, don't!" she cried. "*I* looked at it when he was walking away, and I know what you're thinking."

"What is he goin' to do?" the man asked from his daze.

"Nothing. He said he wouldn't do nothing if I didn't. If he hadn't said it I might believe it!"

Laban shifted his weight where he stood from one foot to the other.

"He passed the night at David's. He's passed two nights there."

"Was it the snorting man?"

"I reckon."

"I heard about him at the Cross Roads. Why didn't David tell us yesterday?" he asked.

"Maybe he hadn't thought it out. David thinks slow. He likes to be sure before he speaks. He was sure enough this morning!" the woman ended bitterly.

"What did he say?"

"He said it was living in sin for us to keep together if *he* was alive."

Laban pondered it. "I reckon if we come together without knowing he was alive, it ain't no sin."

"Yes it is!" she shrieked.

"We was married just like anybody; we didn't make no secret of it; we've lived together four years. Are you goin' to unlive them years by stoppin' now?"

"Don't you s'pose I been over all that a million times? My mind's sore workin' with it; there ain't a thought in me that don't ache from it. But David's right. We've got to part. I put your things in this poke here," she said, and she gave him a bag made from an old pillow tick, with a few clothes lumping it half full. "I'll carry the baby, Laban!" She pulled back from him with the child in her arms. "Or no, you can carry her; you'll have to leave *her*, too, and you've got a right to all the good you can get of her now. Don't touch anything. I'll stay at David's, to-night, but I'll come back in the morning, and then I'll see what I'll do—stay, or go and live with David. Come!"

"And what about Joey?" Laban asked, half turning with the child when they were outside.

"I declare I forgot about Joey! I'll see, tomorrow. It seems as if my very soul was tired now. Joey will just think we've gone over to David's for a minute; he'll go to bed when he comes; he'll have had his supper at Peter Hingston's, anyway." As they walked away, she said, "You're a good man Laban Billings, to feel the way you always do about Joey. You've been a true father to him; I wonder what his *own* father'd have been."

"No truer father to him than I've been a husband to you Nancy," the man said, and as they walked along together, so far apart, his speech came to him, and he began to plead their case with her as before an adverse judge. Worn as she was with the arguments for and against them after the long day of iteration, she could not refuse to let him plead. She scarcely answered him but he knew when they reached Gillespie's cabin that she had seen them in the fierce light of her conscience where there was no shadow of turning.

David was alone; Jane, he said, had gone to the Reverdies, and was going with the woman to the Temple.

Nancy did not seem to hear him. She took the sleeping baby from its father's arms. "Laban has come with me to say good bye before you, David. I hope you'll be satisfied."

"I hope your conscience will be satisfied, Nancy. It doesn't matter about me. Laban, do you see this thing like I do?"

"I see it like Nancy does."

"God will bless your effort for righteousness. Your path is dark before you now, but His light will shine upon it."

The old man paused helplessly, and Nancy asked, "Does Jane know?"

"Not yet. And I will confess I'm not certain what to do, about her, and about the neighbors. This is a cross to me, too, Nancy.

I have lived a proud life here; there has never been talk about me or mine. Now when you and Laban are parted, there will be talk."

"There's no need to be," Laban said, "not at once. They want me back at the Cross Roads, the Wilkinses do. I can go now as well as in the morning. I forgot to tell you," he added to his wife. "It was drove out of my mind."

"Oh, I don't blame you," she answered.

"I can have work there all the fall."

David Gillespie rubbed his forehead, and said tremulously: "I don't know what to say. I suppose I am weak. It'll be *one* kind of a lie. But Laban—I thank you"—

"I can come back here Sundays and see Nancy and the baby," Laban suggested.

The old man's voice shook. "You'll be making it harder for yourself," was all he could say.

"But perhaps—perhaps there'll be light—that light you said —by and by"—

"Let us pray that there'll be no light from the Pit. I am a sinful man, Laban, to let you do this thing. I ought to have strength for all of us. But I am older now—I'm not what I was—the day has tried me, Nancy."

"Good bye, then, Laban," the woman said. "And don't you think hard of David. I don't. And I'm not sure I'll ever let you come. Say good by as if it was for life." She turned to her brother. "We can kiss, I reckon?"

"Oh, I reckon," he lamented, and went indoors.

Laban opened his arms as if to take her in them; but she interposed the baby.

"Kiss her first. Me last. Just once. Now, go! I won't be weak with you like David is. And don't you be afraid for *me*. *I* can get along. *I'm not a man!*" She went into the cabin, with her baby over her shoulder; but in a little while she came back without it, and stared after the figure of Laban losing itself in the night. Then she sat down on the doorstep and cried; it seemed as if she never could stop; but the tears helped her.

When she lifted her head she caught the sounds of singing from the village below the upland where the cabin stood. It was the tune that carried, not the words, but she knew them from the tune; as well as if she were in the Temple with them she knew what the people were singing. While she followed the lines helplessly, almost singing them herself, she was startled by the presence of a boy, who had come silently round the cabin in his bare feet and stood beside her.

"Oh!" she cried out.

"Why, did I scare you, mom?" he asked tenderly. "I didn't mean to."

"No, Joey. I didn't know any one was there; that's all. I didn't expect you. Why ain't you at home in bed? You must be tired enough, poor boy."

"Oh, no, I ain't tired. Mr. Hingston is real good to me; he lets me rest plenty; and he says I'll make a first rate miller. I helped to dress the burrs this morning—the mill-stones, you know," the boy explained, proud of the technicality. "Oh, I tell you I just like it there," he said, and he laughed out his joy in it.

"You always was a glad boy, Joey," his mother said ruefully.

"Well, you wouldn't thought so if you seen me over at our house. It seemed like there was somebody dead; I dasn't hardly go in, it was so dark and still. Whyn't you there? Didn't pop come home?"

"Yes, but he had to go back to the Cross Roads; he's got work there all the fall."

"Well! We do seem to be gittin' along!" He laughed again. "I reckon you come over here because it seemed kind o' lonesome. Goin' to stay all night with uncle?"

"Yes. You won't mind being there alone?"

"Oh, no! Not much, I reckon."

"You can stay here too, if you want to"—

"Oh, no! Mom," he confessed shyly, "I brung Benny Hingston with me. I thought you'd let him stay all night with me."

"Why, certainly, Joey"—

"He's just behind the house; I wanted to ask first"—

"You know you can always bring Benny. There's plenty of room for both of you in your bed. But now when you go back with him be careful of the lamp. I put a fresh piece of rag in and there's plenty of grease. You can blow up a coal on the hearth; I covered the fire; only be careful."

"Oh, we'll be careful. Benny's about the carefullest boy the' is in Leatherwood. Oh, I do like bein' in the mill with Mr. Hingston." He laughed out his joy again, and then he asked doubtfully, "Mom?"

"Yes, Joey."

"Benny and me was wonderin'—we'd go straight back home, and not light any lamp at all—if you'd let us go to the Temple. There's a big meetin' there to-night." The mother hesitated, and the boy urged, "They say that strange man—well, some calls him the Snorter and some the Exhorter—is goin' to preach." The mother was still silent, and the boy faltered on, "He dresses like the people do Over-the-Mountains, and he wears his hair down his back"—

The mother gasped. "I don't like your being out late, Joey. I'd feel better if you and Benny was safe in bed."

"Oh, well." The boy's voice sank to the level of his disappointment; but after a silent interval he caught it up again cheerily, "Oh, well, I reckon Benny woon't care much. We'll go right back home. We can have a piece before we go to bed?"

"Yes"—

"Benny thinks our apple-butter is the best they is. Can we have some on bread, with sugar on top?"

His mother did not answer at once, and he said again, as if relinquishing another ideal, "Oh, well."

Nancy rose up and kissed him. "Yes, go to the Temple. You might as well."

"Truly, mom? Oh, Benny, hurrah! She's let me! Come along!"

He ran round the cabin to his comrade, and she heard them shouting and laughing together, and then the muted scamper of their bare feet on the soft road toward the settlement.

The mother said to herself, "He'd got to see him sooner or later." She drew her breath in a long sigh, and went into the cabin. "What a day, what a day! It seems a thousand years," she said aloud.

"Are you talking to me, Nancy?" her brother asked from somewhere in the dark.

"No, no. Only to myself, David. Where did I put the baby? Oh! I know. I've let Joey go to the Temple to hear his father preach. Lord have mercy!"

VI

THE DISCOURSE of Dylks the second night was a chain of biblical passages, as it had been the first night. But an apparent intention, which had been wanting before, ran through the incoherent texts, leaping as it were from one to another, and there binding them in the intimation of a divine mission. He did not say that he had been sent of God, but he made the texts which he gave, swiftly and unerringly, say something like that for him to such as were prepared to believe it. Not all were prepared; many denied; the most doubted; but those who accepted that meaning of the inspired words were of the principal people, respected for their higher intelligence and their greater wealth.

He had come to the Temple with Peter Hingston and he went home with him from it. Hingston's quarter-section of the richest farmland in the bottom bordered his mill-privilege, with its barns and corncribs and tobacco sheds, and his brick house behind the mill was the largest and finest dwelling in the place. His flocks and herds abounded; his state was patriarchal; and the neighborhood loved and honored him, for some favor and kindness done nearly every man there: for money when the crops failed; for the storage of their wheat and corn in the deep bins of his mill when the yield was too great for their barns; for their use of his sheds in drying their tobacco before their own were ready. His growing sons and daughters until they were grown men and women obeyed his counsel as they had obeyed his will while children. But he was severe with no one; since his wife had died his natural gentleness was his manner as it had always been his make, and it tempered the piety, which in many was forbidding and compelling, to a wistful kindness. His faith admitted no misgiving, for himself, but his toleration of doubts and differences in others extended to the worst of skeptics. He believed that revelation had never ceased; he was of those who looked for a sign, because if God had ever given Himself in communion with his creatures it was not reasonable that he should afterwards always withhold Himself. A friendly humor looked from his dull eyes, and in never quite coming to a formulated joke stayed his utterance as if he were hopeful of some such event in time. He stood large in bulk as well as height, and drew his breath in slow, audible respirations.

The first people of the community tacitly recognized him as the first man in it, though none would have compared him in education with his nearest friend Richard Enraghty, who had been the schoolmaster and was now the foremost of the United Brethren. He led their services in the Temple, and sometimes preached for them when it came their turn to occupy the house which they shared with the other sects. Hingston was a Methodist, but perhaps because their sects were so akin in doctrine and polity their difference made no division between the friends: Enraghty little and fierce and restless, Hingston large and kind and calm. What they joined in saying prevailed in questions of public interest; those who yielded to their wisdom liked to believe that Enraghty's opinion ruled with Hingston. Matthew Braile alone had the courage to disable their judgment which he liked to say was no more infallible than so much Scripture, but the hardy infidel who knew so much law, and was inexpugnable in his office, owned that he could not make head against their gospel. He could darken their counsel with citations from *Common Sense* and *The Age of Reason*, but the piety of the community remained safe from his mockery.

The large charity of Hingston covered the multitude of the Squire's sins; he would have argued that he had not been understood perhaps in the worst things he said; but the fiercer godliness of Enraghty was proof against the talk of a man whose conversation was an exhalation from the Pit. He had bitterly opposed Matthew Braile's successive elections; he had made the pulpit of the Temple an engine of political warfare and had launched its terrors against the invulnerable heathen. He was like Hingston in looking for a sign; in that day of remoteness from any greater world the people of the backwoods longed to feel themselves near the greatest World of all, and well within the radius of its mysteries. They talked mostly of these when they met together, and in the solitude of their fields they dwelt upon them; on their weekdays and workdays they turned over the threats and promises of the Sabbath and expected a light or a voice from on high which should burst their darkness and silence.

To most of them there was nothing sacrilegious in the pretensions which could be read into the closely scriptured discourse of Dylks when he preached the second time in the Temple. The affability which he used in descending from the pulpit among them, and shaking hands and hailing them Brother and Sister, and personally bidding each come to the mercy seat, convinced them of his authority; no common man would so fearlessly trust his dignity among those who had little of their own. They thronged upon him gladly, and the women, old and young alike, trembled before him with a strange joy.

"Where is your father, Sister Gillespie?" he demanded of the girl who wavered in his strong voice like a plant in the wind.

"I don't know—he's at home," she said.

"See that he comes, another time. I send him my Peace and tell him that it will not return to me. Say that I said he needs me."

He went out between Enraghty and Hingston, and as they walked away, he sank his voice back in words of scripture; farther away he began his hymn:

> "Plunged in a gulf of dark despair,
> We wretched sinners lay"—

and ended with his shout of "Salvation!"

VII

THE CABIN of the Reverdys stood on a byway beyond the Gillespies. Sally had joined the girl on her way out of the Temple, and was prancing beside her as they went homeward together. "Oh, ain't it just great? I feel like as if I could fly. I never seen the Power in Leatherwood like it was tonight. He's *sent*, you can tell that as plain as the nose on your face. How happy I do feel! I believe in my heart I got Salvation this minute. Don't you feel the Spirit any? But you was always such a still girl! I did like the way the women folks was floppin' all round. *I* say, if you feel the Power workin' in you, show it, and help the others to git it. What do you s'pose he meant by your paw's needin' him?"

"I don't know. Perhaps *he* will," the girl answered briefly.

"Goin' to tell him? Well that's right, Janey. I kep' wonderin' why he didn't come tonight. If Abel hadn't be'n so beat out with his work at the Cross Roads today, you bet I'd 'a' made *him* come; but he said I'd git enough glory for both. I believe his talkin' with Squire Braile don't do him no good. You b'lieve Washington and Jefferson was friends with Tom Paine? The Squire says they was, but I misdoubt it, myself; I always hearn them two was good perfessin' Christians. Kind o' lonesome along here where the woods comes so clos't, ain't it? Say, Janey: I wisht you'd come a little piece with me, though I don't suppose the bad spirits would dast to come around a body right on the way home from the Temple, this way"—

They had reached the point where Sally must part with the girl, who stopped to lift the top rail of the bar to the lane leading from the road to her father's cabin. She let it drop again. "Why, I'll go the whole way with you, Sally."

"Will you? Well I declare to gracious, you're the best girl I ever seen. I believe in my heart, I'll rout Abel out and make him go back home with you."

"You needn't," the girl said. "I'm not afraid to go alone in the dark."

"Well, just as you say, Janey. What do you do to keep from beun' afraid?"

"Oh, I don't know. I just think, I suppose."

"Well, *I* just want to *squeal*." As they went on, Sally kept talking in her loud, loose voice to keep her courage up. "Well I declare if we ain't there a'ready. If you just say the word I'll have Abel out in half a minute and"—

"No," the girl said. "Good night."

"Well, good night. I've got half a mind to go back with you myself," Sally called as she lifted her hand to pull the latch string of her door.

Jane Gillespie found her father standing at the bars, when she went back. He mechanically let them down for her.

"I thought you would be in bed, father," she said gently, but coldly.

"I've had things to keep me awake; and it's hot indoors," he answered, and then he demanded, "Well?"

If it was his way of bidding her tell him of her evening's experience, she did not obey him, and he had to make another attempt on her silence. "Was Hughey there?"

"Hughey? I don't know."

"Didn't he ask to come home with you?"

"I didn't see him. Sally Reverdy came with me."

"Yes, I know that."

She was silent for another moment and then she said, "Father, I have a message for you. He said, 'I send my Peace to him; and it will not return unto me.' He said you needed him."

Gillespie knew that she meant Dylks and he knew that she kept out of her voice whatever feeling she had in delivering his message.

In the dark she could not see her father's frown, but she was aware of it in his answer. "You went there against my will. Well?"

"I believe."

"You believe? What do you believe?"

"Him. That he is sent."

"Why?"

"I can't tell you. He made me; he made all the people there."

Her father was standing between her and the door. He stood aside. "Go to bed, now. But be quiet. Your Aunt Nancy is there."

"Aunt Nancy?"

"Laban came, but he went back to the Cross Roads, and she's over for the night with the baby."

"The baby? Oh, I'll be careful!" A joy came into her voice, and the strain left it in something like a laugh.

Early in the morning she crept down the ladder from the loft; her father had looped his cot up against the cabin wall, and gone out. Nancy was sitting up in the bed she had made for herself on the floor, coiling a rope of her black hair into a knot at her neck. The baby lay cooing and kicking in her lap. The morning air came in fresh and sweet at the open door.

"Oh, Aunt Nancy, may I take her?"

"Yes; I'll get the breakfast. Your father'll be hungry; he's been up a good while, I reckon."

"I'll make the fire first, and then I'll take the baby."

The girl uncovered the embers on the hearth and blew them into life; then she ran out into the cornfield, and gathered her apron full of the milky ears, and grated them for the cakes which her aunt moulded to fry for breakfast. She took the baby and washed its hands and face, talking and laughing with it.

"You talk to it a sight more than you do to any body else, Jane," the mother said. "Don't put anything but its little shimmy on; it's goin' to be another hot day."

"I believe," the girl said, "I'll get some water in the tub, and wash her all over. There'll be time enough."

"It'd be a good thing, I reckon. But you mustn't forget your milkin'. I dunno what *our* cow'd do this morning if it wasn't for

Joey. But he'll milk her, him and Benny Hingston, between them, somehow. Benny stayed with him last night."

"I did forget the milking," the girl said, putting the baby's little chemise on. "But I'll do it now. Sissy will have to wait till after breakfast for her washing." She got the tin bucket from where it blazed atilt in the sun beside the back door of the cabin, and took her deep bonnet from its peg. She did not ask why the boys slept alone in the cabin, but her aunt felt that she must explain.

"Laban's got work for the whole fall at the Cross Roads. He went straight back last night. I come here." She had got through without telling the lie which she feared she must. "I'm goin' home after breakfast."

Jane asked nothing further, but called from the open door, "Sukey, Sukey! Suk, Suk, Suk!" A plaintive lowing responded; then the snapping sound of a cow's eager hoofs; the hoarse drumming of the milk in the bucket followed, subduing itself to the soft final murmur of the strippings in the foam. Jane carried the milk to the spring house before she reappeared in the cabin with a cup of it for the baby. "It's so good for her to have it warm from the cow," she said, as she tilted the tin for the last drop on the little one's lips. "I wish you'd leave her here with me, Aunt Nancy."

"It's about time she was weaned," the mother said. "I reckon you better call your father now. He must be ready for his breakfast, bendin' over that tobacco ever since sun-up."

Jane took down the tin dinner horn from its pegs, and went to the back door with it, and blew a long, surd blast, crumbling away in broken sounds.

The baby was beating the air with its hands up and down, and gurgling its delight in the noise when she came back. "Oh, honey, honey, honey!" she cooed, catching it up and hugging it to her.

The mother looked at them over her shoulder as she put the cakes of grated corn in the skillet, and set it among the coals on the hearth. "It's a pity you ha'n't got one of your own."

"I don't want one of my own," the girl said.

"I thought, a spell back," the woman took up the subject again after a decent interval, "that you and Hughey Blake was goin' to make a match." The girl said nothing, and her aunt pursued, "Was he there, last night?"

"I didn't notice."

"Many folks?" her aunt asked with whatever change or fulfilment of a first intent.

From kneeling over to play with the baby the girl sank back on her heels, with her hands fallen before her.

"I don't know."

"What did he preach?"

"The Word of God; God's own words. All Scripture; but it was like as if it was the first time you ever heard it."

The girl was looking at the woman, but seemed rapt from the sight of her in a vision of the night before.

"I reckon Satan could make it sound that way," Nancy said, but her niece seemed not to hear her. Nancy stood staring at her, with words bitter beyond saying in her heart; words that rose in her throat and choked her. When she spoke she only said, "Get up, Jane; your father'll be here in a minute."

"I'm not going to eat anything. I'm going into the woods." She staggered to her feet, and dashed from the door. The child looked after her with outstretched arms and whimpered pitifully, but she did not mind its call.

"Where's Jane?" her father said, coming in at the back door.

"Gone into the woods," she said.

"To pray, I reckon."

He sat down at the table-leaf lifted from the wall, and his sister served him his breakfast. He ate greedily, but his hand trembled so in lifting his cup that the coffee spilled from it.

When he had ended and sat leaning back from the board, she asked him: "What are you going to do?"

The old man cleared his throat. "Nothing, yet. Let the Lord work His will."

"And let Joseph Dylks work *his* will, too! I'll have something to say about that."

"Be careful, woman. Be careful."

"Oh, I'll be careful. He has as much to lose as I have."

"No, not half so much."

VIII

Where Matthew Braile sat smoking most of the hot forenoon away on the porch of his cabin there came to him rumor of the swift spread of the superstition running from mind to mind in the neighborhood, and catching like fire in dry grass. The rumor came in different voices, some piously meant to shake him with fear in the scorner's seat which he held so stubbornly; some in their doubt seeking the help of his powerful unfaith; but he required their news from them all with the same mocking. They were not of the Scribes and Pharisees, the pillars of the Temple, the wise and rich and proud who had been the first to follow Dylks, but the poorer and lowlier sort who wavered before the example of their betters, and were entirely willing to submit it to the searching of the old Sadducee's scrutiny.

The morning after Abel Reverdy had finished his work at the Cross Roads, and had returned to the cares patiently awaiting him at home he rode his claybank so hesitantly toward the squire's cabin that his desire to stop and talk was plain, and Braile called to him: "Well, Abel, what do they think of the Prophet over at Wilkins's? Many converts? Many dipped or sprinkled, as the case required?"

Reverdy drew rein and faced the Squire with a solemnity presently yielding to his natural desire to grin at any form of joke, and his belief that when the squire indulged such flagrant irreverence as this he must be joking. Yet he answered evasively: "You hearn't he says now he hain't never go'n' to die?"

"No. But I'm not surprised to hear it; about the next thing on the docket. Did he say that at the Cross Roads?"

"Said it right here in Leatherwood. Sally told me the first thing when I got home. You wusn't at the Temple last night, I reckon?"

"Well, not *last* night," Braile said with an implication that he had been at the Temple all the other nights, which made Reverdy laugh with guilty joy.

"One o' the Hounds—no, it was Jim Redfield hisself—stopped on the way out, and he says, 'What's this I hear? You say you ain't goin' to die.' And Dylks he lifts his hands up over his head and he says, 'This shell will fall off,' and Jim he says, 'I've got half a mind to *crack* your shell,' and the believers they got round, and begun to hustle Jim off, but Dylks he told them to let him alone, and he says, 'I can endure strong meat, but I must be fed on milk for a while.' What you s'pose he meant, Squire?"

Braile took his pipe out and cackled toothlessly. "I'm almost afraid to think, Abel. Something awful, though. You say Sally told you?"

"Yes."

"I should think Sally would know what he meant, if any body." He looked at Abel and Sally's husband joined him in safe derision. "Tell you anything else?"

"Well, no, not just in so many words. But it 'pears he's been teachin' round all sorts of things in private, like. Who do you reckon he says he is?"

"Not John the Baptist, I hope. I don't know where we should get the locusts and wild honey for him in *this* settlement. Might try grasshoppers, but the last bee-tree in the Bottom was cut down when I was a boy. I got a piece of the comb, I remember."

"I don't know if he said John the *Baptist*; but it was John, anyway. And they say—or that's what Sally hearn tell—that when he was off with Enraghty and Hingston on some 'pointments down round Seneca there was doin's that 'uld make your hair stand up."

"You don't happen to know just what the doings were?"

"Well, no, I don't, Squire. But they was doin's to deceive the very elec', from all I hearn."

"That's just what Hingston and Enraghty both are—the very elect. What deceived *them ?*"

"Oh, pshaw, now, Squire! You know I don't mean they was deceived! That's just a Bible sayin'. You see Brother Briggs was sick and Brother Enraghty went along with Dylks and Brother Hingston to preach in his place."

"Couldn't Dylks have done the preaching?"

"I reckon he could. But there was three 'pointments, and maybe Dylks couldn't fill 'em all, and maybe he didn't want to. Fust Brother Enraghty preached in the Temple at Seneca, and then at Brother Christhaven's house off south of that, and then at David Mason's, the local preacher, but Brother Mason has got the consumption, and *he* couldn't preach; so Brother Enraghty had to do *all* the preachin'."

"I see. Well?"

"Well, that wasn't anything out o' the common, but what Dylks done to the Devil beat all the preachin', I reckon."

"How d'it get out? Devil tell?"

"No. Brother Enraghty told, and Sally she got it putty straight from the wife of the man that he told it to."

"Go on," Braile said. "I can hardly wait to hear."

"Well, sir, they had just got acrost the Leatherwood, and Brother Enraghty felt as if he was lifted all at once into heaven; air diff'ent, and full of joy. Dylks's face got brighter and brighter, and his voice sounded like music. When they got to the top of the hill where you can look back and see the Temple, Dylks turned his horse and stretched out his hands, and says he, 'How ignorant them people is of my true natur'. But time will show 'em.' Well, not just them words, you know; more dictionary; and they preached with a great outpourin' at Seneca. They didn't go to bed that night at all, accordin' to the woman's tell that Enraghty told her man: sot up tell mornin', prayin', and singin' hymes and readin' the Bible. Next mornin' when they started out Brother Enraghty seen a bright ring round Dylks's head and whenever Dylks got down to pray the ring just stayed in the air over the saddle tell he got back, and then it dropped round his head ag'in."

Reverdy stopped for the effect, but Braile only said, "Go on! Go on!"

"Well, sir, so they kep' on all that day and all the next night, prayin', and singin' and readin' the Bible. The next mornin' when they started Brother Enraghty felt kind o' cold all over, and his teeth chattered, and Dylks looked at him hard in the face, and says he, 'Time is precious now. This is the time for work. I now reveal unto you that you are Paul the Apostle.'"

"And what did Paul the Apostle say? Did he own up that he was Paul?"

Reverdy halted in his tale. "Look here, Squire! I don't feel just right, havin' you say such things. It sounds—well, like profane swearin'."

"Any worse than Dylks or Enraghty? You go right ahead, Abel; I'll take the responsibility before the law."

"Well," Reverdy continued with a reluctance that passed as he went on, "what Dylks told him was that he would increase his faith so't he could see the sights of his power, and glorify him among men, and then Enraghty he commenced to git warm ag'in, and Dylks he turned up his eyes, and kep' still, and it was so bright all round him that it made the daylight like dusk, and Dylks made him hark if he didn't hear a kind of rush in the air; and Dylks said it was the adversary of souls, but he would conquer him. They come into a deep holler in the woods and there they see the devil standin' in their way, and Dylks he lights and hollers out, 'Fear not, Paul; this day my work is done,' and he went towards Satan, and Satan he raised his burnin' wings and bristled his scales, and stuck out his forked tongue and dropped melted fire from it; and he rolled his eyes in his head, hissin' and bubblin' like sinners boilin' in hell's kittles. Then Dylks he got down on his knees and prayed, and got up and give his shout of Salvation, and the devil's wings fell, and he took in his tongue, and his eyes stood still, and Dylks he blowed his breath at him, and Satan he turned and jumped, and every jump he give the ground shook, and Dylks and the balance of 'em follered him till the devil come to Brother Mason's house, and then he jumped through the shut winder out of sight. They found Brother Mason's son David in bed sick, but he got up and took Dylks in his arms and called him his Savior, and everybody got down on their knees and prayed, and their faces was shinin' beautiful, and Dylks he walks round David Mason, and rubs his hands over him, and says, 'I bind the Devil for a thousand years,' and he hugged David, and said, 'The perfect work is done.' And he wouldn't stay to preach there, but told 'em they must come back with him to the Temple here in Leatherwood. On the way back he wouldn't talk at all, hardly, but just kep' sayin', 'The perfect work is done,' and he didn't give his shout no more; just snorted."

Braile's pipe had gone out, but he pulled slowly at it two or three times, before he said, "Well Abel, I don't wonder Sally is excited. I suppose *you* would be, if *you* believed a word of this yarn?"

"Well, it's poorty cur'ous doin's, Squire," Reverdy said, daunted between his natural bent and his wish to be of the Squire's thinking. "Don't *you* believe it?"

"Oh, yes, *I* believe it. But you know *I* believe *any*thing. If Dylks did it, and Enraghty says he did it, why there we've got gospel for it—right from St. Paul himself."

He said no more, and Reverdy lingered a moment in vague disappointment. Then he sighed out, "Well, I must be goun', I reckon," and thumped his bare heels into the claybank's ribs and rode away.

Day by day the faith in Dylks spread with circumstance which strengthened it in the converts; they accepted the differences which parted husband, wife, parent and child, and set strife between brothers and neighbors as proof of his divine authority to bring a sword; they knew by the hate and dissension which followed from his claim that it was of supernatural force, and when the pillars of the old spiritual temple fell one after another under his blows, they exulted in the ruin as the foundation of a new sanctuary. They drove the worshippers out of the material Temple, Methodists and Moravians and Baptists who had used it in common, and they met to dedicate it solely to the doctrine of the prophet who came teaching that neither he nor they should ever die, but should enter in the flesh into the New Jerusalem which should come down to them at Leatherwood. His steps in passing from teacher to prophet and to Messiah were contested by a few with bitter and strenuous dissent, but on the night when Dylks proclaimed before the thronging assembly in the stolen Temple "I am God and there is none else," they pressed round him, men and women and children, and worshipped him. "I am God and the Christ in one," he proclaimed. "In me, Father, Son and Holy Ghost are met. There is no salvation except by faith in me. They who put their faith in me shall never taste death, but shall be translated into the New Jerusalem, which I am going to bring down from Heaven." He snorted; the few unbelievers protested in abhorrence; but the Sisters in the faith shrieked, and the Brothers shouted "We shall never die!" Dylks came down from the pulpit among them, and Enraghty called out, "Behold our God!" and they fell on their knees before him. As it had been from the beginning the wisest and best, the first in prayer and counsel, were foremost in the idolatry; and young girls, and wives and mothers joined in hailing Dylks as their Creator and Savior and beseeching him to bless and keep them. The believers were in such force that none of the Hounds, veteran disturbers of camp-meetings and revivals, who were there, dared molest them; the members of the sects expelled from the Temple of their common worship held aloof from the tumult in dismay, and made no attempt to reclaim the sanctuary. One man, not of any church, but of standing in the community, tried to incite the sectaries to assert their rights, but found no following among them. They left the Temple together with certain others who had been trembling toward belief in Dylks but whom the profanation repelled; when they were gone the tumult sank enough to let Enraghty announce another meeting a week hence, and then dismiss the congregation.

"An' afore that we're goin' to have a murricle," Sally Reverdy told Squire Braile sitting early the next morning at the receipt of gossip on his cabin porch with his pipe between his teeth. Her cow had not come up the night before, and Abel had not found her in the woods pasture when he went to look. "An' I couldn't wait all day, an' I just slipped over to git some milk of Mis' Braile," she explained to the Squire as she paused with the bucket in her hand. "I told her I'd bring it back the first chance't I git at our cow; I reckon Abel will find her some time or 'nuther; and I 'lowed you had plenty."

Braile had already heard her explaining all this to his wife, but now he kept her for the full personal detail of the last night's event at the Temple. She ended an unsparing report of the wonders seen with a prophecy of the wonders to come.

"Why," Braile said, "I don't see what you want of a miracle, more than what you've had already. The fact that your cow didn't come up last night, and Abel couldn't find her in the woods pasture this morning is miracle enough to prove that Dylks is God. Besides, didn't he say it himself, didn't Enraghty say it?"

"Well, yes they did," Sally assented, overborne for the moment by his logic.

"And didn't you all believe them?"

"Well, *we* all did," Sally said. "But look here, Squire Braile: what about them that didn't believe it?"

"Oh, then there were some there that didn't believe it! Well, I suppose nothing less than more miracles will do for *them*. Who were they?"

"Well, of course, there was Jim Redfield; he's been ag'inst him from the first, and there was old George Nixon, and there was Hughey Blake, and a passel of the Hounds that I don't count."

"Why, certainly not; the Hounds would doubt anything. But I'm surprised at Redfield and Nixon and Hughey Blake. What reason did they give for the faith that wasn't in them? When a man stood up and snorted like a horse and said he was God why didn't they believe him? Or the other fellows that didn't snort but said they knew it was God from a sound that he made?"

"Oh, pshaw, now, Squire Braile!" Sally gurgled. She did not yield quite with Abel's helplessness at a joke, but the Squire's blasphemous irony had its force with her too, though she felt it right to bring herself back to her religious conviction with the warning: "Some day you'll go too fur."

"Yes, I'm always expecting the lightning to strike in the wrong place. Didn't Nixon or Redfield or Hughey Blake say anything? Or did they just look ashamed of you, down there on your knees before a man that you worshipped for a God because he snorted like a horse? Didn't anybody in their senses say anything, or couldn't those that were out of their senses hear anything but their own ravings?"

The old man had pleased himself with his mockeries, but now he let the scorn which his irony had hidden blaze out. "Wasn't anybody ashamed of it all? Weren't you ashamed yourself, Sally?"

"Well, I dunno," Sally said easing herself from one foot to another and shifting the milk-bucket from her right hand to her left. "Where everybody is goun' one way, you don't know what to think exactly. Jane Gillespie was there, and she went on as bad as the best."

"Jane Gillespie?"

"Yes. She come with me, and she was goin' to come home with me, as fur's the door, and she would ha' done it, if it hadn't ha' been for her father. He bruk through the believers and drug her up from the floor where she was kneelin', and stoopin' her forehead over to the ground, and pulled her out through the crowd. 'You come home with me!' says he, kind o' harsh like; and if it hadn't ha' been for Nancy Billun's Joey I'd ha' had to git through the woods alone, and the dear knows I'm always skeered enough. But Joey and Benny Hingston they come with me, or I don't feel as if I'd been here to tell it."

"You'd have been safe from the devil, though; he stayed with Dylks. Didn't David say anything to the girl?"

"Just, 'You come home with me,' and he looked so black that

Hughey Blake he kind o' started from where he was standin' with the unbelievers, and he says, 'Oh, don't, Mr. Gillespie!'—like that—and Jane she said, 'It's my father, Hugh,' and she went along with him, kind o' wild lookin', like she was walkin' in her sleep. I noticed it at the time."

"Didn't Dylks do anything—say anything?"

"Well, not that *I* seen or hearn. But some o' them that was standun' nigh him was talkun' about it when we all got out, and they was sayun' he said, 'Go with your earthly father; your heavenly father will keep you safe.' I don't know whether he did or not; but that's what they was sayin'."

"And did Gillespie say anything back?"

"Not 't anybody heared. Just give Dylks a look like he wanted to kill him, and then Dylks snorted, and yelled 'Salvation!' Squire," Sally broke off, "some of us Believers was talkun' it over, when we started home, and wonderun' what ought we to call him. Jest Dylks don't sound quite right, and you can't say Almighty, to a body, exactly, and you can't say Lord. What should you think was the right way?"

Braile got back to his irony. "Well, that's an important question, Sally. I should call him Beelzebub, myself; but then I'm not a believer. That night when he first came, didn't he tell the people to call him just Dylks?"

"Yes, he did, but that was for the present, he said."

"Has he given himself any other name?"

"Well, no."

"Then I should let it go at Dylks," he said.

"Just plain Dylks? *Mr.* Dylks wouldn't do; or Brother Dylks, wouldn't. Father Dylks don't sound quite the thing"—

"Might try Uncle Dylks," Braile said, cackling round his pipe-stem, and now Sally perceived that it was in vain to attempt serious discussion of the point with him.

She said, "Oh, pshaw, Squire Braile," and lankly let herself down sidewise from the porch, and flopped away on the road. Then she stopped, and called back, "Say, Squire, what do you think of the Good Old Man?"

"What good old man?"

"Why, Dylks. For a name. That's what most of 'em wants to call him."

"Sounds like a good name for them that like a name like it."

"He calls *us* the Little Flock."

"Well, well! Geese or sheep?"

"Oh, pshaw, now! I wouldn't belong to the Herd of the Lost, anyway. That's what he calls the unbelievers."

"You don't tell me! Well now I *will* be scared in the dark."

Failing of any retort, Sally now flopped definitively beyond calling back.

Braile with a sardonic smile watched her going, but when his wife after waiting for her to be quite gone came out to him, he was serious enough.

"Did that fool tell you of the goings on at the Temple last night?"

"As much as I would let her. I suppose it had to come to something like that. It seems as if the people had gone crazy."

"Yes," the squire sighed heavily, "there's no doubt about that. And it's a pity. For such a religious community Leatherwood Creek used to be a very decent place to live in. They were a lot of zealots, but they got on well with one another; that Temple of theirs kept them together, and they didn't quarrel much about doctrine. Now with the Dylksites driving the old fashioned believers out of the sanctuary and dedicating it to the exclusive worship of Dylks, the other denominations are going to fight among themselves; and there'll be no living with them. And that isn't the worst of it. This new deity isn't going to be satisfied with worship merely. Money, of course, he'll want and get, and he'll wear purple and fine linen, and feed upon fried chicken every day. Still the superstition might die out, and no great harm done, if the faith was confined to men. But you know what women are, Martha."

"They're what men make 'em," Mrs. Braile said sadly.

"It's six of one and half a dozen of another, I'm afraid. But this god of theirs is a handsome devil, and some poor fool of a girl, or some bigger fool of a married woman is going to fall in love with him, and then"—

"Did you just think of that? Well, you can't help it by lettin' your coffee get cold."

Braile tilted his chair down and rose from its rebound to follow his wife stiffly indoors. "The question is, Who will it be? Which poor girl? Which bigger fool? And nothing can be done to prevent it! The Real God put it into human nature, and all Hell couldn't stop it. Well, I suppose it's for some wise purpose," he ended in parody of the pious resignation prevailing on the tongues of the preachers.

IX

DAVID GILLESPIE woke later than his daughter, and when he had put away the shadows of his unhappy dreams which had filled his sleep he took up the burden of waking thoughts which weighed yet more heavily on him. The sight of his child groveling at the feet of that blasphemous imposter and adoring him as her God pitilessly realized itself to him as a thing shameful past experience, and beyond credence, and yet as undeniable as his pulse, his breath, his seeing and hearing. The dread which a less primitive spirit would have forbidden itself as something too abominable, possessed him as wholly possible. He had lived righteously, and he had kept evil from those dear to him, both the dead and the quick, by the force of his strong unselfish will; now he had seen his will without power upon the one who was dearest, and whom he seemed to hold from evil only by the force of his right hand. But his hand could not be everywhere and at all times; and then?

The breakfast which the girl had got for him and left on the hearth was warm yet, when he put it on the table, and she could not have been gone more than a few minutes, but she had gone, he did not know where, without waiting to speak with him after the threats and defiances which they had slept upon. When he had poured the coffee after the mouthfuls he forced down, he acted on the only hope he had, and crossed the woods pasture to his sister's cabin.

She understood the glance he gave within from the threshold where he paused, and she said, "She ain't here, David." Nancy had cleared her breakfast away, and was ironing at the shelf where she had eaten; the baby was playing on the floor.

Gillespie looked down at it. "I didn't know but what she'd come over to dress it; she cares so much for it."

"It cares for her, too. But what brings you after her?"

"She's gone somewhere without her breakfast. We had high words last night after I brought her home."

"I'm afraid you'll have higher words yet, David. Joey was at the Temple."

"Nancy, I don't know what to do about her."

"You knew what to do about *me*, David." She gave her stab, and then she pitied him, not for the pain she was willing he should feel from it, but for the pain he was feeling before. "I know it isn't like that. I'm sorry for you—both. You haven't come to the end of your troubles."

"I can't understand the girl," he said desolately. "Up to a year ago she was like she had always been, as biddable as a child, and meek and yielding every way. All at once she's got stiff-necked and wilful."

"She couldn't tell you why, herself, David. We are all that way—good little girls, and then all of a sudden wilful women. I don't know what changes us. It's harder on us than it is on you. It came on me like a thief in the night and stole away my sense. It gave Joseph Dylks his chance over me; if it had been sooner or later, I should have known he was a power of darkness as far as I could see him. But my eyes were holden, in my self conceit, and I thought he was an angel of light."

"He's got past being an angel now," Gillespie said, forcing himself to the real matter of his errand, far from the question of his daughter's estrangement from her old self. "Did Joey tell you about—last night?"

Nancy did not quit the psychological question at once. "Up to that time we think our fathers and brothers are something above the human; then we think they're not even up to the common run of men. We think other men are different because we don't know them. Yes," she returned to his question with a sigh,

"Joey told me something about it—enough about it. I suppose it isn't right to let him be a spy on his father; but I have to. If I didn't he might want to go, from the talk of those fools, and get to believin' with them. He said there was boys and girls kneelin' with the rest—little childern, almost, and shoutin' and prayin' to Joseph. Did you see 'em?"

"Yes, it was dreadful, Nancy. But it was worse to see the women, the grown-up girls, and the mothers of the children. It looked like they had been drinking. It fairly turned me sick. And my own daughter grovelling on her knees with the worst! If I didn't know Dylks for the thing he is, without an idea beyond victuals and clothes, I might ha' thought he had thrown a spell on 'em, just for deviltry. But they done it all themselves; *he* just gave them the *chance* to play the fool."

Nancy resumed from her own more immediate interest, "Well, I let Joey go; and I don't know whether it helps or hurts to have him come home feelin' about him, and all the goings on, just like I would myself. He always says he's glad I wasn't there, and he pities the poor fool women more than he despises his father. Or I ortn't to say despise; Joey don't despise anybody; he's all good, through and through; I don't know where he gets it. He's like Laban, and yet he ain't any kin to Laban."

"It must be hard on you, Nancy. I don't know how you can bear up the way you do. It is like a living streak of fire in me."

"That's because there's some hope left in you. I can bear what I've got to because the feeling is all burnt out of me. It's like as if my soul was dead."

"You mustn't say that, Nancy."

"I say anything I please, now; anything I think. I'm not afraid any more; I hain't got anything left to be afraid of."

"Well, I have," David returned. "Something I'm ashamed to be afraid of—his hold on Jane. I don't understand it. We've always thought alike and believed alike, and now to see her gone crazy after a thief and liar like that! It's enough to drive me mad the other way. I don't only want to kill *him*; I want to kill"—

"David!" she stopped him, and in his pause she added,

"You're worse than what I ever was. Where is your religion?"

"Where is *her* religion? I raised her to fear God, the Bible God that I've prayed to for her since she was a little babe, but now since she's turned to this heathen image I begin to turn from *Him*. What's *He* been about if He's All Seeing and All Powerful, to let loose such a devil on a harmless settlement like this where we were all brethren and dwelt together in unity, no matter whether we believed in dipping or sprinkling? We loved one another—in the Scripture sense—and now look! Families broken up, brothers not speaking, wives and husbands parting, parents cursing the day their children were born, and children flying in the face of their parents. Did you hear about Christopher Mills, how he come crying to his father and mother and tried to make them believe in Dylks, and when his father said it was all a snare and a delusion, Christopher went away telling them their damnation was sealed?"

"No," the woman said with bitter pleasure in the mockery, "but I heard how our new Saint Paul Enraghty went over to his uncle's the other day, and said he should never see corruption, and should never die, and told his uncle he couldn't shoot him. Them that was there say the old man just reached for his rifle, and was going to shoot Saint Paul in the legs, and then Paul begged off and pretended that he was only in fun!"

She laughed, but David Gillespie looked sadly at her. "I don't believe I like to hear you laugh, Nancy."

"Why, are you turning believer too, David? It'll be time for me next," she mocked. "I couldn't laugh at Joseph, may be, but Saint Paul Enraghty is a bigger rascal or a bigger fool than he is. Some say that Joseph is just crazy, and some that he's after money, and that Enraghty's put him up to everything."

"Yes," David moodily assented to the general tenor of her talk. "The way they've roped in between 'em that poor fool Davis who'd been preaching for the United Brethren, and now preaches Dylks! First he wouldn't hardly go into the same house and then he wouldn't leave it till he could come with Dylks. *I* don't know how they do it! Sometimes I think the decentest man left in the place is that red-mouthed infidel Matthew Braile! Some times I'm a mind to go to his house and get him to tell me what Tom Paine would do in my place."

"You *are* pretty far gone, David. But I don't wonder at it; and I don't believe I think so badly of Matthew Braile either. He may be an infidel, but he believes in some kind of a God that wants people to do right; he don't believe in mortal sin, and may be that's where he's out; and I hear tell he don't think there's going to be any raising of the body, or any Last Day, or any Hell; but he keeps it to himself unless folks pester him. I was afraid once to have Joey talk with him, before the plow went over me. But now I let Joey go to him all he wants to. He lets Joey come and pet the coon Joey give him because he heard that the squire's little boy used to want one. From all I can make out they don't do much but talk about the little boy; he seems to take comfort in Joey because Joey's like him, or the Squire thinks so."

"If Jane had died when she was his little boy's age, I wouldn't feel as if I had lost her half as much as I do now."

Nancy lifted herself from her ironing board and looked at her brother. "You told me what the duty of a woman was that found out she had two husbands. Don't you know what the duty of a man is that has a daughter turned idolater?"

"No, I don't, Nancy," David answered doggedly.

"Then, why don't you wrestle with the Lord in prayer? Perhaps He'd make you some sign."

"Oh, prayer! The thought of it makes me sick since I saw them fools wallowing round at Dylks's feet, and beseeching that heathen image to save them."

"Then if you hain't got any light of yourself, and you don't believe the Lord can give you any, what do you expect smoking flax like *me* to do for you?"

"I don't expect anything, Nancy. If she was a child I could whip it out of her, but when your child has got to be a woman you can't whip her."

They left the hopeless case, and began to talk of the things they had heard, especially the miracle which Dylks had promised to work. "He appointed it for to-night," Gillespie said, "but I don't believe but what he'll put it off, if the coast ain't clear when the time comes. He always had the knack of leaving the back door open when he saw trouble coming up to the front gate."

"You can't tell me anything about Joseph Dylks," Nancy said. She was ironing, and at the last word she brought the iron down with the heavy thump that women give with it at an emphatic word in their talk. "What I wonder is that a man like you, David, could care what people in such a place as this would say if they found out that I was livin' with Laban when I knowed Dylks was alive. There wouldn't be any trouble with his followers, I reckon. He'd just tell 'em he never saw me in his life before, and that would do them."

"Nancy," her brother turned solemnly upon her, "as sure as I'm standing here I don't care for that any more. If you say the word, I'll go and tell Laban myself to come back to you."

"You're safe there, David. If you've parted with your conscience, I've got it from you. I wonder you don't go and follow after Joseph Dylks too. All the best and smartest men in the place believe in him. Just look at Mr. Enraghty! A man with more brains and book learnin' than all the rest put together; willin' to be the Apostle Paul because Joseph Dylks called him it, and gets up in the Temple where he used to preach Christ Jesus and Him crucified, and tells the people to behold their God in Joseph Dylks! There's just one excuse for him: he's crazy. If he ain't he's the wickedest man in Leatherwood, the wickedest man in the whole world; he's worse than Joseph Dylks, because he knows better. Joseph is such a liar that he could always make himself believe what he said. But it's no use your staying here, David!" she suddenly broke off to turn on her brother. "If you're a mind to let Jane come, I'll try what I can do with her."

The old man faltered at the door. "Are you going to tell her, Nancy?"

"I'm not going to tell *you*, whether I am or not, David!"

Her words began harshly, but ended with his name tenderly, almost pitifully, uttered.

She called after him as he moved from her door, heavily, weakly, more like an old man than she had noted him yet, "I'll talk to Jane, and whatever I say will be for her good." She watched him out of sight from where she was working; then she went to the door, with some mind to call more kindly yet to him; but he was not to be seen, and she went back to her ironing, and ironed more swiftly than before, moving her lips in a sort of wrathful revery. From time to time she changed her iron for one at the hearth, which she touched with her wetted finger to test its heat, and returned to her table with an unconscious smile of satisfaction in its quick responsive hiss. In her movements to and fro she spoke to the baby, which babbled inarticulately up to her from the floor. Then she seemed to forget it, and it was in one of these moments of oblivion that she was startled by a sharp cry of terror from it. A man was looking in at the door.

X

THE MAN stood with one foot on the log door-step outside and the other planted on the threshold of the cabin.

Nancy came toward him with her iron held at arm's length before her. "What do you want?" she demanded fiercely.

"Give me to drink," he said, with a grin.

"Go round to the well," she answered.

The man bent his body a little forward, and looked in, but he did not venture to lift his other foot to the threshold. "Where is your husband?" he asked.

"I have no husband. What is it to you?"

" 'Thou hast well said . . . he whom thou now hast, is not thy husband.' You don't look a bit older, and you're as handsome as ever, Nancy. I suppose that's his," he said, turning his eye towards the little one on the floor, lifted by her hands half upright, and peering at him, in conditional alarm.

"It's mine," she retorted.

"Oh, anybody could see that. It's the image of you. And so is our Joey. You don't let your young ones favor your husbands much, Nancy; and yet you was not always so set against me. What's your notion letting Joey come to the Temple?"

"To see for himself what you are."

"That's what I thought, maybe. Well, he don't seem to take to me much, if I can judge from his face when he looks my way. I hai'n't been able to give him all the attention I may later. But you needn't be troubled about him. I won't do anything to make you anxious. Nancy, I wish you could feel as friendly to me as I do to you. Will you let me have something to drink out of?"

"Go round," she said, "and I'll bring the gourd to you."

Dylks laughed, but he obeyed, and found his way to the well where he lowered the bucket at the end of the sweep, and stood waiting for Nancy to follow him with the dipper fashioned from a long-necked gourd, as the drinking cup oftenest was in the Western country of those days. She held it out to him, with her head turned and he carried it to his lips from the brimming bucket.

He drank it empty, and then turned it over with a long, deep "Ah—h—h!" of satisfaction. "That was good! Good as the butter-milk would have been that you didn't think to offer me. Well, I thank you for the water, anyway, you Woman of Samaria." He held the gourd toward her but she did not take it, and he laughed again. "If you could have had your way without sin you'd have made it poison, I reckon. Don't you know I could drink poison the same as water?"

"*You* don't," she said, and as he swung the gourd in tacit question what to do with it since she did not offer to take it, she bade him, "Put it down."

He did so, and she set her foot on the thin bowl and crushed it like an egg shell. He laughed. "Is that the way you feel about me, Nancy? Pity for the gourd, but don't you believe that if I was to will it so, it would come good and whole again?"

"*You* don't believe it," she said.

"It's not for me to believe or to unbelieve," he answered. "I am that I am."

"Oh yes," she taunted him, "you've tried saying such things, and you're not afraid because it ha'nt killed you yet. You think if you *was* just a man it would kill you."

"Who can tell what I think? Perhaps something like what you say has gone through my mind. Why, Nancy, if you would listen once, I could convince you of it, too. Come, now, look at it in this light! If God lets a man say and do what the man pleases— and He *has* to do it every now and then according to what the Book tells,—why ain't the man equal with God? You believe, maybe, that you would be struck dead if you said the things that

I do; but why ain't I struck dead? Why, either because it ain't so, at all, or because I'm God. It stands to reason, don't it? What is God, anyway? If he was so mighty and terrible, wouldn't he have ways of showing it in these times just as much as in those old times that we read about in the Book? Don't you know that if there was anything besides you and me, here now, it would have sent the lightning out of this clear sky and blasted me when I said, I was God? Well, now we'll try it again. Listen! *I am God*, Jehovah, ruler of heaven and earth!" He stood a moment, smiling. "There you see! I'm safe and sound as ever. May be you think it would be worse if *you* said I was God. Lots have said it. Last night all Leatherwood was hanging to my arms and legs down there in the Temple, worshipping me. If I hadn't been God it would have made me sick! No mere man could stand the praising God gets in the churches all the time. Why that proves I'm what I say I am, if nothing else does. I saw it from the first; I felt it; I knew it." He ended with his laugh.

She stayed herself by the trunk of the tree overhanging the well. "Yes, you've got all Leatherwood with you, or as good as all, and I don't wonder it's made you crazy. But don't you be so sure. Some day there's going to be a reckoning with you, and you're going to wake up from this dream of yours." She seemed to gather force as she faced him. "I could feel to be glad it *was* a dream; I could feel to pity you. But don't you believe but what it's going to turn against you. Some day, sooner or later, some man's going to show the people what you are; some woman"—

"There you've said it," he broke in. "That's what I've come for. You're the only woman that could hurt me, not because you think you know me the best, but because you're the bravest woman that ever was. That's why I've got to have you with me in my dispensation. Male and female created He them in His image. I can swing all Leatherwood by myself, but Leatherwood's nothing. If I had you with me we could swing the world! Nancy, why don't you come to me?" He flung his arms wide and bent his stalwart shape toward her. "Leatherwood's nothing, I tell you. Why, you ought to see the towns Over-the-Mountains, you ought to see Philadelphia, where I came from the last thing. Everywhere the people are waiting for a sign, just as they've always been, and we would come with a sign—plenty of signs: the perfect Godhead, male and female, for the greatest sign of all. Why, I wonder there's a Christian woman living, with the slur that the idea of just one male God throws on women! Don't you know that the Egyptians and the Greeks and the Romans, and everybody but the Hebrews, had a married God, and that the Godhead was husband and wife? If you had ever read anything at all you would know that."

The bad, vulgar beauty of his face, set in its flowing beard and hair, glowed on her.

"You needn't look that way at me, Joseph Dylks," she answered. "I don't want any book-l'arning to know what *you* are. You're what you always was, a lazy, good-for-nothing— Oh, I don't say you wasn't handsome; that was what done it for me when I made you my God; but I won't make you my God now, though you're as handsome as ever you was; handsomer, if that's any comfort to you."

"Nothing to what your coming to me would be, Nancy."

"You'll have to do without, then. You think you can twist me round your finger, like you used to, if you willed it, but I've outlived you, you and your will. Now I want you to go, and not ever come near me again; or I'll have Laban here, the next time."

"Laban? Laban? Oh, the man who is not thy husband! I'm not afraid of your having Laban, here; let him come. I've converted worse sinners than Laban." He had remained, bent forward with his gaze still on her; now he lifted himself, and said, as if it were another word of his spell, "Come, Nancy!"

She answered, "If I thought there was any mercy in you"—

"Why, I'm All-merciful, as well as All-powerful, Nancy!" he jeered.

"No," as if concluding her thought, she said, "it's no use! You couldn't do a right thing if you wanted to; you can only do wrong things. I see that."

"What is right and what is wrong? When you stand by my

side in your half of the godhead, you will know that there is no difference. Why, even a poor human being can make wrong right by wanting it enough, and with God there is nothing but one kind of thing, the thing that God allows. It don't matter whether it's letting the serpent tempt that fool woman in Eden, or Joseph's brethren selling him into Egypt, or Samuel hewing Agag in pieces, or the Israelites smiting the heathen, or David setting Uriah in the forefront of the battle, or Solomon having hundreds of wives: it's all right if God wills it. You'll say it's proved right by what happens to them that do wrong. Be God yourself and the right and the wrong will take care of themselves. I want you to come and help me. Why, with the sister and daughter of old David Gillespie both following me"—

She suddenly shrank from the grandeur of judging of him, to the measure of her need of his forbearance. "Oh, why can't you let David alone? What's he ever done to you?"

"What have I ever done to him?" Dylks demanded, temporizing on her ground.

"Why can't you let Jane alone?"

He gave his equine snort, as if the sense of his power could best vent itself so. "Why can't she let *me* alone? That girl bothers me worse than all the other women in Leatherwood put together. She won't *let* me let her alone."

"She was all right before you came. Why can't you let her go back to Hughey Blake?"

"Hughey Blake? Oh! Then it wasn't"— A light of malign intelligence shone in his eyes. "Well, I haven't got anything against Hughey Blake."

"Oh, if you'd only let her go back to Hughey! If you'd only let her alone, I'd"—

"You'd what?" He bounded toward her, and at her recoil he laughed and said, "I didn't mean to scare you."

"I wasn't scared. You can't scare *me*, Joseph Dylks. It's past that, long ago, with you and me. But if I only knowed what you was up to—what you would really take to let David alone; to let her go back to Hughey Blake— But there ain't any pity in you!"

"Don't I tell you I'm *full* of pity? Look here, Nancy; I don't ask you to come with me, to be one with me, to go halves in the godhead, all at once. It's been step by step with me: first exhorter, then prophet, then disciple, then the Son, then the Father: but it's been as *easy!* You don't know how faith, the faith of the elect, helps along; and you would have that from the beginning; they would take you on my word, you wouldn't have to say or do anything. But that's not what I'm expecting now," he hurried to add, smiling at the cloud of refusal in her face. "I'm not fooling; all I ask now is to have you come and see me do a miracle at Brother Hingston's tonight. I'll do *two* miracles if you'll come, and one will be sending Jane Gillespie away from me and back to Hughey Blake. You'll want to see that, even if you don't want to see me turn a bolt of cloth into seamless raiment by the touch of my hand."

"You are a wicked man, Joseph Dylks," the woman solemnly answered. "And I'm sorry I asked you anything. You *couldn't* do good, if you tried." She pulled her sunbonnet across her face, as if to hide it for shame, and went back slowly toward the cabin.

"Salvation!" Dylks shouted after her, and gave his equine snort. He began to sing, as he took his way through the woods,

"Plunged in a gulf of dark despair
We wretched sinners lay."

At first he sang boldly, filling the woods with the mocking of his hymn. But at the sound of footsteps crackling over the dry fallen twigs toward him intermittently, as if they paused in question, and then resumed their course toward him, his voice fell, brokenly silencing itself till at the encounter of a man glimpsed through the trees, and pausing in a common arrest, it ceased altogether.

"Who are you?" Dylks demanded of the slight, workworn figure before him.

"Laban Billings," the man faltered.

"Well, then, Laban Billings, make way for the Lord thy God," Dylks powerfully returned, and as if he had borne the man down before him, he strode over the place where he had stood and lost himself in the shadows beyond.

Laban hurried on, stumbling and looking back over his shoulder, till he found himself face to face with Nancy at the door of the shed behind the cabin. She was looking too in the direction where Dylks had ceased from their sight in the woods. They started from each other in mutual fright.

"Nancy!" he entreated. "I didn't see you. I—I wasn't comin' to see you, indeed, indeed I wasn't. I just thought I might ketch sight of the baby— It's pretty hard to do without you both!— And I was just passin'— Well, they've knocked off work at the Corners, so's to come to the miracle at Hingston's Mill tonight— But I'll go right away again, Nancy."

"You needn't, Laban. Come in and see the baby."

"Nancy!" he uttered joyfully. Then he faltered, "Do you think it will be right"—

"Oh, who knows what's right?" she retorted. Then at his stare, she demanded, "Didn't you run across anybody in the woods?"

"Yes."

"What did he look like?"

"Like what they tell the Leatherwood God looks like. They're half crazy about him at the Corners. They don't hardly talk about anything else."

"Did you think he looked like God?"

"More like Satan, I should say. He's handsome enough for Satan."

"It was Joseph Dylks."

"Yes, I s'picioned that."

"And he's been here, wanting me to go away with him— Over-the-Mountains."

Laban made a dry sound in his throat and it was by a succession of efforts that he could say, "And—and—and"—

"Oh, could you *ask*, Laban?" she lamented. "You're my husband, don't you know it?" At the sound of her lament a little voice of fear and hope answered from the cabin. The father-hunger came into the man's weak face, making it strong. "Come in and see our baby, Laban."

She put out her hand to him innocently like a little girl to a little boy, and he took it. "I know it's just for the baby; and I feel to thank you, Nancy," he said, and together they went into the cabin.

At sight of him the baby crowed recognition. "She knowed you in a minute," the mother said, and she straightened the skirt of the little one which the father had deranged in lifting the child from the floor. "I don't believe she'll ever forget you; I *reckon* she won't if I have any say in it. Me and Joey talks about you every night when we're gettin' her to sleep." She gurgled out a half-sob, half-laugh, as the little one pulled and pushed at his face, which he twisted this way and that, to get her hand in his mouth. "She always cared more for you than she did for me. I'll set you a piece, Laban; I was just going to get me a bite of something; I don't take my meals very regular, with you not here."

"Well, I *am* a little hungry with the walk from the Corners, after such an early breakfast."

"Well, you just keep her."

"Oh, *I'll* keep her," he exulted.

She bustled about the hearth getting the simple meal, which she made more than she had meant, and they had a joyful, strange time together at the leaf she stayed from the wall.

He kept the baby in his lap while he ate. Then he walked the floor till she fell asleep in his arms. When he lifted himself from laying her in the rough cradle which he had himself made for her, he said, without looking at the mother, "Now, I must be going, Nancy."

"Don't go on account of me, Laban," she said with the same fierce courage she had shown in driving him from her before. "If it's for me"—

"Nancy, I've thought it all out since I been away. And I reckon I ain't your husband, in the sight of God. You was right about that; and I won't ever come back again till—as long as"— He glanced wistfully at the little one in the cradle, and then he turned to go out of the door. "And—and—good bye, Nancy."

She followed him to the door. "Kiss me, Laban!"

He put away the arms she lifted toward him. "No," he said, "I reckon it wouldn't be right," and he turned and walked swiftly away, without looking back.

XI

THE WOMAN stood watching the man, as long as she could see him, and long after, with her left hand lifted to the jamb of the door, higher than her head. Then from the distance where he passed from sight over the brow of the hill, the figure of another man appeared, and slowly made its way down to the cabin. As she knew while he was still far off, it was Matthew Braile who, as long as he sat in the seat of the scorner, with his chair tilted against the wall, seemed a strong middle-aged man; but when he descended from his habitual place, with the crook of his stick, worn smooth by use, in his hard palm, one saw that he was elderly and stiff almost to lameness. He carried himself with a forward droop, and his gaze bent ponderingly on the ground, as if he were not meaning to look her way, and would pass without seeing her.

"Squire Braile!" she called to him, and as he straightened himself and turned round toward her, she besought him, "Do you believe there's any God?"

"Oh!" he answered, and he smiled at the challenge from the somewhat lonely elevation which he knew the thoughts of his neighbors kept aloof from the sordid levels of politics and business. "Why, Nancy, haven't we got one, right here in Leatherwood?"

"That's what makes me think there ain't any, Squire Braile. If you're not in too much of a hurry, I wish you'd stop and talk to me a minute. I'm in trouble."

"Most women are; or men, for the matter of that. What is it,

Nancy? I'm rather stronger on law than gospel; but if I can be any help, why you know your Joey's an old friend of mine, and I'll be glad to help you."

He came toward her where she had stepped from the threshold and sat crouched on the hewn log, and stood looking down at her.

"You may think it's pretty strange, my asking *you* for help. Won't you set? I can't let you come inside because the baby's just got to sleep."

"Well," he assented, "if you're not afraid to be seen with such an infidel in the full light of day," he jested, confronting her from the log where he sank beside her. "What would Brother Gillespie say?"

She ignored his kindly mockery, and again she began, "What makes you believe there's a God? You don't believe in the Bible?"

"Not altogether, Nancy."

"Do you believe in the Bible God?"

"As much as the Bible'll let me."

"Then, do you believe in the miracles?"

"What are you after, Nancy Billings?"

"If you saw a miracle, would you believe it?"

"That would depend on who did it. Now, I want you to let *me* do a little of the catechising. I've liked you and Laban ever since you came to Leatherwood, and you know how your Joey has all but brought my boy back to me. Well, do *you* believe in God?"

"No!"

"Why don't you?"

"A God that would let Joseph Dylks claim to be Him, and let them poor fools kneel down to him and worship him? Would an all-wise and all-powerful God do that?"

"What makes you say all-powerful? Haven't you seen time and time again when good didn't prevail against evil, and don't you suppose He'd have helped it if He could? And why do you call Him all-wise? Is it because men are no-wise? That wouldn't prove it, would it? And about the miracles, what does a miracle prove? Does it prove that the person who does it is of God, or just that faith is stronger than reason in those who think it's happened?"

"But sin: do you think there's such a thing?" Nancy pursued.

"There you are, catechizing *me* again! Yes, I think there's sin, because I've known it in myself, if I haven't in others."

"And what is it: sin?"

"Well, Nancy, it seems to vary according to the time and place. But I should say it was going against what you knew was right at the time being."

"And do you always know?"

"Always!" the old man answered solemnly. "I never was mistaken in my life, whether I went for or against it, and I've done both."

The woman drew a hapless sigh. "Yes, I reckon it's so."

Braile was putting out his stick to help himself in rising, after the silence she let follow. She came from it, and reached a staying hand toward him. "And supposin'—supposin'—there was a woman—that there was a woman, and her husband left her, and he kept away years and years, till she thought he was dead, and she married somebody else, and then he come back, would it be a sin for her to keep on with the other one when she knowed the first one was alive?"

"I reckon that's what would be called a sin, Nancy. Not that I'd be very quick to condemn her"—

"And supposin' that the first one hadn't claimed her yet, and she'd made the other one leave her, and then the first one come and wanted her to join him in the wickedest thing that ever was, and she wasn't as strong as she had been, and she felt to need the protection-like of the other one: would it be a sin for her to take him back?"

Braile made again as if to rise. "I reckon you'd better talk to Mis' Braile about a thing like that. You see, a man"—

She stayed him again with a beseeching gesture. "Squire Braile, do you believe that God is good?"

"Ah, now, I'm more at home in a question like that. You might say that if He lets evil prevail, it's either because He can't help it, or because He don't care, or even because He thinks it's best for mankind to let them have their swing when they choose to do evil. I incline to think that's my idea. He's made man, we'll say, made him in His own image, and He's put him here in a world of his own, to do the best or the worst with it. The way I look at it, He doesn't want to keep interfering with man, but lets him play the fool or play the devil just as he's a mind to. But every now and then He sends him word. If we're going to take what the Book says, He sent him Word made flesh, once, and I reckon He sends him Word made Spirit whenever there's a human creature comes into the world, all loving and all unselfish —like your Joey, or—my—my Jimmy"—

The old man's voice died in his throat, and the woman laid her hand on his knee. He trembled to his feet, now. "When I think of such Spirits coming into this world, I'm not afraid of all the devils out of hell Dylksing round."

He walked on down the road, and Nancy went indoors and went about her household work. She cleaned the dishes and trimmed the hearth; she spun the flax which tufted her wheel; then she took the rags of some garments past repair, and in the afternoon shadow of her threshold she cut them into ribbons and sewed them end to end and wound them into balls, for weaving into carpets.

People, as the evening drew on, went by, singly, in twos, or in groups, silent for the most part, but some talking seriously. These looked at Nancy without speaking, but some asked, "Ain't you goin' to the Miracle?" and she shook her head for answer.

She had brushed her hair and put it up neatly after her indoors work was done, but she was in what she would have called her everyday clothes, and the passers had on their Sunday clothes; the girls wore their newest plaids of linsey-woolsey, and the young men wore tall beaver hats, and long high-collared coats, with tight pantaloons, which some pretenders to the latest fashions had strapped under their boots. They had on their Sunday faces, too, some severe, some sly, some simple and kind, but all with an effect of condition for whatever might be going to happen.

They went as the people of Leatherwood went to the Temple on the Sabbaths before their meetings had been turned from the orderly worship of the Most High to the riot of emotions raised by the strange man who proclaimed himself God. In their expectation of the Sign which he had promised to give them, both those who believed and those who denied him found themselves in a sort of truce. They were as if remanded to the peace of the time before the difference which had rent the community into warring fragments. In this truce brothers were speaking who had not spoken since they accepted or refused the new God; families walked together in the harmony which he had lately counselled; children honored their believing or disbelieving parents; fathers and mothers ceased to abhor their children as limbs of Satan, according to their faith or unfaith. "Let everybody come to the Sign," he had exhorted them when he promised them the miracle, "just as if they had never seen or heard me before, and let His creatures judge their Creator with love for one another in their hearts."

In all there was an air of release, and the young people looked as if they were going to one of the social gatherings they would have called a frolic, in the backwoods phrase. Nancy heard a girl titter in response to her companion's daring whisper, "Wonder if Mis' Hingston's going to pass round the apples and cider." They walked in couples, openly or demurely glad of being together for the time; and as if the miracle before them were the wonder of coming home through the woods with their arms around each other, whether the miracle of the seamless raiment was wrought or not.

It was their elders who were more singly set upon the fulfillment of the sign, and who went with a more passionate expectation in the doubt or the faith which differenced them; the children were more bent upon the affair of the evening than the young girls and the young men. They had been privileged in being allowed to go with their fathers and mothers when they had not been punished in being left at home and they subdued themselves as they could to the terms of keeping step beside them with the bare feet that felt winged and ached to fly. Old and young they passed Nancy's cabin thinly or at intervals; they glanced kindly or unkindly askance at her when they did not question her, and very possibly they read in her sitting there boldly aloof from them a defiance of the question which had begun to gather about her in the common mind since Laban had left her for his work at the Cross Roads, with none of those Saturday night returns which had at first been expected. It was known that Laban was of the same opposition to Dylks as Nancy and her brother, and it could not be that Dylks had caused the break between her and Laban which no one would have noticed if it had been an effect of religion. It could only be that Laban had left her, or that her temper had driven him away.

With the last came a crowd of boys, whose lagging she understood when her own boy jumped down from the cabin door beside her.

"Did I scare you, mother?" he asked, at her start.

"No; I was expecting you, and you always come in at the back. You'll want your supper, I'll be bound. What made you so late, and all out of breath, so?"

"I been running. We just got the last of the tobacco in, this evening, and Mis' Hingston made me stay and eat with Benny; she said she'd excuse me to you. I just left the other boys up over the hill, and run through the woods to get here in time and ask you."

"To ask me what, Joey dear?" She put her arms fondly round the boy's knees, and pulled him down to her.

"The boys said you let me go to the Temple all I want to; but I told them the Miracle was different, and I'd have to ask you first. I told Mis' Hingston, and I told the boys. Me 'n' Benny got them to come round. Kin I, mother? Mis' Hingston thought may be—may be—you might come yourself. But I told her I didn't believe you would."

"No, I won't go, Joey. What makes *you* want to go?"

"Oh, I don't know. All the boys are goin'. And I never seen a miracle, yet."

"Do you believe he can do a miracle?" she asked.

"Well, it would be some fun to see what he would do if he didn't. I'd like to hear what he'd say."

"And what would you think if he did do it? That he was—God?"

"Oh, *no*, mother! He couldn't be, Mr. Dylks couldn't. I ain't ever thought for a minute that he was *that*."

"And if he failed—if he tried, and put himself to shame before everybody, how would you feel?"

"Well, mother, nobody as't him to." Nancy was silent for so long, that the boy said discouragedly, "But if you don't want me to go"—

Her face hardened from the pity of her inward vision of the man's humiliation, as if his own son had judged him justly. "Yes, you can go, Joey. But be careful, be careful! And don't stay too late. And if anything happens"—

"Oh, surely, mother, nothing will *happen*," he exulted, and he broke from her hold and ran down the road where the group of boys had waited for him, and as he ran he leaped into the air, and called to them, "She's let me; she's let me!" and the boys leaped up in response, and called back, "Hurrah, hurrah!" and when he had come up with them, they all tried to get their arms round him, and trod on his heels and toes in pushing one another from him.

In the August twilight which now began to pale the hot sunset glow, as if she had waited to come alone, in her pride or in her shame, the woman who was bearing the body of the miracle to the place where the wonder was to be wrought, came last of all to pass Nancy where she sat at her door. She was that strong believer who in her utter trust, when she heard that cloth would be needed for the seamless raiment of his miracle, had offered to provide it; and now, neither in pride nor in shame, but in defiance of her unbelieving husband, she was bearing away from her house the bolt of linsey-woolsey newly home from the weaver, which was to have been cut into the winter's clothing of her children. She had spun the threads herself and dyed them, and they had become as if they were of her own flesh and blood. She carried the bolt wrapped about with her shawl, bearing it tenderly in her arms, as if it were indeed her flesh and blood, her babe which she was going to lay upon an altar of sacrifice.

XII

THE CROWD at Hingston's Mill grew with the arrival of the unbelievers as well as the believers in Dylks. They came from all sides, sometimes singly and sometimes in groups, and the groups came disputing as often as agreeing among themselves. When a group was altogether believing they exchanged defiances with a party of those religious outcasts the Hounds, disturbers of camp-meetings and baptisms, and notorious mockers, now, of the Leatherwood god in his services at the Temple. But the invitation given to see the promised miracle had been *to all*; the Hounds had felt in it the tenor of a challenge, and they had accepted it defiantly. They jeered at the believers as these arrived, sometimes hailing them by name; they neighed and whinnied, and shouted "Salvation!" and in the intervals of silence they burst out with the first lines of the Believers' hymn. There were those who mocked, "I am God Almighty," "The Father and the Son are one, and I am both of 'em put together," and "Oh, Dylks, save us!" "Don't leave us, Dylks!" "Make the Devil jump, Joseph! Make him rattle his scales for us!" "Fetch on your miracle!" The believing women turned away; some of the younger tittered hysterically at a droll profanation of their idol's name, and then one of the ruffians applauded. "That's right, sisters! We like to have you enjoy yourselves. Promised to let anybody in particular see you home tonight?" The girls tried to control themselves, and laughed the more, and the Hound called, "Say, girls, let's have a dance—a dance before the Lord."

Jane Gillespie had come with her father in the family pride

which forbade them to reject each other publicly. The girl stood a little apart from her father, and near her hung, wistfully, fearfully, the young farmer whom the neighborhood gossip had assigned her for an acceptable if not accepted lover. She looked steadfastly away from Hughey Blake, with her head lifted and her cheeks coldly flushed under the flame of her vivid hair: she was taller than the other girls, and showed above the young man.

"Say, Hughey," one of the Hounds spoke across the space they had left between them and the decent unbelievers, "Can't you gimme a light? Reach up!" He held out a cigar, in the joke of kindling it at the girl's hair.

Hughey Blake turned, and his helpless retort, "You ought to be ashamed of yourself," redoubled the joy of the Hounds. The girl glanced quickly at him, with what meaning he could not have made out, and it might have been fear of her which kept him hesitating whether to cross over and fall upon his tormentor. He looked at her as if for a sign, but she made as if she had heard nothing; then while he still hesitated a slender, sinewy young fellow came down the open ground, with a soft jolt in his gait like that of a rangy young horse. He wore high boots with his trousers pushed carelessly into their tops, and for a sign of weekday indifference to the occasion, a checked shirt, of the sort called hickory; he struck up the brim of his platted straw hat in front with one hand, and with the other on his hip stood a figure of backwoods bravery, such as has descended to the romance of later times from the reality of the Indian-fighting pioneers.

"You fellows keep still!" he called out. "If you don't I'll make you."

Retorts of varied sense and nonsense came from the Hounds, but without malice in their note. One voice answered, "I'd like to see you try, Jim Redfield!"

The other jolted closer toward the line of the Hounds, and leaned over. "Did I hear somebody speak?" he asked.

"I reckon not, Jim," the voice of his challenger returned. "Come to join the band?"

"I didn't come to worry helpless women," Redfield said.

"That's right, Jim. There's where we're with you. D'you reckon Apostle Hingston'll let us in to see the miracle if we'll keep the believers straight while the Almighty is at it?"

"I can't say for Mr. Hingston," Redfield returned. "But if I was in his place I'd want to keep my jug out of sight when you fellows were on duty."

Redfield passed the Gillespies as he lounged back to his place with a covert glance at the girl, who made no sign of seeing her champion.

The woman who was bringing the body of the miracle came round the corner of the mill, and showed herself in the open space with the bolt of cloth borne carefully in her arms.

"Why, it's a baby!" came from that merriest of the Hounds whom Redfield had turned from an enemy into a troublesome friend of the believers. "Reckon the women'll have something to say to that if he tries to turn e'er a baby into seamless raiment."

The fellow got the laugh he had tried for, and when Redfield looked toward him again he said, "All right, Jim. I'm keepin' 'em quiet the best I can. But the elect *will* make a noise, sometimes."

The woman with her bundle passed through the open door of the house behind the mill. The public entrance was at the front where by day the bags of grain were lifted by rope and tackle to the upper story, and the farmers who brought them climbed up by the inner stairways. The believers had expected that they were to come in by way of the dwelling, but now the burly figure of the miller, with the light of a candle behind it, showed black in the doorway, and he spoke up, in his friendly voice: "Neighbors, we want you all to go round to the front of the mill and come in there. The miracle is going to be done on the bolting-cloth floor, where there will be room for all that wants to see. We don't mean to keep anybody out, whether they believe or don't believe. The only thing we want is for you all to be quiet, and not make trouble. And now, come in as quick as you can, so you can be sure we haven't had time to do anything to the cloth that the seamless raiment is going to be made out of."

"Hounds and everybody?" called that gayest voice among the outcasts.

"Hounds and everybody," the miller humorously assented, and his black bulk melted into the dark as the candle disappeared within.

The dim light from tin lanterns threw the pattern of their perforations on the walls and roofs of the interior, and showed the tracery of the floury cobwebs. The people could scarcely see their way to the stairs by the glimmer, and there was more talking with nervous laughter than there had been outside. One of the Hounds called out, "I don't want any of you girls to kiss *me!*" and gave the relief of indignation to the hysterical emotion of the believers; the more serious of the unbelievers found escape in their helpless laughter from their tense expectation of triumph in the failure of the promised miracle.

The wide space on the bolting-cloth floor, before the bins, mounded high with new wheat, and the rows of mill stones, motionless under their empty hoppers, was lighted by candles in tin sconces, but these were so few that they shone only on the foremost faces and left those behind a gleam of eyes or teeth. The familiar machinery had put on a grewsome strangeness which had its final touch from the roll lying on the table like something dead. A table had been set in front of the barrels under the bolting cloths, and the muslin funnels, empty of flour, hung down into the barrels with the effect of colossal legs standing in them. The air of the hot night was close within; a damp odor from the water flowing under the motionless mill wheels seemed to cool it, but did not; the perspiration shone on the faces where the light fell on them.

The miller and his family had places in the front line of the spectators, and with them was the woman who had given the cloth for the miracle; and who stood staring at the stuff, which she had known so intimately in every thread and fibre, with an air of estrangement.

When the stumbling feet of the last arrivals ceased on the stairs, the miller stood out facing the crowd, and told them that he expected the Good Old Man, now, any minute, together with the Apostle Paul, whom they all knew by his earthly name as their neighbor Mr. Enraghty. He asked them to be as still as they could, and especially after the Good Old Man came, to be perfectly silent; not to whisper, and not to move if they could help it. There was nothing, though, he said, to hinder the believers from joining in their favorite hymn; and at once the wailing of it began to fill the place. When it ended, the deep drawn breath of some wearied expectant made itself heard with the shifting of tired feet easing themselves. The minutes grew into an hour, with no sign of Dylks or Enraghty, and the miller was again forced to ask the patience of his neighbors. But there began to be murmurs from the unbelievers, and more articulate protests from the Hounds. Some children, whom the believers had brought with them to see the divine power manifest itself, whimpered, and were suffered to lie down at the feet of their fathers and mothers, and forget their disappointment in sleep. A babe, too young to be left at home, woke and cried, and was suckled to rest again, with ironical applause from the Hounds.

At the end of two hours of waiting, relieved with pleas and promises from the miller, there was no word from Dylks, and no token of his bodily presence. With the scoffing of the unbelievers, the prayers of the faithful rose. "Come soon, oh Lord!" "Send thy Power!" "Remember thy Little Flock!" Upon these at last broke falteringly, stragglingly, a familiar voice, the voice of Abel Reverdy, kindly and uncouth as himself, and expressive, like his presence, of an impartial interest in the feelings of both the faithful and the unfaithful. He was there in the company of his wife, who held a stedfast place among the believers, while Abel ranged freely from one party to the other, and could not well have known himself of either, though friendly with both. He was of a sort of disapproving friendship even with the Hounds, and now his voice said, in impartial suggestion, "Why not somebody go and fetch him?"

"Good for you, Abel!" came from the Hound who was oftenest spokesman for the others. "Why don't you go yourself, Abel?"

Other voices applauded, and Abel was beginning to share a general confidence in his fitness for the mission, when his wife spoke up, " 'Deed and 'deed, I can tell you he ain't agoun' to do no such a thing, not if we stay here all night, murricle or no murricle. I ain't agoun' to have him put his head into the Lion of Judah's mouth, and have it bit off, like as not. I can't tell from one minute to another whether he's a believer or not, and if anybody is to go for the Good Old Man it's got to be a studdy believer, and not a turn-coat of many colors like Abel."

If Sally had satisfied her need of chastising her husband for his variableness, and found a comfort in her scriptural language, not qualified by its wandering application, Abel loyally accepted her open criticism. "That's so, Sally, I ain't the one to send. I misdoubted it myself, or I'd 'a' gone without sayin' nothin' in the first place. But, as Sally says," he addressed the crowd, "it ought to be a believer."

"Then why not Sally?" a scorner suggested. She did not refuse, and there was a whispering between her and those next her, in debate of the question. But it was closed by the loud, austere voice of one of the believing matrons in the apostolic mandate, "Let your women keep silence in the churches." The text was not closely apt; it was not a precept obeyed in the revivals of any of the sects in Leatherwood; it was especially ignored in the meetings of the Dylks believers; but its proclamation now satisfied the yearning always rife in them to affiliate their dispensation with the scriptural tradition.

"Well, that settles it, Sister Coombs," Sally promptly assented, "I wusn't agoun' to any way, and I ain't agoun' to now, if I stay here all night, or the Good Old Man don't ever come."

"Why not Jim Redfield?" a Hound demanded, and the miller tried to be stern in calling out, "No trifling!" but lost effect by gently adding, "Friends." The unbelievers laughed, but the miller's retreat from the bold stand he had taken was covered by Redfield's threat that if those fellows kept on he would give them something to laugh about.

As he stepped into the neutral space between the friends and enemies of Dylks he had a sort of double fearfulness for the women, because he was not only not of their faith, but because he was of no religious sect in a community where every one but an open infidel like Matthew Braile was of some profession. He came to the Baptist services with his mother, but he had not been baptized, and he was not seen at the house to house prayer meetings, where the young people came with the old, or at the frolics where dancing was forbidden, but not kissing in their games or in their walks home through the woods. He was not supposed to be in love with any one, and he lived alone on a rich bottomland farm with his mother, in a house which his father had built where his grandfather's log cabin had stood. He was of a tradition which held him closer to the wilderness than most of the people of Leatherwood; in the two generations before him the Redfields had won and held their lands against the Indians, and had fought them in the duels, from tree to tree, which the pioneers taught the savages, or learned from them, risking their lives and scalps in the same chances. He was of the sort of standing which old family gives, even where all families are new, and he was now making his way politically, in spite of his irreligion; he meant to go to the legislature, eventually, and in a leisurely sort he was reading law, and reciting his Blackstone to Matthew Braile. As he came and went from the old infidel's house, he was apt to stop at the tavern porch, where the few citizens who could detach their minds from the things of another world gave them in cloudy conjecture to the political affairs of this, or to scrutiny of the real motives actuating the occasional travelers who apparently arrived for a meal's victuals or a night's lodging. With these Redfield had scarcely a social tie, but he could talk with them almost to the point of haranguing them, for they were men; at the store, where his mother's errands sometimes took him, he shrank from the women as timid as they when they dismounted from their saddles or wagons, and slipped in with their butter and eggs, and passed out again deeply obscured in their sunbonnets.

They were mostly women past the time of life when men look

at them curiously, but once Redfield was startled by meeting a young girl, as he was trying to go out, and began losing himself with her in that hopeless encounter of people who try to give way to each other and keep passing to the same side at once. Her face and her red hair burned one fire, but at last she stopped stone still, and let him go by, with a sort of angry challenge in her blue eyes. He knew that it was Jane Gillespie without knowing her to speak with, as he would have said, and he knew that against her father's will she was one of the followers of Dylks. The idolatry was not yet open and scandalous, but since then he had heard his mother denouncing her as a worthless hussy with the other women who had worshipped Dylks in that frenzy at the Temple. He walked up and down, passing near where she stood with her father and Hughey Blake, and lost his breath at each approach and caught it again at each remove. It so vividly seemed that he must speak to her, though he did not know what he wished to say, that it was as if he really had done so, when he heard one of the Hounds saying, "Well, and what are you goin' to do about it, Jim?"

Then he heard himself boasting, "I'm going after Dylks myself; and if he'll come peaceably, and do his miracle I'll take him for my god, and if he won't, God have mercy on him!"

He was answering his jeering questioner in his words, but his eyes were on the girl; her own eyes were lowered after a glance at her father and Hughey Blake, and his vow remained in his ears a foolish vaunt. While he stood unable to return to his place, a voice which no one knew, came from the darkness outside.

"Behold," it said, "I am the Presence of the Most High, and I come to you with my Peace. The miracle that ye wait to see has been wrought already unseen of you. The cloth before you has been touched by my Power, and turned into the seamless raiment which ye seek as a sign. But it shall not be shown to you now. Ye shall see it seven days and seven nights hence on the eighth night at the Temple. Till then, have patience, have faith. Thus saith the Lord."

The voice died from the medley of scriptural phrase and a

shiver of awe passed over those who had heard. One of the believing women called out, "Praise ye the Lord!" Then a yell of mockery broke from the Hounds and some one shouted, "Let's have a look!" and the crowd rushed upon the roll of cloth which lay on the table, where the woman who had brought it in her arms had put it, and had stood patiently, anxiously, trustfully waiting.

She spread her arms out over it, with a piteous gesture, like a mother trying to keep her child from harm. "Oh, don't, oh, don't!" she implored. "It's *my* cloth! I spun it, I wove it, every thread! It's all we've got for our clothes this winter! Don't touch it, don't tear it!"

Her prayer was like a signal for its denial. One of the Hounds pushed her away and caught the cloth up. "We won't hurt it, Sister Bladen. We just want to see what a seamless garment looks like, anyway. Maybe it'll fit some of us. Here, boys, take a hold!"

He held by the outer edge of the cloth, and flung the bolt unfurling itself toward his fellows over the heads of the believing men who had crowded forward to save it from the desecration, while the woman tried to seize it from him, beseeching, imploring, "Oh, don't hurt it, Bill Murray! Oh, be careful! Don't let it drop! Oh, don't, don't, don't!"

"We can't do it any hurt, Sister Bladen, if it's got a miracle inside of it," one of the ruffians mocked. "*You* tell her we won't hurt it, Jim Redfield! She'll trust *you !*"

The women believers were sobbing; the men gathered themselves for a struggle with the surprise sprung upon them, but held back as if in a superstitious hope of help from the god whom the women seemed not to trust in his failure of them.

"Here, you fellows!" Redfield shouted over the tossing heads before him. "What do you want to spoil her cloth for?"

His look and voice had their effect with the angry, pushing, shuffling, elbowing, wailing, weeping crowd, in a pause like the arrest of curiosity.

"Let go that cloth, Bill," he said, not with authority, but in a tone of good fellowship.

The miller interposed with his friendly voice, and it seemed as if the unbelievers would give way in pity of the poor woman who had brought the cloth. Suddenly the bolt of stuff which Murray had conditionally yielded was twitched from Redfield in boisterous fun, and then in the frenzy more of mischief than of malice it was seized by the Hounds, and torn into shreds. "Find the seamless raiment!" they yelled to one another. The unbelievers stood aside; the believers did nothing, in a palsy of amaze; the poor woman, to whom her toil and pride in it had hallowed the stuff, sank down staying herself on her hands from the floor, in hapless despair. Her moaning and sobbing filled the place after the tumult of destruction had been stricken silent. "Oh, I don't care for the miracle," she kept lamenting, "but what are my children going to wear this winter? Oh, what will *he* say to me!" It was her husband she meant.

XIII

THE RIOT in Hingston's mill, after the failure of Dylks to appear personally and work the promised miracle, left the question of his divinity where it had been. With no evident change in their numbers on either side, the believers assented, the unbelievers denied. The faithful held that the miracle had been wrought and the seamless raiment had been torn to pieces by the mob; some declared that they had seen the garments, and tried to keep them from the sacrilege but had been overpowered. The unfaithful laughed at the pretence, and defied the faithful to show any scrap of the cloth having the form of clothing. The pieces remained with the poor woman who had brought the cloth for the miracle; she carried them home, weeping, and she and her husband remained like the rest, believing and unbelieving as before; but at every chance she scanned the desecrated fragments in secret, and pieced them together, trying to follow the lines of imaginary garments in them.

Throughout the week the excitement raged, silently for the most part in the breasts of the two parties, but sometimes breaking out in furious affirmation and denial at such points of common meeting as the store, the tavern, and the postoffice. There the unbelievers outnumbered the believers, who met for mutual support and comfort at one another's houses, but appeared nowhere in force until the Sunday night following; then they came three to one of the enemy, and filled the Temple to overflowing. Dylks was expected to meet them from the concealment or the absence in which he had passed the days; the unbelievers said that he was hiding in fear and shame; the believers that he was preaching to the heathen in other neighborhoods, and would come in power and glory with a great multitude of the converted following him. But the meeting in the Temple was opened by Enraghty, who, in front of the pulpit, rose saying, "The Good Old Man will not be here, tonight, but I will fill his place." A thrill of exultation and disappointment ran through the congregation, according as they believed or disbelieved, but they all waited patiently.

Among the many families which had come in internecine enmity, Gillespie and his daughter strained in the unlove which was like hate up to the door of the Temple. He had taunted her with Dylks's failure to work the miracle and with his absence during the week. "If I could get my hands on him, I would pull him out of his hole, and make him face the people he's deceived. I'd show him whether he was God or not."

"If you touched him, your hands would be withered," she said in an ecstasy of faith. "If you will bring me a single hair of his head I will deny him."

"I'll remember that," he threatened bitterly, and in the loss of all the dignity of their relation as parent and child he cast a look of contemptuous triumph on her when Enraghty rose and said that he would take the place of Dylks for the night.

"Bring me one hair of his head," she said again.

The people of both sides had supposed that Dylks was sitting behind the pulpit, as his habit was, with his head out of sight bowed in meditation. But when Enraghty, after a few words, sat down to await the coming of the spirit, suddenly the minister whose turn to preach would have come that night, sprang to his full height in the pulpit and denounced Enraghty's pretence. The believers rose shouting to their feet, and crying, "He is my God!" stormed out of the Temple in the night, where their voices were heard repeating "He is my God!" till they swelled together in the hymn which was their confession of Dylks. A few of the unbelievers remained in the Temple, amazed, but the greater part followed the believers into the night.

They had the courage of their triumph through Dylks's failure to work the miracle he had promised, and then his failure to show himself in the Temple; but they pushed on with no definite purpose except perhaps to break up some meeting of his followers, when one of the Hounds, yelping and baying in acceptance of their nickname, broke upon them from the woods they were passing with word that they had found Dylks in Enraghty's house, where the believers were already gathering.

"We've treed him," he said. "The whole pack's round the place, and there's no limb in reach for him to jump to. I reckon it'll be the best coon hunt we've ever had in Leatherwood, yit."

Redfield put himself in touch rather than in sight amidst the darkness which the disembodied voices broke upon. "Enraghty's house? Then we've got him. Come on!"

The women of the unbelievers had fallen behind and finally gone home, but all the believers, the women as well as the men, had followed their apostle, and now their voices, in praying and singing, came from the house still hidden by a strip of woodland. In the bewilderment which had fallen upon David Gillespie amid the tumultuous rush from the Temple, he had been parted from his daughter; now he fumbled forward on the feet of an old man, and found himself beside Redfield. "I want you to let me at him first, Jim. I just want one hair of his head."

"Why, don't you know it's death to touch him?" Redfield jeered.

"I know that," Gillespie assented in the same mood. "But I'll risk dying for that one hair."

"What do you want with one hair? I'll get you a handful," Redfield said.

"One'll do to work the miracle I'm after."

"What miracle? None o' your seamless raiment, is it?"

"It's bringin' a crazy girl to her senses. She's said if I fetched her a single hair of his she'd renounce him."

"Oh!" Redfield said with respectful understanding. Then he added, "I'll get you the hair."

The unbelievers crowded to the house in the light from the

uncurtained windows. One of them stood tiptoe peering in while the others waited. "It's chuck full," he reported. "No room for sinners, I reckon."

"Oh, if Dylks is in there he'll work one of his miracles and *make* room," another of the Hounds retorted. Redfield stood trying the door. "Locked? Hammer on it! Break it in! Here! Give him a shoulder!"

The mob pushed forward, laughing and shouting, and crushed Redfield against the door. The panel cracked and groaned; Redfield called to the crowd to hold back, but suddenly the door opened, and the fanatical face of Enraghty showed itself above Redfield's back.

"What do you want?" he demanded. "This is the Lord's house."

"Then it's as much ourn as what it is yourn," some one shouted back.

"We want to *see* the Lord," another called. "Just one look, just one lick."

The old schoolmaster lost his self-control. "There are some of you out there that I've licked before now for your mischief."

"Yes, we know that," came back. "You didn't lick us enough. We'd like to have you give us some more."

The hindmost of the Hounds surged against those in front, and the whole mob fell forward upon Redfield; he staggered over the threshold to save himself, and struck Enraghty backward in his helpless plunge.

"Oh, look out there!" the nearest of the mob called back. "You're hurtin' Mr. Enraghty!"

"Well, we don't want to hurt old Saint Paul!" a mocker returned; but they pressed on wilfully, helplessly; they pushed those in front, who might have held back, and filled the entryway and the rooms beyond. In a circle of his worshippers, kneeling at his feet, stood Dylks, while they hailed him as their God and entreated his mercy. At the scramble behind them, they sprang up and stood dazed, confronting their enemies.

"We want Dylks! We want the Good Old Man! We want the

Lion of Judah! Out o' the way, Little Flock!'' came in many voices; but when the worshippers yielded, Dylks had vanished.

A moment of awe spread to their adversaries, but in another moment the riot began again. The unbelievers caught the spirit of the worst among them and stormed through the house, searching it everywhere, from the cellar to the garret. A yell rose from them when they found Dylks half way up the chimney of the kitchen. His captors pulled him forward into the light, and held him cowering under the cries of "Kill him!" "Tie him to a tree and whip him!" "Tar and feather him!" "Ride him on a rail!"

"No, don't hurt him!" Redfield commanded. "Take him to a justice of the peace and try him."

"Yes," the leader of the Hounds assented. "Take him to Squire Braile. He'll settle with him."

The Little Flock rallied to the rescue, and some of the Herd joined them. As an independent neutral, Abel Reverdy, whom his wife stirred to action, caught up a stool and joined the defenders.

"Why, you fool," a leader of the Hounds derided him amiably, "what you want to do with that stool? If the Almighty can't help himself, you think *you're* goin' to help him?"

Abel was daunted by the reasoning, and even Sally stayed her war cries.

"Well, I guess there's sumpin' *in* that," Abel assented, and he lowered his weapon.

The incident distracted his captors and Dylks broke from them, and ran into the yard before the house. He was covered with soot and dust and his clothes were torn; his coat was stripped in tatters, and his long hair hung loose over it.

His prophecies of doom to those who should lay hands upon him had been falsified, but to the literal sense of David Gillespie he had not yet been sufficiently proved an impostor: till he should bring his daughter a strand of the hair which Dylks had proclaimed it death to touch, she would believe in him, and David followed in the crowd straining forward to reach Redfield, who with one of his friends had Dylks under his protection. The old man threw himself upon Dylks and caught a thick strand of his hair, dragging him backward by it. Redfield looked round. He said, "You want that, do you? Well I promised." He tore it from the scalp, and gave it into David's hand, and David walked back with it into the house where his daughter remained with the wailing and sobbing women-worshippers of the outraged idol.

He flung the lock at her feet. "There's the hair that it was death to touch." She did not speak; she only looked at it with horror.

"Don't you believe it's *his?*" her father roared.

"Yes, yes! I know it's his; and now let's go home and pray for him, and for *you*, father. We've both got the same God, now."

A bitter retort came to the old man's lips, but the abhorrent look of his daughter stayed his words, and they went into the night together, while the noise of the mob stormed back to them through the darkness, farther and farther away.

XIV

THE CAPTORS of Dylks chose the Temple as the best place for keeping him till morning, when they could take him for trial to Matthew Braile; but they had probably no sense of the place where he had insolently triumphed so often as the fittest scene of his humiliation. They stumbled in a loose mob behind and before and beside him through the dim night, and tried to pass Redfield's guard to strike him with their hands or the sticks which they tore from the wayside bushes. At a little distance, a straggling troop of the believers followed, men and women, wailing and sobbing, and adoring and comforting their god with promises of fealty, in terms of pathetic grotesqueness. A well known voice called to him, "Don't you be afraid, God Almighty! They can't hurt a hair of your head," and the burst of savage mirth which followed Sally Reverdy's words, drowned the retort of a scoffer, "Why, there ain't hardly any left *to* hurt, Sally."

The noise of the talking and laughing and the formless progress of the mob hushed the nearer night voices of the fields and woods; but from a distance the shuddering cry of a screech-owl could be heard; with the melancholy call of a killdee in a pasture beside the creek. The people, friends and foes together, made their way unlighted except by the tin lantern which some one had caught from where it stood on Enraghty's gate-post.

With this one of the unbelievers took his stand at the door of the Temple after Redfield had passed in with his prisoner, and lifted it successively to the faces of those trying to enter. He allowed some and refused others, according as they were of those who denied or confessed Dylks, and a Hound at his elbow explained, "Don't want any but goats in here, tonight."

99

The common parlance was saturated with scriptural phrase, and the gross mockery would have been taken seriously if the speaker had not been so notoriously irreverent. As it was the words won him applause which Redfield and his friends were not able to quell. The joke was caught up and tossed back and forth; the Little Flock outside raised their hymn, the scoffers within joined in derision, and carried the hymn through to the end.

Dylks sat shrunken on the bench below the pulpit, his head fallen forward and his face hidden. Redfield and one of his friends sat on each side, and others tried to save Dylks from those who from time to time pushed forward to strike him. They could not save him from the insults which broke again and again upon the silence; when Redfield rose and appealed to the people to leave the man to the law, they came back at him with shrieks and yells. "Did the law keep my family from bein' broke up by this devil? My wife left me and my own brother won't speak to me because I wouldn't say he was my Savior and my God."

"I'm an old woman, and I lived with my son, but my son has quit me to starve, for all he cares, because I believe in the God of Jacob and he believes in this snorting, two-legged horse."

"My sister won't live with me, because I won't fall down and worship her Golden Calf."

"He's spread death and destruction in my family. My daughters won't look at me, and my two sons fought about him till they were all blood."

The accusings and upbraidings thickened upon him, but Dylks sat silent, except for a low groan of what might have seemed remorse. He put his hand to the place on his head where the hair had been torn away, and looked at the blood on his fingers.

A woman stole under the guard of his keepers, and struck him a savage blow on the cheeks, first one and then the other. "*Now* you can see how it feels to have your own husband slap you because you won't say you believe in such a God as you are, you heathen pest!"

The guards struggled with her, and a man stooped over Dylks and voided a mouthful of tobacco juice in his face; another lashed him on the head with a switch of leatherwood: all in a squalid travesty of the supreme tragedy of the race. As if a consciousness of the semblance touched the gospel-read actors in the drama, they shrank in turn from what they had done, and lost themselves in the crowd.

The night wore away and when the red sunrise began to pierce the dusk of the Temple, where some had fallen asleep, and others drowsed as they walked to and fro to keep themselves awake, Redfield conferred with his lieutenants. Then they pulled their captive to his feet, not roughly, and moved with him down the aisle and out of the door. They left some of the slumberers still sleeping; of the others not all followed them on their way to Matthew Braile's, up through the woods and past the cornfields and tobacco patches; but with those of the Little Flock who had hung night-long about the Temple, singing and praying to their idol, they arrived, some before and some after the prisoner, at the log-cabin of the magistrate. He was sitting after his habit in his split-bottomed chair tilted against the porch wall, waiting for the breakfast which his wife was getting within. As the crowd straggled up to the porch, he tilted his chair down, and came forward with a frown of puzzle. "What's this?" he demanded; then, catching sight of a woman's eager face among the foremost, his frown relaxed and he said, "Don't all speak at once, Sally."

" 'Deed and 'deed, I'm not agoun' to speak at all, Squire Braile; but if you want to know you can see for yourself that they've got the Good Old Man, here, and from the tell I've hearn they want you to try him; they've been hittun' him over the face and head all night." She looked defiantly round on the unbelievers who so far joined in the squire's grin as to burst into a general laugh, and a cry of "Good for you, Sally. You're about right."

Braile referred himself to Redfield, who mounted to the porch with the other guards, and the tattered and bedraggled Dylks among them. "What are you doing with this man, Jim?"

"We've brought him to you to find out, Squire Braile. You know who he is, and all the mischief he's been making in this settlement. We don't need to go into that."

"Wish you'd step in there," the squire said, nodding toward the room opposite the kitchen, "and bring me out the Laws of Ohio. You know where it is."

His recognition of Redfield as a law-student pleased the Herd of the Lost, and one of the guards said, "All right, Jim. We'll hold him."

As Redfield disappeared within the squire called after him, "Bring out my table, too, will you. We'll have the trial here."

"That's all right as fur as it goes, Squire," one of the crowd before the cabin called out, "but there ain't room enough for us up there."

"Well," the squire answered, "you've got the whole State of Ohio down there. I reckon you can find room in it, if you stand close."

He turned the joke on the crowd which acquiesced with cheers. When Redfield returned with the large book and the small table he had been sent for the squire drew up to them and proclaimed silence in the Court. Then he said, "Who complains against this man? You, James Redfield?"

"I arrested him, but I don't complain of him more than the rest. You know what he's been doing in Leatherwood, as well as other places, for the last month or six weeks. We want his mischief stopped; we want to see what the law can do about it. We could have lynched him, but that ain't the right way, and so we all feel."

"Well, we've got to make a start, somewhere," the justice returned. "What's he accused of? What do *you* accuse him of?"

"Well, for one thing," Redfield said, rather reluctantly, "he professes to be Almighty God."

"And he *is* God, the Most High Jehovah, Maker of Heaven and Earth," came in a varying cry, from the believers who had gathered increasingly on the skirts of their enemies.

Their voices seemed to put life and courage into the prisoner, who for the first time lifted his fallen face and looked at the justice with a light of hope in his dulled eyes.

"You hear that," the old squire addressed him. "Is that your name? Are you God?"

"Thou sayest," the prisoner answered, with a sudden effrontery.

"That will *do!*" the old man shouted. He might have been willing to burlesque the case from his own disbelief, but he could not suffer the desecration of the hallowed words; and Dylks shrank from his eyes of fierce rebuke. "Stand away from him," he added to the guards. "Now, then, have you folks got any other charge against him? Has he stolen anything? Like a mule, for instance? Has he robbed a hen-roost? Has he assaulted anybody, or set a tobacco-shed on fire? Some one must make a charge; I don't much care what it is."

The old man scowled round on the people nearest him and down on the crowd below. The believers waited in anxious silence; the unbelievers applauded his humor with friendly laughter, and a kindlier spirit spread through them; they were beginning to see Dylks as a joke.

"Redfield," the squire turned to the young man, "let's have a look at the Laws of Ohio, in such case made and provided." He opened the book which Redfield put on the table before him, and went carefully through the index; then he closed it. "There don't seem," he said, "to be any charge against the prisoner except claiming to be the Almighty; he pleads guilty to that, and he could be fined and imprisoned if there was any law against a man's being God. But there isn't, unless it's some law of the Bible, which isn't in force through reenactment in Ohio. He hasn't offended against any of our statutes, neither he nor his followers. In this State every man has a right to worship what God he pleases, under his own vine and figtree, none daring to molest him or make him afraid. With religious fanaticism our laws have nothing to do, unless it be pushed so far as to violate some public ordinance. This I find the prisoner has not done. Therefore, he stands acquitted."

A roar of protest, a shout of joy went up from the crowd according to their belief and unbelief. After his first plea Dylks had remained silent in becoming meekness and self-respect; now he looked wildly round in fear and hope; but he did not speak.

"Clear the way, you!" the squire called to the people about him and below him, and he got slowly to his feet. He took the arm of the prisoner at one side, and said, "Here, Jim Redfield, you take this fellow's other arm," and as the young man helplessly obeyed, "Now!" he commanded, and with Dylks between them, they left the porch and passed through the severing crowd of friends and foes before the cabin. While they hesitated in doubt of his purpose, Braile led the way with the prisoner, acquitted, but still in custody, toward the turnpike road where the country lane passing the cabin joined it a little way off.

The crowd straggled after in patient doubt, but when the squire halted with his captive and bade Redfield move back, the suspicions of the unbelievers began to stir.

"Now, put!" the squire said in a low voice and loosed his hold. Dylks lifted his head alertly as he was accustomed to do when he gave his equine snort, but now he made no sound. He leaped forward and ran with vast bounds up the smooth turnpike toward the wall of woodland, where the whiteness of the highway ceased in the shadow of the trees. He far outdistanced the foremost of his pursuers, who stopped to gather the broken stone heaped along the roadside, and under the rain of these and the storm of curses that they sent after him, he escaped into the forest.

"Well, Abel," the squire said to Reverdy, whom he found, not unexpectedly, at his elbow when he looked round, "he may not be much of a god, but he's a good deal of a race horse, even if he didn't give his snort."

"Look here, Squire Braile," Redfield broke out in the first realization of his defeat, "I'm not sure your decision was just right."

"Well, you can appeal the case to the Supreme Court, Jim," the old man returned. "It's my *breakfast* time," and he stamped stiffly away down the pike and up the road to his cabin, followed by the blessings of the Little Flock.

The Little Flock had remained in stupefaction at the junction of the country road and the turnpike, helplessly watching the flight of their idol from the Herd of the Lost. When Dylks vanished in the dusk of the forest, and the last of those who had followed him came lagging breathlessly back, and dropped from their hands the broken stone which they had unconsciously brought with them, the Little Flock involuntarily raised their hymn, as if it had been a song of triumph; an inglorious triumph, but an omen of final victory, and of the descent of the New Jerusalem in Leatherwood.

"Never mind!" one of the Herd panted. "We'll have him out of that gulf of dark despair, yit!"

"The Lord will put forth His might," one of the Flock defied him. "But if you fellows want to feel the arm of flesh, here and now, come on!"

The Squire put himself between the forces. "I want you to keep the peace; I command the peace," he said with magisterial dignity.

"Oh, all right, Squire," a Hound applauded him. "We know you're on our side."

"Brother Braile is on the side of righteousness," the champion of the Flock declared.

The squire turned a frowning face upon him. "If the law could have held your god, he'd have been on his way to the county jail by this time. Now you fellows, both sides, go home, and look after your corn and tobacco; and you women, you go and get breakfast for them, and wash up your children and leave the Kingdom of Heaven alone for a while."

The weight of condemnation was for the Little Flock, but there remained discomfort for the Herd of the Lost. "And you," the Squire turned to them, "you let these folks worship any stock or stone they've a mind to; and you find out the true God if you can, and stick to Him, and don't bother the idolators. I reckon He can take care of Himself. I command you all to disperse. Go home! Get out! Put!"

The saints and the sinners felt alike the mystical force of the law in his words and began to move away, not without threats and defiances, more or less straggling, and not altogether ceasing even after they had lost sight of one another in their parting ways.

Redfield stayed to walk home with the old man. "Of course, Squire Braile," he said, "this ain't the last of Dylks, and it ain't the last of *us*. It's a sin and a shame to have the thing going on among us. You know that as well as I do. It's got to be stopped. If he'd got his just dues from you"—

"You young fool," the squire retorted, kindly, "haven't you gone far enough yet in your Blackstone to know that justice is one thing and law is another? I gave Dylks his legal deserts."

"Blackstone says the law is the perfection of reason."

"Well, you think it don't seem to be so in the State of Ohio. But I reckon it is, and so long as we look after our own souls, we can't do better than let others look after theirs in their own way. Come in and have some breakfast!" He paused before his cabin with the young man.

"No, not *this* morning, Squire Braile." Redfield lingered a moment, and then he said, askingly, "I didn't see old Mr. Gillespie anywhere this morning."

"I didn't notice. Where it comes to a division in public, he doesn't usually take sides against his daughter."

"He won't have to, after this."

"What do you mean?"

"Didn't you know she told him once that if he would bring her a hair of Dylks's head she would deny him? I helped him to a whole lock of it."

"Oh, *you* did that?" There was condemnation in the squire's tone, and as if he had been going to express a more explicit displeasure, he hesitated. Then he said, "Well, I must be going in," and turned his back upon Redfield, who turned again into the turnpike road and took his way homeward past the long and deep stretch of woods where Dylks had found refuge.

XV

In the middle of the woods there was a dense thicket of lower growths on a piece of dry land lifted above the waters of a swamp. The place was the lair of such small wild things as still survived in the wilderness once the haunt of the wolf and the wild cat, and the resort of the bear allured by the profusion of the huckleberries which grew there. But, except in the early fall when the annual squirrel-hunt swept over the whole country side and the summer drought had made the swamp easily passable to the gunners, the place was unmolested. Even the country boy who seeks the bounty of nature wherever she offers it, and makes the outlying property of man his prey where nature has been dispossessed, did not penetrate the thicket in his search for hazelnuts or chinquapins; it was proofed against his venture by its repute of rattlesnakes and copperheads and the rumor of ghosts and witches. Few men or boys knew the approach to the interior by the narrow ridge of dry land lifted above the marsh, and Dylks did not stop in his flight till he reached the thicket and saw in it his hope of securer refuge. He walked round it through the pools which the frog and turtle haunted, twice before he found this ridge, overhung by a tangle of grape-vines. There his foot by the instinct which the foot has where the eye fails of a path, divined the scarcely trodden way, and he found himself in a central opening among the thickly growing bushes. It was warm here, without the close heat of the woodland, and dry except for the spring of clear water that bubbled up in the heart of it, and trickled out over green mosses into the outer waters of the swamp.

The man stooped over and drank his fill, and then made his greedy breakfast on the berries that grew abundantly round, and nodded hospitably to his hand. All the time he wept, and moaned to himself in the self-pity of a hunted, fearful wretch. Then he drank again from the spring, and without rising from his knees pushed himself back a little from it, and fell over in an instant sleep.

He slept through the whole day, and at night, falling early in the shadows of the forest which thickened over his retreat, he supped, as he had breakfasted, on the wild berries and spring water, but with protesting from a stomach habitually flattered by the luxury of fried chicken and ham, and corn-pone and shortened biscuit, and hot coffee, which his adorers put before him when he laid aside his divinity and descended to the gratification of his carnal greed. He was a gross feeder, and in the midst of his fear and the joy of his escape, he thought of these things and lusted for them with a sort of thankless resentment. He looked about for something he might kill, and he found a wounded pigeon which had fluttered into his refuge from the shot of some gunner. But he could not bring himself to eat it raw, and if he could have kindled a fire to cook it, he reflected, it would have betrayed him to his pursuers who must now be searching the woods for him. He wrung the pigeon's neck and flung it into the bushes, and then fell down and wept with his face in the grass. He had slept so long that now he could not sleep, and when his tears would come no more, he sat up and watched the night through till the dawn grayed the blue-black sky. The noises of the noiseless woods made themselves heard: the cry of a night hawk, the hooting of an owl, the whirring note of the whip-poor-will; the long, plunging down-rush of a dead branch breaking the boughs below it; even the snapping of twigs as if under the pressure of stealthy feet. These sounds, the most delicate of the sounds he heard, shook him most with fear and hope, and then with despair. The feet could be the feet of his enemies seeking him out, or of his friends coming to succor and save him; then they resolved themselves into the light pressure from little paws, the paws of the wildcat, or the coon, and there was nothing to be feared or hoped from them. The constellations wheeled over him in the clear sky, and the planets blazed. He made out the North Star from the lower lines of the Dipper; the glowing and fading of the August meteors that flitted across the heavens seemed to leave a black trace on his straining eyes. Texts of Scripture declaring how the splendors of the day and night showed forth the glory of the Being whose name he had usurped to the deceit and shame of those who trusted him, glowed and faded in his mind like those shooting stars in the sky. At one time he thought he had cried aloud for destruction in the sin which could not be forgiven, but it was only a dull, inarticulate moan bursting from his tortured breast.

The place where the hair had been torn from his head burned like fire; it burned like the wound of a man whom he had once heard tell how it felt to be scalped by an Indian; the man had recovered, but the wound had always hurt; and Dylks pitied himself that it should be so with him, and cursed himself for his unguarded boast that any one who touched a hair of his head should perish. He promised that if God would show him a little mercy, and send a raven with something for him to eat, something warm, or send him a cup of coffee, somehow, or even a raw egg, he would go forth before the people, get up in the Temple amidst his believers and declare himself a false prophet and a false god. He would not care what they did to him if only he had something cooked to eat, something hot to drink.

Towards morning he slept, and then for days and nights, how many he did not know, it seemed to him that he did not wake but dreamed through a changing time when he was dimly aware of contending voices: voices of his believers, the Little Flock, and voices of his unbelievers, the Herd of the Lost, pleading and threatening in the forest round his place of refuge. His followers were trying to bring him food and raiment, and his enemies were preventing them and boasting that they would keep guard over his refuge till they starved him out. Then all again was a blur, a texture of conscious and unconscious misery till a night came when the woof broke and trailed away from him, and he lifted himself on his elbow and after he had drunk a long draft from the spring, found tremulous strength to get to his feet. He tried some steps in the open space, where the light of the full moon fell, and found that he could walk. He reached the tangled entrance to his covert, and stealthily put the vines aside. He peered out into the shadows striped with moonshine and could see no one, and he was going to venture farther, when he stopped stone still at the figure of a man crouched in the middle of the causeway. The man's head was fallen forward and his gun lay across his lap; he must be one of the guards that his enemies had set on his refuge to keep him there and starve him out; and he must be asleep. Dylks stooped and peered into his face and knew the man for one of the Hounds who had often disturbed his meetings, and now he looked about in the rage that surged up through his penitence and self-pity for a stone or a club to strike him senseless, or dead if need be. But there was no such weapon that he could see, and the risk of a struggle was greater than the risk of trying to pass the man without waking him. After long doubt he tried with one foot and then the other, and the man did not wake; then he crept slowly by, and then with softly dragging steps he got farther from the sleeper and pushed on through the woods in the direction of the turnpike, as he imagined it. But he came out into a clearing where a new cabin of peeled logs showed clear in the open under the moon.

In the single room of the house a woman lay sleeping with a little child in its cradle beside her bed. She rose up and put out her hand instinctively to still the child, but it was sleeping quietly, and then she started up awake, and listened for the voice which she had dreamt was calling her. There was no voice, and then there was a voice calling hoarsely, weakly, "Nancy! Nancy!"

In her dream she had thought it was the voice of her husband stealing back to her in the night, and it was in the terror of her dream that she now sprang from her bed, with her heart aching for pity of him, to forbid him and rebuke him for breaking his promise, and to scold him away. But as she stood listening, and the voice came again she knew it was not the voice of Laban. She ran to the ladder which led to the cabin loft, and called up through the open trap-door, "Jane! Jane! Come down here to the baby, will you. I've got to leave her a minute."

"What for?" the girl answered sleepily. Then, "Oh, I'll come. She ain't sick, is she, Aunt Nancy? Oh, I do hope she ain't sick!"

"No. She ain't sick," Nancy said, as she put her hands up to help the girl place her feet aright on the rungs of the ladder. "But—listen!" she whispered as the voice outside called again. "It's that miser'ble wretch! It's Joseph Dylks! I've got to go to him! Don't you say a word, Jane Gillespie! He's Joey's father, and he must be at death's door, or he wouldn't come to mine."

She left the girl standing dazed, and ran out and round the cabin. In the shadow that it cast in the moon, Dylks crouched close in the angle made by the chimney.

"Oh, Nancy!" he implored her, "do give me something to eat! Something warm. Coffee, if you've got it. I've been sick, and I'm starving."

She knew without seeing it in the shadow how he was stretching out pleading hands to her, and she had mercy upon him. But she said stonily, "Wait a minute. Don't be a cry-baby," and ran back to the door, and called to the girl within, "Rake open the fire, Jane, and set the kittle on." Then she ran again to Dylks and stood over him. "Where you been? Don't you know they'll kill you if they ketch you?"

"Yes, I know it, Nancy. But I knew this would be the last place they would come for me. Will the coffee be ready soon? Oh, I'm so faint! I reckon I'm going to die, Nancy."

"I reckon you ain't goin' to die before you get your coffee. It'll be ready as soon as the kittle boils."

She stood looking grimly down at him, while he brokenly told, so far as he knew it, the story of the days he had passed in hiding.

"I reckon," she said, with bitter scorn, "that *I* could have fetched you out. I'd 'a' brought you some hot coffee to the door of your den, and you'd 'a' come when you smelt it."

"Yes, that's true," he owned in meek acceptance of her scorn.

The child cried, and she went in, but she had no need to comfort it except with a word. Jane had come to the little one, and was stooping above it, and cooing to it motherwise, and cuddling it to her body while it drowsed away to silence.

"You mind her, Jane," the mother said, and she lifted the pot of coffee from the bed of coals sending a dim glow into the room to meet the dawn at the open door. She put some sugar into the bowl she got from its shelf, and covered it with a piece of cold corn-pone, and then went out to Dylks who had remained on his knees, and now stretched out his trembling hands toward her.

She did not speak, but poured the bowl full of the steaming coffee, and watched him while he gulped half of it down. Then he reached eagerly for the bread. "Is it hot?" he asked.

"No, it ain't," the woman said. "You can eat cold pone, I reckon, can't you?"

"Oh, yes; oh yes, and glad to get it. Only I thought"— He stopped and washed down the mouthful he had torn from the cake with a draft of the coffee which emptied the bowl. She filled it mechanically from the pot in her hand, and he drank again more slowly, and devoured the pone as he drank.

"Now," he said, "I should be all right if it wasn't for my head where they tore out my hair. It burns like fire."

She bent over him and looked at the wound unflinchingly. "I can't see very good in this light; if I only had some goose-grease—but I reckon hog's lard will do. Hold on till I can wash it."

"Oh, Nancy," he moaned gratefully.

She was gone rather long, and there was talk within and the cooing and babble of the child. When she came out with a basin of warm water and some lard in a broken saucer in her hands, and a towel caught under her arm, he suggested, "I heard you talking with some one, Nancy."

"And I suppose it scared you," she answered unsparingly. "Well, you may thank your stars it wasn't Laban. I do believe he'd kill you, meek as he is."

Dylks drew a quivering breath. "Yes, I reckon he would. I suppose you must have told him about me."

"Of course, I did. Here! Hold still!" She had begun to wash his wound, very gently, though she spoke so roughly, while he murmured with the pain and with the comfort of the pain. "If you want to know," she continued, "it's Jane. She's been with me ever since that night they caught you. You made her ashamed before her father, and between her shame and his pride her and him don't speak, or hain't, since then. She stays with me and Joey stays with him."

"Our Joey?" he asked plaintively.

"*My* Joey!" she returned, and she involuntarily twitched at the hair she was smoothing.

"Oh!" he cried from the pain, but she did not mind his pain.

"There!" she said, beginning to put on the lard. Then she bound over the wound the soft pledget of old linen she had brought, and tied round his head a cotton rag to hold the dressing in place. She said, "There!" again. "I reckon that will do."

He moaned gratefully. "It's the first time I've been out of pain for I don't know how many days and nights. Nancy!" he burst out in all recognition of her goodness, "I oughtn't to have left you."

She had been kneeling before him in dressing his hurt, and then in critically regarding her handiwork, she got to her feet. "I know you oughtn't," she retorted, "but I'm glad you done it. And I'm thankful every breath I draw. And now I want you to *go*. And don't you think I done what I done out of love for you, Joseph Dylks. I'd 'a' done it for any hurt or hungry dog."

Dylks got to his feet too, with little moans for the stiffness in his joints. "I know you would, Nancy," he said humbly, "but all the same I won't forget it. If there was anything I could do to show" —

"There's something you could do besides drownin' yourself in the creek, which I don't ask you: in the first place because I don't want your death on my hands, and in the next place because you're the unfittin'est man to die that I can think of; but there's something else, and you know it without my tellin' you, and that is to stop all this, now and forever. Don't you pretend you don't know what I mean!"

"I know what you mean, Nancy, and the good Lord knows I would be glad enough to do it if I could. But I wouldn't know how to begin."

"Begin," she said with a scornful glance at the long tangle of his hair, "begin by cuttin' off that horse's tail of yours, and then stop snortin' like a horse."

He shook his head hopelessly. "It wouldn't do, Nancy. They wouldn't let me draw back now. They would kill me."

"They?"

"The—the—Little Flock," he answered shame-facedly.

"The Herd of the Lost will kill you if you don't." She said it not in mocking, but in realization of the hopeless case, and not without pity. But at his next words, she hardened her heart again.

"I don't know what to do. I don't know where to go. I have nowhere to lay my head."

"Don't you use them holy words, you wicked wretch! And if you're hintin' at hidin' in my house, you can't do it—not with Jane here—*she* would kill you, I believe,—and not without her."

"No, Nancy. I can see that. But where can I go? Even that place in the woods, they're watching that, and they would have me if I tried to go back there again."

From an impulse as of indifference rather than consideration she said, "Go to Squire Braile. He let you off; let him take care of you."

"Nancy!" he exclaimed. "I thought of that."

She gathered up the basin and the towel she had brought, and without looking at him again she said, "Well, go, then," and turned and left him where he stood.

XVI

MATTHEW Braile was sitting in his wonted place, with his chair tilted against his porch wall, smoking. Dylks faltered a moment at the bars of the lane from the field of tall corn where he had been finding his way unseen from Nancy's cabin. He lowered two of the middle bars and when he had put them up on the other side he stood looking toward the old man. His long hair hung tangled on his shoulders; the white bandage which Nancy had bound about his head, crossed it diagonally above one eye and gave this the effect of a knowing wink, which his drawn face, unshaven for a week, seemed to deprecate.

Braile stared hard at him. Then he tilted his chair down and came to the edge of his porch, and called in cruel mockery, "Why, God, is that *you?*"

"Don't, Squire Braile!" Dylks implored in a hoarse undertone. "They're after me, and if anybody heard you"—

"Well, come up here," the squire bade him. Dylks hobbled slowly forward, and painfully mounted the log steps to the porch, where Braile surveyed him in detail, frowning and twitching his long feathery eyebrows.

"I know I don't look fit to be seen," Dylks began, "but"—

"Well," the squire allowed after further pause, "you *don't* look as if you had just come 'down from the shining courts above in joyful haste'! Had any breakfast?"

"Nancy—Nancy Billings—gave me some coffee, and some cold pone"—

"Well, you can have some *hot* pone pretty soon. Laban there?"

"No, he's away at work still. But Squire Braile"—

"Oh, I understand. I know all about Nancy, and her first husband and how he left her, and she thought he was dead, and married a good man, and when that worthless devil came back she thought she was living in sin with that good man—in *sin !*— and drove him away. But she's as white as any of the saints you lie about. It was *like* you to go to her the first one in your trouble. Well, what did she say?"

"She said"— Dylks stopped, his mouth too dry to speak; he wetted his lips and whispered, "She said to come to you; that you would know what it was best for me to do; to"— He stopped again and asked, "Do you suppose any one will see me here?"

"Oh, like as not. It's getting time for honest folks to be up and going to work. But I don't want any trouble about you this morning; I had enough that *other* morning. Come in here!" He set open the door of one of the rooms giving on the porch, and at Dylks's fearful glance he laughed, not altogether unkindly. "Mis' Braile's in the kitchen, getting breakfast for you, though she don't know it yet. Now, then!" he commanded when he sat down within, and pushed a chair to Dylks. "Tell me all about it, since I saw you going up the pike."

In the broken story which Dylks told, Braile had the air of mentally checking off the successive facts, and he permitted the man a measure of self-pity, though he caught him up at the close. "Well, you've got a part of what you deserve, but as usually happens with us rascals, you've got too much, at the same time. And what did Nancy advise?"

"She told me to come to you"—

"What did Nancy *advise ?*" the squire repeated savagely.

"She advised me to stop all this"—he waved his hands outward, and the Squire nodded intelligently—"to tell them it wasn't true; and I was sorry; and to go away"—

He stopped, and Braile demanded, "Well, and are you going to do it?"

"I want to do it, and—I can't."

"You can't? What's to hinder you?"

"I'm afraid to do it."

"Afraid?"

"They would kill me, if I did."

"They? Who? The Herd of the Lost?"

"The Little Flock."

The men were both silent, and then after a long breath, the squire said, "I begin to see"—

"No, no! You don't *begin* to see, Squire Braile," Dylks burst out sobbing, and uttering what he said between his sobs. "Nobody can understand it that hasn't been through it! How you are tempted on, step by step, all so easy, till you can't go back, you can't stop. You're tempted by what's the best thing in you, by the hunger and thirst to know what's going to be after you die; to get near to the God that you've always heard about and read about; near Him in the flesh, and see Him and hear Him and touch Him. That's what does it with *them*, and that's what does it in you. It's something, a kind of longing, that's always been in the world, and you know it's in others because you know it's in you, in your own heart, your own soul. When you begin to try for it, to give out that you're a prophet, an apostle, you don't have to argue, to persuade anybody, or convince anybody. They're only too glad to believe what you say from the first word; and if you tell them you're Christ, didn't He always say He would come back, and how do they know but what it's now and you?"

"Yes, yes," the squire said. "Go on."

"When I said I was God, they hadn't a doubt about it. But it was then that the trouble began."

"The trouble?"

"I had to make some of them saints. I had to make Enraghty Saint Paul, and I had to make Hingston Saint Peter. You think I had to lie to them, to deceive them, to bewitch them. I didn't have to do anything of the kind. They did the lying and deceiving and bewitching themselves, and when they done it, they and all the rest of the believers, they had me fast, faster than I had them."

"I could imagine the schoolmaster hanging on to his share of the glory, tooth and nail," the squire said with a grim laugh.

"But old Hingston, good old soul, he ought to have let go, if you wanted him to."

"Oh, you don't know half of it," Dylks said, with a fresh burst of sobbing. "The worst of it is, and the dreadfulest is, that you begin to believe it yourself."

"What's that?" the squire demanded sharply.

"Their faith puts faith into you. If they believe what you say, you say to yourself that there must be some truth in it. If you keep telling them you're Jesus Christ, there's nothing to prove you ain't, and if you tell them you're God, who ever saw God, and who can deny it? You can't deny it yourself"—

"Hold on!" the old man said. He had risen, and he began to walk up and down, swaying his figure and tilting his head from side to side, and frowning his shaggy eyebrows together in a tangled hedge. Suddenly, he stopped before Dylks. "Why, you poor devil, you're not in any unusual fix. It must have been so with all the impostors in the world, from Mahomet up and down! Why, there isn't a false prophet in the Old Testament that couldn't match experiences with you! That's the way it's always gone: first the liar tells his lie, and some of the fools believe it, and proselyte the other fools, and when there are enough of them, their faith begins to work on the liar's own unbelief, till he takes his lie for the truth. Was that the way, you miserable skunk?"

"It was exactly the way, Squire Braile, and you can't tell how it gains on you, step by step. You see all those educated people like Mr. Enraghty, and all those good men like Mr. Hingston taking it for gospel, and you can't deny it yourself. They convince you of it."

"Exactly! And then, when the Little Flock gathers in all the mentally lame, halt and blind in the settlement, you couldn't get out of it if you had the whole Herd of the Lost to back you, with the Hounds yelping round to keep your courage up; you've got to stay just where you put yourself, heigh?"

"There wouldn't," Dylks said, drying his eyes on a tatter of his coat sleeve, "be so much trouble if it wasn't for the miracles."

"Yes," Braile replied to the thoughtful mood which he had fallen into, rather than to Dylks, "the ignorant are sure to want a sign, though the wise could get along without it. And you have to promise them a sign; you have to be fool enough to do that, though you know well enough you can't work the miracle."

"You ain't sure you can't. You think, maybe"—

"Then, why," the squire shouted at him, "why in the devil's name, *didn't* you work the miracle at Hingston's mill that night? Why didn't you turn that poor fool woman's bolt of linsey-woolsey into seamless raiment?"

Dylks did not answer.

"Why didn't you do it? Heigh!"

"I thought maybe—I didn't know but I did do it."

"What do you mean?"

"When I came up outside and told them that the miracle had been worked and the seamless raiment was inside the bolt, I thought it must be there."

"Why, in the name of"—

"I had prayed so hard for help to do it that I thought it must be."

"You prayed? To whom?"

"To—God."

"To yourself?"

Dylks was silent again in the silence of a self-convicted criminal. He did not move.

Braile had been walking up and down again in his excitement, in his enjoyment of the psychological predicament, and again he stopped before Dylks. "Why, you poor bag of shorts!" he said, "I could almost feel sorry for you, in spite of the mischief you've made. Why, *you* oughtn't to be sent to the penitentiary, or even lynched. *You* ought to be put amongst the county idiots in the poor-house, and"—

There came a soft plapping as of bare feet on the puncheon floor of the porch; hesitating about and then pausing at the door of the opposite room. Then there came with the increased smell of cooking the talking of women. Presently the talking stopped and the plapping of the bare feet approached the door of the room shutting the two men in. The squire set it slightly ajar, in spite of Dylks's involuntary, "Oh, don't!" and faced some one close to the opening.

"That you, Sally? You haven't come to borrow anything at *this* hour of the night?"

"Well, I reckon if you was up as early as Mis' Braile, you'd know it was broad day. No, I hain't come to borry anything exactly, but I was just tellin' *her* that if she'd lend me a fryun' of bacon, I'd do as much for her some day. She ast me to tell you your breakfast was ready and not to wait till your comp'ny was gone, but bring anybody you got with you."

Sally peered curiously in at the opening of the door, and Braile abruptly set it wide. "Perhaps you'd like to see who it is."

Sally started back at sight of the figure within. When she could get her breath she gasped, "Well, for mercy's sakes! If it ain't the Good Old Man, himself!" But she made no motion of revering or any offer of saluting her late deity.

"Well, now, if you've got some bacon for Abel's breakfast you better stop and have yours with us," the squire suggested.

"No, I reckon not," Sally answered. "I ain't exactly sure Abel would like it. He ain't ever been one of the Flock, although at the same time he ain't ever been one of the Herd: just betwixt and between, like." As she spoke she edged away backward. "Well, I must be goun', squire. Much obleeged to you all the same."

The squire followed her backward steps with his voice. "If you should happen to see Jim Redfield on his way to his tobacco patch, I wish you'd tell him to come here; I'd like to see him."

He went in again to Dylks.

"What are you going to do with me, Squire Braile," he entreated. "You're not going to give me up?"

"I know my duty to my Maker," the old man answered. "I'll take care of you, Jehovah Dylks. But now you better come in to breakfast—get some *hot* pone. I'll bring you a basin of water to wash up in."

He re-opened the door in the face of Sally Reverdy, who gasped out before she plapped over to the steps and dropped away, "I just seen Jim Redfield, and I tole him you wanted him, and he said he would be here in half an hour, or as soon as he could see that the men had begun on his tubbacco. I didn't tell him who you had here, and I won't tell anybody else; don't you be afraid."

"Well, that's a good girl, Sally. Abel couldn't have done better himself," the squire called after her and then he turned to Dylks. "Come along now, and get your *hot* pone. Jim Redfield won't hurt you; I'll go bail for him, and I'll see that nobody else gets at you. I've got a loft over this room where you'll be safe from everything but a pet coon that your Joey gave me after my little boy— And I reckon the coon won't bite you. *I* wouldn't, in his *place.*"

XVII

Redfield came rather later than he had promised, excusing himself for his delay. "I was afraid the frost had caught my tobacco, last night; but it seems to be all right, as far as I can see; I stayed till the sun was well up before I decided."

"It *was* a pretty sharp night, but I don't believe there was any frost," the squire said. "At least Dylks didn't complain of it."

"Dylks?" Redfield returned.

"Yes. Didn't you know he was out again?"

"No, I didn't. If I had that fellow by the scruff of the neck!"

The squire knew he meant the sleeping sentinel at the thicket where Dylks had been hidden, and not Dylks. But he said nothing, and again Redfield spoke.

"Look here, Squire Braile, I think you did a bad piece of business letting that fellow go."

"I know you do, Jim, but I expect you'll think different when you've seen him."

"Seen him? You mean you know where he is?"

"Yes."

"Well, all I've got to say is that if I can lay hands on him he won't give me the slip again."

"Suppose we see," the squire said, and he opened the door into the room where Dylks was cowering, and remarked with a sort of casualness, as if the fact would perhaps interest them both, "Here's one of the Lost, Dylks. I thought you might like to see him. Now, sit down, both of you and let's talk this thing over."

He took a place on the side of the bed and the enemies each faltered to their chairs in mutual amaze.

122

"Oh, sit down, sit down!" the squire insisted. "You might as well take it comfortably. Nobody's going to kill either of you."

"I don't want to do anybody any harm," Dylks began.

"You'd better not!" Redfield said between his set teeth; his hands had knotted themselves into fists at his side.

"I'm all weak yet from the fever I had there, with nothing but water and berries," Dylks resumed in his self-pity. "I *did* think some of my friends might have come"—

"I took good care of that," Redfield said. "They did come, at first, with something to eat, but they knew blame well we'd have wrung their necks if we'd 'a' caught 'em. We meant to starve you out, that's what, and we did it, and if it hadn't been for that good for nothing whelp sleeping over his gun you wouldn't have got out alive."

"Well, that's all right now, Jim, and you'd better forgive and forget, both of you," the squire interposed. "Dylks has reformed, he tells me; he's sorry for having been a god, and he's going to try to be a man, or as much of a man as he can. He's going to tell the Little Flock so, and then he's going to get out of Leatherwood right off"—

Dylks cleared his throat to ask tremulously, "Did I say that, Squire Braile?"

"Yes, you did, my friend, and what's more you're going to keep your word, painful as it may be to you. I'll let you manage it your own way, but some way you're going to do it; and in the meantime I'm going to put you under the protection of Jim Redfield, here"—

"*My* protection?" Redfield protested.

"Yes, I've sworn you in as special constable, or I will have as soon as I can make out the oath, and have you sign it. And Dylks will get out of the county as soon as he can—he tells me it won't be so easy as we would think; and when he does, it will be much more to the purpose than riding on a rail in a coat of tar and feathers. Why!" he broke off, with a stare at Dylks as if he saw his raggedness for the first time. "You'll want a coat of *some* kind to show yourself to the Little Flock in; the Herd of the Lost won't mind; they don't want to be so proud of you. I must look up something for you; or perhaps send to Brother Hingston; he's about your size. But that don't matter, now! What I want is your promise, Jim Redfield, and I know you'll do what you say, that you won't tell anybody that the Supreme Being is hiding in my loft, here, till I say so, and when I do, that you'll see no harm comes to him from mortals—from Hounds, and such like, or even the Herd of the Lost. Do you promise?"

Redfield hesitated. "If he'll leave the county, yes."

"And *you*, 'Jehovah, Jove or Lord' ?"

"I will, as quick as I can, Squire Braile; I will, indeed."

The squire rose from the edge of the bed. "Then this court stands adjourned," he said formally.

Redfield went out with him, leaving Dylks trembling behind. He said, "I ain't sure you ain't making a fool of me, Squire Braile."

"Well, *I* am," the squire retorted. "And don't you make one of yourself, and then there won't be any."

Redfield still hesitated. "I'd just like to had another pull at that horse-tail of his," he said wistfully.

"Well, I knew old man Gillespie hadn't quite the strength. But I thought maybe Hughey Blake helped pull"—

"Hughey Blake," Redfield returned scornfully, "had nothing to do with it."

"Well, any way, I hear it's converted Jane Gillespie, and she was worth it, though it was rather too much like scalping a live Indian."

"She's worth more than all the other girls in this settlement put together," Redfield said, without comment on the phase of the act which had interested the squire, and went down the cabin steps into the lane.

Braile turned back and opened the door of the room where Dylks was lurking.

"Better come out, now," he said, not ungently, "and get into a safe place before folks begin to be about much. Or wait, I'll put the ladder up first." He brought the ladder from the kitchen where he exchanged a fleeting joke with his wife, still at her work of clearing the breakfast things away, and set it against the wall under the trap door of the loft. "Now then!" he called and Dylks came anxiously out.

"Ain't you afraid"—he began.

"No, but *you* are, and that'll do for both of us. There's nobody round, and if you'll hurry, nobody'll see you. Push the lid to one side, and get in, and you'll be perfectly safe," he said as Dylks tremulously mounted the ladder. "I don't say you'll be very comfortable. There's a little window at one end, but it don't give much air, and this August sun is apt to get a little warm on the clapboards. And I don't suppose it smells very well in there; but the coon can't help that; it's the way nature scented him; she hadn't any sweet brier handy at the time. And be careful not to step on him. He's not very good-tempered, but I reckon he won't bite you if you don't bite *him*."

The kitchen door opened and Mrs. Braile put her head out. She saw the ladder and the two men. Then she came out into the porch. "Well, Matthew Braile, I might have knowed from the sound of your voice that you was up to some mischief. Was you goin' to send that poor man up into that hot loft? Well, I can tell you you're not." She went into the room they had left, and they heard her stirring vigorously about beyond its closed door, with a noise of rapid steps and hard and soft thumpings. She came out again and said, "Go in there, now, Mr. Dylks, and try to get some rest. I've made up the bed for you, and *I'll* see that nobody disturbs you. Matthew Braile, you send and tell Mr. Hingston, or *go*, if you can't ketch anybody goin' past, and tell him he's here, and bring some decent clothes; he ain't fit to be seen."

"Well, he don't want to be," the squire said in the attempt to brave her onset. "But I reckon you're right, mother. I should probably have thought of it myself—in time. I'll send Sally or Abel, if they go past—and they nearly always do—or some of the hands from the tobacco patches. Or, as you say, I may go myself, towards evening. He won't want to be troubled before then."

XVIII

At the first meeting in the Temple after the open return of Dylks to his dispensation, the Little Flock had apparently suffered no loss in number. Some of his followers had left him, but his disciples had been busily preaching him during his abeyance, and the defection of old converts was more than made up by the number of proselytes. The room actually left by the Flock was filled by the Herd of the Lost who occupied all the seats on one side of the Temple, with Matthew Braile and his wife in a foremost place, the lower sort of them worsening into the Hounds who filled the doorway, and hung about the outside of the Temple.

The whole assembly was orderly. Those of the Little Flock who conducted the services had a quelled air, which might have been imparted to them by the behavior of Dylks; he sat bowed and humble on the bench below the pulpit, while Enraghty preached above him. It was rumored that at the house-meetings the worship of Dylks had been renewed with the earlier ardor; there had been genuflections and prostrations before him, with prayers for pardon and hymns of praise, especially from the proselytes. Dylks was said to have accepted their adoration with a certain passivity but to have done nothing to prevent it; there was not the more scandalous grovelling at his feet which had stirred up the community to his arrest. There was as much decorum as could consist with the sacrilegious rites which were still practiced with his apparent connivance.

He now sat without apparent restiveness under the eyes of the two men who had the greatest right to exact the fulfillment of his promise, to forbid this idolatry, to end the infamy of its continuance and to go out from among the people whose instincts and conventions his presence outraged. Near Redfield sat David Gillespie with his eyes fixed on Dylks in a stare of hungry hate, and with him sat his daughter, who testified by her removal from the Little Flock her renunciation of her faith in him. Redfield showed greater patience than Gillespie, and at times his eyes wandered to the face of the girl who did not seem to feel them on her, but sat gazing at her forsaken idol in what might have seemed puzzle for him and wonder at herself. Others who had rejected him merely kept away; but she came as if she would face down the shame of her faith in him before the eyes of her little world. Sometimes Dylks involuntarily put his hand to the black silken cap which replaced the bandage Nancy Billings had tied over the place where the hair had been torn out. When he did this, the girl moved a little; her face hardened, and she stole a glance at Redfield.

The schoolmaster went on and on, preaching Dylks insistently, but not with the former defiance. He did not spare to speak of the cruel sufferings inflicted upon their Savior and their God, who had borne it with the meekness of the Son and the mercy of the Father. The divine being who had come to sojourn among them at Leatherwood in the flesh, for the purposes of his inscrutable wisdom might have blasted his enemies with a touch, a word, but he had spared them; he had borne insult and injury, but in the Last Day he would do justice, he the judge of all the earth. Till then, let the Little Flock have patience; let them have faith sustained by the daily, hourly miracles which he had wrought among them since his return to their midst, and rest secure in the strong arms which he folded about them.

Dylks sat motionless. "Well, mother," Matthew Braile hoarsely whispered to his wife, "I reckon you'd better have let me put him up with the coon. The heat might have tried the mischief out of him. He hasn't kept his word."

"No, Matthew, he hasn't," she whispered back, "and I think his lying to you so, is almost the worst thing he's done. The next time you may put him with the coon. Only, the coon's too good for him. But Jim Redfield will look out for him."

"Jim'll have to let him alone. We can't have any more mobbing, and there's no law that can touch Dylks in the State of Ohio. We settled that the first time."

Enraghty abruptly closed his discourse with a demand for prayer, and addressed his supplication to the Savior and the Judge incarnate there among them. The Little Flock sang the hymn which always opened and closed its devotions, and at the end, Hingston, who sat by Dylks on the bench below the pulpit, made a movement as if to rise. But Dylks put out his hand and stayed him. He welcomed Enraghty to the place which he left beside Hingston, and slowly, with the step of one in a dream, mounted the stairs of the pulpit, amidst the silent amaze of the people. He began without preamble, in the blend of scriptural text and crude every day parlance which he ordinarily used.

"Ye have heard it said aforetime that the New Jerusalem would come down here in Leatherwood, but I say unto you that all that has passed away, that the words which were spoken by the prophet might be fulfilled, 'Many are called but few are chosen.' Verily, verily, I said unto you, that heaven and earth shall pass away, but the words I speak now shall not pass away. If the works which have been done in Leatherwood had been done in Tyre and Sidon the New Jerusalem would have come down in both places, for they did not stone the prophets as the Herd of the Lost did in Leatherwood."

"He means that morning when he took up the pike and the fellows chased him into the tall timber," Braile whispered to his wife; "but *I* can't tell what he's driving at."

"Be still!" she said.

Many of the Little Flock groaned and cried aloud; the Herd of the Lost, except for one shrill note of bitter laughter, were silent, and only those who sat near perceived that it was Jane Gillespie who had laughed. Redfield looked round at her, unconscious of his look.

"I go a long way off," Dylks proceeded, "and some of my

beloved, even my Little Flock, cannot follow me; but though they cannot follow me, even the lame, halt and blind shall be with me in the spirit, and shall behold the New Jerusalem where I will bring it down."

Many of the Little Flock at this cried out, "Where will it be, Lord?" "Where will the New Jerusalem come down?" "How shall we see it?"

"With the eyes of faith, even as ye have seen the miracles I have wrought among ye, which were shown to babes and sucklings and were hidden from the wise of this world. But now I go from you, and my feet shall be upon the mountains and shall descend upon the other side and there I will bring down the New Jerusalem, and there ye shall be, in the flesh or in the spirit, to behold the wonder of it."

Some of the Little Flock cried out again. "Oh don't leave us, Father!" "Take us all with you in the flesh!" "We want to be taken up with you!" and then some of them entreated, "Tell us about it; tell us what it will be like."

Dylks lifted his eyes as if in the rapture of the vision. " 'Its light shall eclipse the splendor of the sun. The temples thereof, and the residences of the faithful will be built of diamonds excelling the twinkling beauty of the stars. Its walls will be of solid gold, and its gates silver. The streets will be covered with green velvet, richer in luster and fabric than mortal eye ever beheld. The gardens thereof will be filled with all manner of pleasant fruits, precious to the sight, and pleasant to the taste. The faithful shall ride in chariots of crimson, drawn by jet-black horses that need no drivers; and their joys shall go on increasing forever. The air of the city shall be scented with the smell of shrubs and flowers, and ten thousand different instruments all tuned to the songs of heaven shall fill the courts, and the streets and the temples, and the residences, and the gardens with music like ear hath not heard, swelling the soul of the saved with perpetual delight.' "

Sighs and groans of ecstasy went up from the Flock at each of the studied pauses which Dylks made in recounting the wonders of the heavenly city, fancied one after another at the impulse of their expectation. At the end they swarmed forward to the altar place and flung themselves on the ground, and heaped the pulpit steps with their bodies. "Take us with you, Lord!" they entreated. "Take us all with you in the flesh!" "Don't leave us here to perish among the heathen and the ungodly when you go." Then some began to ask, as if he had already consented, "But what shall we eat, and what shall we drink, and wherewithal shall we be clothed on that far journey?"

Dylks leaned forward against the pulpit desk and showed a few coins drawn from the pocket of Hingston's pantaloons which he was wearing. "These shall be enough, for out of these three rusty old coppers I can make millions of gold and silver dollars."

The frenzy mounted, and the Herd of the Lost who began to tire of the sight, left the temple. Redfield followed out behind Matthew Braile and his wife. "That settles it," he said. "I'll see to Mr. Dylks in the morning."

"Now, I look at it differently. He's going, like he said he would, and we've got to let him go in his own way, and bring down the New Jerusalem Over the Mountains, or anywhere else he pleases, so he don't bring it down in Leatherwood."

"I say so, too, Matthew. He's keeping his word the best he can, poor lying soul. They wouldn't let him back out now."

"I don't want you to trouble him, Jim Redfield, till you have a warrant from me," Braile resumed, braced by his wife's support. "And I want you to keep the Hounds away, and give Dylks a fair start. You know the law won't let you touch him. Now do you hear?"

"I hear," Redfield said sullenly, with the consent which Braile read in his words. "But if there's any more such goings on as we've had here tonight, I won't answer for the rest of his scalp."

He hurried forward from the elderly couple and overtook the Gillespies walking rapidly. Hughey Blake had just fallen away from them and stood disconsolately looking after them.

"Is that you, James Redfield?" David Gillespie asked, peering at him in the night's dimness. "This is the man that helped me to get you a lock of that scoundrel's hair," he said to his daughter.

She answered nothing in acknowledgement of the introduction, but Redfield said, coming round to her side and suiting his step to hers, "I would like to go home with you till my road passes yours."

"Well," she said, "if you ain't ashamed to be seen with such a fool. Nobody *can* see you tonight," she added, bitterly, including him in her self-scorn.

"You needn't imply that I like it to be in the dark. I would like to walk with you in broad day past all the houses in Leatherwood. But I don't suppose you'd let me." She did not say anything, and he added, "I'm going to ask you to the first chance." Still she did not say anything, though her father had fallen behind and left the talk wholly to them.

XIX

Nancy sat at her door in the warm September evening when the twilight was beginning to come earlier than in the August days, and her boy rushed round the corner of the cabin in a boy's habitual breathlessness from running.

"Oh mother, mother!" he called to her, as if he were a great way off, "Guess what!" He did not wait for her to guess. "The Good Old Man is goin' to leave Leatherwood and go Over the Mountains with the Little Flock, and he says he's goin' to bring down the New Jerusalem at Philadelphy, and all that wants to go up with him kin go. Mr. Hingston's goin' with him, and he's goin' to let Benny. Benny don't know whether he can get to go up in the New Jerusalem or not, but he's goin' to coax his father the hardest kind."

He stopped panting at his mother's knees where she sat on the cabin threshold nearly as high as he stood. She put up her hand and pushed the wet hair from his forehead. "How you *do* sweat, Joey! Go round and wash your face at the bench. Maybe Jane will give you a drink of the milk, while it's warm yet, before she lets it down in the well. She's just through milkin'."

The boy tore himself away with a shout of "Oh goody!" and his mother heard him at the well. "Wait a minute, Jane! Mother said I could have a drink before you let it down," and then she heard him, between gulps, recounting to the girl's silence the rumors she had already heard from him. He came running back, with a white circle of milk round his lips. "Mother," he began, "have you ever been Over the Mountains?"

132

"No, I've never been anywhere but just here in the country, and where you was born, back where we moved from."

"Well, mother, how old am I now?"

"You're goin' on twelve, Joey, dear."

"Yes, that's what I thought. Benny ain't on'y ten. And he ain't as big for his age as what I am. He's been to the circus, though; his father took him to it at Wheeling that time when he went on the steamboat. I wisht I could go to a circus."

"Well, maybe you kin when you grow up. Circuses ain't everything."

"No," the boy relucted. "Benny says the New Jerusalem will be a good deal like the circus. That's the reason he coaxed his father to let him go. Is Philadelphy as far as Wheeling?"

"A good deal further, from what I've heard tell," his mother said; she smiled at his innocently sinuous approach to his desire.

He broke out with it. "Mother, what's the reason I can't go with Benny, and Mr. Hingston, and the Little Flock? They'd take good care of me, and I wouldn't make Mr. Hingston any trouble. Me 'n' Benny could sleep together. And the Good Old Man he's always been very pleasant to me. Patted my head oncet, and ast me what my name was."

"Did you tell him it was Billings?" his mother asked uneasily.

"No, just Joseph, and he said, Well, that was his name, too. Don't you think the Good Old Man is good?"

"We're none of us as good as we ought to be, Joey. No, he ain't a good man, I'm afraid."

"My!" the boy said, and then after a moment: "I don't want to go, mother, unless you want to let me go."

His mother did not speak for a while, and it seemed as if she were not going to speak at all, so that the boy said, with a little sigh of renunciation, "I didn't expect you would. But I'd be as careful! And even if the Good Old Man ain't so very good, Mr. Hingston is, and he wouldn't let anything happen to me."

The woman put her hand under the boy's chin, and looked into his eager eyes which had not ceased their pleading. At last she said, "You can go, Joey!"

"Mother!" He jumped to his feet from crouching at hers. "Oh, glory to God!"

"Hush, Joey, you mustn't say things like that. It's like swearing, dear."

"I know it is, and I didn't mean to. Of course it's right, in meetin', and it kind of slipped out when I wasn't thinkin'. But I won't say any bad things, you needn't be afraid. Oh, I'll be as good! But look a' here, mother! Why can't you come, too?"

"And leave your little sister?" She smiled sadly.

"I didn't think of that. But couldn't Jane take care of her? She's always carryin' her around. And Uncle David could come here, and live with them. He wouldn't want to stay there without me, or no one."

"It wouldn't do, Joey dear."

"No," the boy assented.

"You can go and tell Benny I said you might go, if his father will have you."

"Oh, he *will*; he said so; Benny's ast him! And he said he'd take good care of us both."

"I'm not afraid. You know how to take care of yourself. And, Joey"—

She stopped, and the boy prompted her, "What, mom?"

"When I said the Good Old Man wasn't a good man, I didn't want to set you against him. I want you to be good to him."

"Yes, mother," the boy assented in a puzzle. "But if he ain't good"—

"He ain't, Joey. He's a wicked man. Sometimes I think he's the wickedest man in the world. But I want you to watch out, and if ever you can help him, or do anything for him, remember that I wanted you to do it: a boy can often help a man."

"I will, mother. But I don't see the reason, if he's so very wicked, why"—

"That's the very reason, Joey dear. And go and tell Benny now that I let you go. And—don't tell him what I said about the Good Old Man."

"Oh, I woon't, I woon't, mom! Oh glory— Oh, I didn't

mean to say it, and I didn't, really, did I? But I'm so glad, and Benny'll be, too! Can I tell him now? Tonight?"

"Yes. Run along."

He hesitated; then he leaped into the air with a joyful yell, and vanished round the corner of the cabin into the dusk.

His mother did not leave her place on the threshold, but sat with her face bowed in her hands. By and by Jane Gillespie came to the door from within, and then Nancy lifted her head and made room for her to sit beside her. She told her what had passed, and Jane said, "If I was a man I would— Well, I know what I would do!"

She did not sit down, but stood behind Nancy and talked down over her shoulder. "Yes," Nancy said, "that's what I used to say when I was a girl. But now I'm glad I ain't a man, for I wouldn't know what to do."

"Well, I wouldn't 'a' left a hair in his head. I'd 'a'—I'd 'a' half killed him! Oh, when I think what a fool that man made of me!"

"Don't let Jim Redfield make a fool of you, then."

"Who said I'm letting him?" the girl demanded fiercely.

"Nobody. But don't."

"Aunt Nancy! If it was anybody but you said such a thing! But *I* know! It's because you're so set on Hughey Blake. Hughey Blake!" she ended scornfully, and went back into the cabin.

Nancy rose from her place with a sigh. "Oh, I 'spose you're right about my lettin' Joey go. *I* don't know why I let him."

———

XX

THE MEETINGS of the Little Flock had continued ever since the reappearance of Dylks, and in the earlier spirit. But the spring was broken, and since he had said that the New Jerusalem would not come down at Leatherwood, many had lost not faith but hope. Few could have the hope of following him as far as far-off Philadelphia, and sharing the glories which he promised them there. For a pioneer community the people were none of them poor; some were accounted rich, and among the richest were many followers of Dylks. But most of the Flock were hard-working farmers who could not spare the time or the money for that long journey Over the Mountains, even with the prospect of the heavenly city at the end. Yet certain of the poorest set their houses in order, and mortgaged their lands, and went with the richest, when on a morning after the last great meeting in the Temple, the Little Flock assembled for parting, some to go and some to stay.

Nancy did not come with her boy for the farewell. They had kissed each other at the cabin door, and then he had run light-heartedly away, full of wild expectation, to find Benny Hingston at the cross-roads and then race with him to join the crowd before the Temple, where the Little Flock stood listening to the last words which the Good Old Man would speak to them in Leatherwood. Many wept; Dylks himself was crying. The enemies of their faith did not molest them except for a yelp of derision now and then, and a long-drawn howl from the Hounds, kept well back by the Herd of the Lost, under the command of

Redfield. He stood in the chief place among these, and at his right hand Matthew Braile leaned on his stick.

When the last prayer had been said, and they who were going had kissed or shaken hands with those who were staying, and friends and foes had both scattered, Braile said to the young man whom he now faced, "Well, that's the last of him."

Redfield's jaw was still set from the effort of seeing the affair through in as much decency as he had been able to enforce. "It ain't the last of *them*. But I reckon, now he's gone, they'll behave themselves. None of the saints that are left will make trouble."

"No, with Enraghty out of the way and that kind old fool Hingston, with his example of mistaken righteousness, we can get along fairly enough with the old dispensation. Well, Abel," he called to Reverdy, who was lounging about in the empty space which the crowd had left, unwilling to leave the scene of so much excitement for the dull labors of the field, "you thought you wouldn't go to see the New Jerusalem come down, after all. How's the Good Old Man goin' to work it without you?"

"He's had to work things 'thout me for a good while now, squire," Abel returned, not with perfect satisfaction in the part assigned him by the irony of the squire. "Ever sence that night at Mr. Enraghty's, I been putty much done with him. A god that couldn't help hisself in a little trouble like that, he ain't no god for me."

"Oh, I remember. But what about Sally? She didn't go with the Little Flock, either?"

"I reckon me 'n' Sally thinks putty much alike about the Little Flock," Abel said with as much hauteur as a man in his bare feet could command. "We hain't either of us got any use for Little Flocks, any more."

"Well, I'm glad of it. But I thought she might have come to see them off."

Abel relented. "Sally ain't very well, this mornin'. Up all night with the toothache." Redfield had turned from them, and Abel now remarked, "I *was* wonderin' whether I couldn't borry a little coffee from Mis' Braile for breakfast; I been so took up 'ith all these goin's on that I hain't had no time to go to the store."

"Why, certainly," the squire replied, "and you'd better come and have breakfast with us on the way home. I came down without mine so as to see the Ancient of Days off, and make sure of it."

"Pshaw, squire, it don't seem quite right to have you usin' them old Bible sayin's so common like."

"Well, Abel, perhaps it isn't quite the thing. But you must make allowance for my being in such high spirits. I haven't breathed so free in a coon's age. I *would* like to have stowed Dylks for a little while in the loft with ours! But Mis' Braile wouldn't hear of it. Well, we've seen the last of him, I hope. And now we're hearing the last of him." He halted Abel in their walk, at a rise in the ground where they caught the sound of the hymn which the Little Flock, following Dylks for a certain way, were singing. " 'Sounds weel at a distance,' as the Scotchman said of the bag-pipes. And the farther the better. I don't believe I should care if I *never* heard that tune again." They reached Braile's cabin, and he said, "Well, now come in and have something to stay your stomach while you're waiting for Sally to make the coffee you're going to borrow."

"No, I reckon not, squire," Abel loyally held out.

"Well, then, come in and get the coffee, anyhow."

"I reckon that's a good idea, squire," Abel assented with a laugh for the joke at his cost. As they mounted the steps, Braile stopped him at the sound of voices in the kitchen.

A prevalent voice was the voice of Sally. "Well, just one *sup* more, Mis' Braile. You do make the *best* coffee! I believe in my heart that it's took my toothache all away a'ready, and I suppose poor Abel'll be goin' up home with some of that miser'ble stuff he gits at the store, and expectin' to find me there in bed yit. I thought I'd jest slip down, and borry a little o' your'n to surprise him with, but when I smelt it, I jest couldn't hold out. I don't suppose but what he stayed to see the Little Flock off, any way, and you say Squire Braile went. Well, I reckon he had to, justice o' the peace, that way. I'm thankful the Good Old Man's gone, for one, and I don't never want to see hide or hair of him ag'in in Leatherwood. There's such a thing as gittin' enough of a thing, and I've got enough of strange gods for one while."

Murmurs of reply came from Mrs. Braile at times, but Sally mainly kept the word.

"Well, and what do you think of Nancy Billun's lettun' her Joey go off with the Little Flock, her talkun' the way she always done about 'em? Of course he's safe with Mr. Hingston and Benny, and they'll bring him back all right, but don't you think she'd be afeared 'ut he might be took up in the New Jerusalem when it riz ag'in?"

"Abel," the squire said, "I don't like this. We seem to be listening. I don't believe Sally will like our overhearing her; and we ought to warn her. It's no use your stamping your bare feet, for they wouldn't make any noise. I'll rap my stick on the floor." He also called out, "Hello the house!" and Sally herself came to the kitchen door. She burst into her large laugh. "Well, I declare to goodness, if it ain't Abel and the squire! Well, if this ain't the best joke on *me!* Did you see Dylks off, Squire Braile? And a good riddance to bad rubbage, *I* say."

XXI

HUGHEY BLAKE, long-haired, barefooted and freckled, hung about the door of Nancy's cabin, where she sat with her little girl playing in the weedy turf at her foot. The late October weather was sometimes hot at noon, but the evenings were cool and the evening air was sweet with the scent of the ripened corn, and the faint odor of the fallen leaves. The grasshoppers still hissed; at moments the crickets within and without the cabin creaked plaintively.

"I just come," Hughey said, "to see if you thought she wouldn't go to the Temple with me, tonight. The Flock lets us have our turn reg'lar now, and we're goin' to have Thursday evenin' meetin' like we used to." In a discouraging silence from Nancy, he went on, "I'm just on my way home, now, and I'll git my shoes there; and I don't expect to wear this hickory shirt, and no coat"—

"Yes, I know, Hughey, but I don't believe it'll be any use. You can try; but I don't believe it will. I reckon you'd find out that she's goin' with Jim Redfield, if any body. She's been off with him 'most the whole afternoon, gatherin' pawpaws—he knows the best places; I should think they could have got all the pawpaws in Leatherwood by this time. You know I've always liked you, Hughey, and so has her father, and you've played together ever since you was babies, and you've always been her beau from childern up. There ain't a person in Leatherwood that don't respect you and feel to think that any girl might be glad to get you; but I'm afraid it's just your cleverness, and bein' so gentle like"—

140

"Do you 'spose, Nancy," the young man faltered disconsolately, "it's had anything to do with my not gettin' her that hair? I could 'a' done it as easy as Jim Redfield; but to tear it right out of his head, that way, I couldn't; it went ag'in my stommick."

"I don't believe it's that, Hughey. If you must know, I believe it's just Jim Redfield himself. He's bewitched her and she's got to be bewitched by somebody; if it ain't one it's another; it was *him* then, and it's Jim, now."

"I see," the young man assented sadly.

"She ain't good enough for you, that's the truth, Hughey, though I say it, her own kith and kin. I can't make you understand, I know; but she's got to have somebody that she can feel the power of."

"I'd do anything for her, Nancy."

"That's just it! She don't want that kind of lovin', as you may call it. I don't believe my brother's a very easy man to turn, but Jane has always done as she pleased with him; he's been like clay in the hands of the potter with her. Many another girl would have been broken into bits before now; but she's just as tough as so much hickory. I don't say but what she's a good girl; there ain't a better in Leatherwood, or anywheres. She's as true as a die, and tender as anything in sickness, and 'd lay down and die where she saw her duty, and 'd work till she dropped if need be; but, no, she ain't one that wants softness in her friends. Well, she won't git any too much of it in Jim Redfield. They're of a piece, and she *may* find out that she's made a mistake, after all."

"Has she—she hain't promised to marry him yit?"

"No, I don't say that. But ever since that night at the Temple he's been round after her. He's been here, and he's been at her father's, and she can't go down to the Corners for anything but what he comes home helpin' her to bring it. You seen yourself, how he always gets her to come home from meetin'."

"Yes," Hughey assented forlornly. "I'm always too late at the door; he's with her before a body can git the words out."

"Well, that's it. I don't say she ain't a good girl, one of the very best, but she's hard, hard, hard; and I don't see what's ever to break her."

The girl's voice came from round the cabin, calling, "Honey, honey, honey!" and the little one started from her play at her mother's feet, and ran toward the voice, which Jane now brought with her at the corner, and chuckling, and jug-jugging, bird-like, for joy, threw herself at Jane's knees.

"See what I brought you, honey. It's good and ripe, but it ain't half as good as my honey, honey, honey!" She put the pawpaw into the child's hands and mumbled her, with kisses of her eyes, cheeks, hair and neck. "Oh, I could eat you, *eat* you!"

She must have seen the young fellow waiting for her notice, but Nancy had to say, "Here's Hughey, Jane," before she spoke to him.

"Oh! Hughey," she said, not unkindly, but as if he did not matter.

He stood awkward and Nancy judged it best for all the reasons to add, "Hughey wants you to go to the Temple with him tonight," and the young fellow smiled gratefully if not hopefully at her.

The girl stiffened herself to her full height from the child she was stooping over. She haughtily mounted the steps beside Nancy, and without other recognition of Hughey in the matter she said, "I've *got* company," and disappeared into the cabin.

"Well, Hughey?" Nancy pityingly questioned.

"No, Nancy," he replied with a manful struggle for manfulness, "I—I— It's meant, I reckon," and slunk away from the girl's brutality as if it were his own shame.

Nancy picked up her little one, and followed indoors.

"Don't you talk to me, Aunt Nancy!" the girl cried at her. "What does he keep askin' me for?"

"He won't ask you any more, Jane," the woman quietly returned.

They joined in putting the little one to bed. Then, without more words, Jane kissed the child, and came back to kiss her again when she had got to the door. "Aunt Nancy, I hate you," she said as she went out and left the woman alone.

Ever since Joey went away with the believers to see the New Jerusalem come down in Philadelphia, Jane had been sleeping at her father's cabin in resentful duty to his years and solitude. She got him his breakfast and left it for him before she went to take her own with Nancy, and she had his dinner and supper ready for his return from the field, but she did not eat with him, and he was abed before she came home at night.

Joey had been gone nearly a month, and no word had come back from any of the Little Flock who went with Dylks. It was not the day of letters by mail; if some of the pilgrims had sent messages by the wagoners returning from their trips Over the Mountains, they had not reached the families left behind, and no angel-borne tidings came to testify of the wonder at Philadelphia. Those left behind waited in patience rather than anxiety; where life was often hard, people did not borrow trouble and add that needless debt to their load of daily cares. Nancy said to others that she did not know what to think, and others said the same to her, and they got what comfort they could out of that.

Now she did not light the little rag-lamp which she and Jane sometimes sat by with their belated sewing or darning if they had not kept the hearth-fire burning. She went to bed in the dark, and slept with the work-weariness which keeps the heart-heavy from waking. She had work in her tobacco patch to do, as well as in the house, where Jane helped her; she would not let the girl help her get the logs and brush together on the clearing which Laban had begun burning to enrich the soil for the planting of the next year's crop with the ashes.

She must have slept long hours when she heard the sound of a cry from the dark without.

"Mother! Mother! *Oh*, mother!" it came nearer and nearer, till it beat with the sound of a fist on the cabin door. In the piecing out of the instant dream which she started from, she thought as that night when Dylks called her, that it must be Laban; he sometimes called her Mother after the baby came, and now she called back, "Laban! Laban!" but the voice said, "It ain't father; it's me, mother; it's Joey!"

"Oh, dear heart!" she joyfully lamented, and flung herself from her bed and reeled still drunk with slumber, and pulled up the latch and flung open the door, and caught her boy to her breast.

"Oh, mother!" he said, laughing and crying, "I'm so hungry!"

"To be sure you're hungry, child; and I'll have you your supper in half a minute, as soon as I can rake the fire open. Lay down on mother's bed there, and rest while I'm gettin' ready for you. The baby won't wake, and I don't care if she does."

"I 'spose she's grown a good deal. But I *am* tired," the boy said, stretching himself out. "Me 'n' Benny run all the way as soon as we come in sight of the crick, and him 'n' Mis' Hingston wanted me to stay all night, but I wouldn't. I wanted to see you so much, mother."

"Did Mr. Hingston come back with you? Or, don't tell me anything; don't speak, till you've had something to eat."

"I woon't, mother," the boy promised, and then he said, "But you ought to see Philadelphy, mother. It's twenty times as big as Wheeling, Benny says, and all red brick houses and white marble steps." He was sitting up, and talking now; his mother flew about in the lank linsey-woolsey dress she had thrown over her night-gown in some unrealized interval of her labors, and had got the skillet of bacon hissing over the coals.

"And to think," she bleated in self-reproach, "that I'll have to give you *rye* coffee! You know, Joey, dear, there hain't very much cash about this house, and the store won't take truck for coffee. But with good cream in it, the rye tastes 'most as good. Set up to the table, now," she bade him, when she had put the rye coffee with the bacon and some warmed-up pone on the leaf lifted from the wall.

She let the boy silently glut himself till he glanced round between mouthfuls and said, "It all looks so funny and little, in here, after Philadelphy."

Then she said, "But you don't say anything about the New Jerusalem. Didn't it come down, after all?" She smiled, but sadly rather than gladly in her skepticism.

"No, mother," the boy answered solemnly. Then after a moment he said, "I got something to tell you, mother. But I don't know whether I hadn't better wait till morning."

"It's most morning, now, Joey, I reckon, if it ain't already. That's the twilight comin' in at the door. If you wouldn't rather get your sleep first"—

"No, I can't sleep till I tell you, now. It's about the Good Old Man."

"Did he—did he go up?" she asked fearfully.

"No, mother, he didn't. Some of them say he was took up, but, mother, *I* believe—he was drownded!"

XXII

"Drownded?" the boy's mother echoed. "What do you mean, Joey? What makes you believe he was drownded?"

"I seen him."

"Seen him?"

"In the water. We was all walkin' along the river bank, and some o' the Flock got to complainin' because he hadn't fetched the New Jerusalem down yit, and wantin' to know when he was goin' to do it, and sayin' this was Philadelphy, and why didn't he; and Mr. Hingston he was tryin' to pacify 'em, and Mr. Enraghty he scolded 'em, and told 'em to hesh up, or they'd be in danger of hell-fire; but they didn't, and the Good Old Man he begun to cry. It was awful, mother."

"Go on, Joey. Don't stop."

"Well, he'd been prayin' a good deal, off and on, and actin' like he wasn't in his right senses, sometimes, talkin' to hisself, and singin' his hymn—that one, you know"—

"Never mind, Joey dear," his mother said, "keep on."

"And all at once, he up and says, 'If I want to, I can turn this river into a river of gold,' and one o' the Flock, about the worst one, he hollers back, 'Well, why don't you do it, then?' and Mr. Enraghty—well, they call him Saint Paul, you know,—he told the other one to shut his mouth; and they got to jawin', and I heard a rattlin' of gravel, like it was slippin' down the bank, and then there was the Good Old Man in the water, hollerin' for help, and his hat off, floatin' down stream, and his hair all over his shoulders. And before I knowed what to think, he sunk, and

146

when he come up, I was there in the water puttin' out for him."

"Yes, Joey."

"I can't remember how I got there; must 'a' jumped in without thinkin'; he'd been so good to me, all along, and used to come to me in the night-time when he 'sposed I was asleep, and kiss me; and cry— But I'd 'a' done it for anybody, anyway, mother."

"Yes. Go"—

"Some of 'em was takin' their shoes and coats off to jump in, and some jest standin' still, and hollerin' to me not to let him ketch holt o' me, or he'd pull me under. But I knowed he couldn't do that, becuz I could ketch him by one arm, and hold him off—me 'n' Benny's practiced it in the crick,—and I swum up to him; and he went down ag'in, and when he come up ag'in, his face was all soakin' wet like he'd been cryin' under the water, and he says, kind o' bubblin'—like this"— The boy made the sound. "He says, 'Oh my son, God help—bub-ub—bless you!' and then he went down, and I swum round and round, expectin' he'd come up somewheres; but he didn't come up no more. It was awful, mother, becuz that didn't seem to be the end of it; and it was. Just didn't come up no more. They jawed some, before they *got* over the mountains," the boy said reminiscently. "They hadn't brung much money; even Mr. Hingston hadn't, becuz they expected the Good Old Man to work miracles, and make silver and gold money out of red cents, like he said he would. All the nights we slep' out o' doors, and some times we had to ast for victuals; but the Good Old Man he always found places to sleep, nice caves in the banks and holler trees, and wherever he ast for victuals they give plenty. And Mr. Enraghty he said it was a miracle if he always knowed the best places to sleep, and the kindest women to ast for victuals. Do you believe it was, mother?"

Nancy said, after an effort for her voice, "He might have been there before, Joey dear."

"Well, that's so; but none of 'em thunk o' that. And what Mr. Enraghty said stopped the jawin' at the time. It all begun agin, worse than ever when we got almost to Philadelphy; and he said some of 'em must take the south fork of the road with Saint Paul and keep on till they saw a big light over Philadelphy, where the New Jerusalem was swellin' up, and the rest would meet 'em there with him and Saint Peter. They said, why couldn't we all go together? And it was pretty soon after that that he slipped into the river. Stumbled on a round stone, I reckon."

The woman sat slowly smoothing the handle of the coffee-pot up and down, and staring at the boy; but she did not speak.

"Benny jumped in by that time, but it wasn't any use. Oh! I seen the ocean, mother; Mr. Hingston took me 'n Benny down on a boat; and I seen a stuffed elephant in a show, or a museum, they called it. Benny said it was just like the real one in the circus at Wheeling. Mother, do you believe he throwed his-self in?"

"Who, Joey?" she faintly asked.

"Why, the Good Old Man. That's what some of 'em said, them that was disappointed about the New Jerusalem. But some said he did fetch it down; and they seen it, with the black horses and silver gates and velvet streets, and everything just the way he promised. And the others said he'd fooled 'em, or else they was just lyin'. And they said he'd got to the end of his string; and that was why he throwed himself in, and when he got in, he was scared of drowndin' and that was why he hollered for help. But I believe he just slipped in. Don't you, mother?"

"Yes, Joey."

"Mother, I don't believe the Good Old Man had a grea' deal of courage. All the way Over the Mountains, he'd seem to scare at any little noise, even in broad day light. Oncst, when we was goin' along through the woods, a pig jumped out of some hazel-nut bushes, and scared him so that he yelled and fell down in a fit, and they was a good while fetchin' him to. Do *you* think he was God, mother?"

"No, Joey."

"Well, that's what I think, too. If he was God, he wouldn't

been afeared, would he? And in the night sometimes he'd come and git me to come and lay by him where he could put his arm round my neck, and feel me, like as if he wanted comp'ny. Well, now, that wasn't much like God, was it? And when he thought I was asleep, I could hear him prayin', 'O merciful Saviour!' and things like that; and if he was God, who could he pray *to?* It wasn't sense, was it? Well, I just believe he fell in, and he was afeared he was drowndin' and that's why he hollered out. Don't you, mother?"

"Yes, I do, Joey."

"And you think I done right, don't you, to try to help him, even if it *was* some resk?"

"Oh, yes."

"I knowed it was *some* resk, but I didn't believe it was much, and I kind of thought you'd want me to."

"Oh yes, yes," his mother said. "You did right, Joey. And you're a good boy, and— Joey, dear," and she rose from the bench where she was sitting with him, "I believe I'll go and lay down on the bed a minute. Bein' up, so"—

"Why, yes, mother! You lay down and I'll clear up the breakfast, or supper if it's it. It'll be like old times," he said in the pride of his long absence from home. His mother lay down on the bed with her face to the wall, and he went very quietly about his work, so as not to wake the baby. But after a moment he went to his mother, and whispered hoarsely, "You don't suppose I could go and see Benny, a minute, after I've got done? It's 'most broad day, and I know he'll be up, too."

"Yes, go," she said without turning her face to him.

He kept tiptoeing about, and when he had finished, he stood waiting to be sure whether she was sleeping before he opened the door. Now she turned her face, and spoke— "Joey?"

"Yes, mother?" he whispered back, and ran to her softly, in his bare feet.

"Did you get to like him any better?"

He seemed not to take her question as anything strange, or to be in doubt of whom she meant.

"Why, there in the water, at the very last, when he kep' goin' down, I liked him. Yes, I must have. But all along, I felt more like sorry for him. He seemed so miser'ble, all the time, and so—well—scared."

"Yes." She had got the boy's hand, and without turning her body with her face she held his hand in hers closely under her arm. "Joey, I told you he was a wicked man. I can't tell you any different now. But I'm glad you was sorry for him. I am sorry too. Joey,—he was your father." She pressed his hand harder.

"Goodness!" he said, but he did not suffer himself to say more.

"He went away and left me when you was a little baby, and he never come back till he come back here. I never had any word from him. For all I could tell he was dead. I never wanted him to be dead," she defended herself to herself in something above the intelligence of the boy. "I married Laban, who's been more of a father to you than what *he* was."

"Oh, *yes*, mother!"

"When your *real* father come here, I made your *true* father go away." Now she turned and faced her son, keeping his hand tighter in hers. "Joey, I want to have you go and tell him to come back."

"Right away, mother?"

"Why, yes?" she said with question in her answer.

"I thought maybe you'd let me see Benny, first," he suggested a little wistfully.

She almost laughed. "You dear boy! Go and see Benny on your way. Take him with you, if his father will let him go. You're both such great travellers. Your father's at the Wilkinses' yit, I reckon; they hain't finished with their cider, I don't believe. Go, now!"

The boy had been poising as if on winged feet, and now he flew. He came back to say at the door, "I don't believe I'll want any breakfast, mother; we had such a late supper."

It was a thoughtful suggestion, and she said "No," but before her answer came he had flown again.

The baby woke, and she cooed to it, and she went about the

one room of the little cabin trying to put it more in order than before. Some pieces of the moss in the chinking of the round logs near the chimney seemed loose, and she packed them tighter. As she worked she sang. She sang a hymn, but it was a hymn of thanksgiving.

The doorway darkened, and she turned to see the figure of her brother black in the light.

"I see, you've heard the news," he said grimly. "I was afraid I might find you making a show of mourning. *I* don't pretend to any. I haven't had such a load off me since that rascal first come back."

She answered resentfully, "What makes *you* so glad, David? He didn't come back to make *you* drive *your* husband away!"

"I was always afraid he might make me kill him. He tried hard enough, and sometimes I thought he might. But blessed be the Lord, he's dead. They're holding a funeral for him in the Temple. The news is all through the Creek. I suppose you know how Jane has fixed it up with James Redfield. I feel to be sorry for Hughey Blake; but he never could have mastered her. She's got an awful will, Jane has. But James has got an awful will too, as strong as Jane"—

Nancy cut him short: "David, I don't care anything about Jane—now."

"No," he assented. "Where's Joey?" he asked, leaning inward with his hands resting on either jamb of the door.

"Gone for Laban."

"Well," David said, with something like grudge. "You hain't lost much time. But I don't know as I blame you," he relented.

"I wouldn't care if you did, David," she answered.

XXIII

LATE in the long twilight of the early spring day a stranger who was travelling in the old fashion on horseback, with his legs swathed in green baize against the mud of the streaming roads, and with his spattered saddle-bags hung over the pommel before him, was riding into Leatherwood. He paused in a puddle of the lane that left the turnpike not far off, and curved between the new-plowed fields in front of a double log-cabin, which had the air of being one of the best habitations of its time though its time was long past; the logs it was built of were squared; the chimneys at either end were of stone masonry instead of notched sticks laid in clay. Against the wall of the porch between the two rooms of the cabin, an old man sat tilted back in his chair, smoking a pipe which he took from his mouth at sight of the stranger's arrest.

"Can you tell me, please, which is my way to the tavern, or some place where I can find a night's lodging?"

The old man dropped his chair forward, and got somewhat painfully out of it to toddle to the edge of his porch. "Why, there isn't a tavern, rightly speaking, in Leatherwood, now, though for the backwoods we had a very passable one, once. I wish," he said after a moment, "that we could offer you a lodging here; but if you'll light and throw your horse's rein over the peg in this post, I would be pleased to have you stay to supper with us. My wife is just getting it."

"Why, thank you, thank you," the stranger said. "I mustn't think of troubling you. I dare say I can get something to eat at your tavern. I've often been over night in worse places, no doubt. I've been travelling through your State, and I've turned a little out of my way to stop at Leatherwood, because I've been interested in a peculiar incident of your local history."

The two men perceived from something in each other's parlance, though one spoke with the neat accent of the countries beyond the Alleghanies, and the other with the soft slurring Ohio River utterance, that they were in the presence of men different by thinking if not by learning from most men in the belated region of a new country.

"Oh, yes," the old man said with instant intelligence, "the Leatherwood God."

"Yes," the other eagerly assented. "I was told, at your county seat, that I could learn all about it if I asked for Squire Braile, here."

"I am Matthew Braile," the old man said with dignity, and the stranger returned with a certain apology in his laugh:

"I must confess that I suspected as much, and I'm ashamed not to have frankly asked at once."

"Better 'light," the squire condoned whatever offence there might have been in the uncandor. "I don't often get the chance to talk of our famous imposture, and I can't let one slip through my fingers. You must come in to supper, and if you smoke I can give you a pipe of our yellow tobacco, afterwards, and we can talk"—

"But I should tire you with my questions. In the morning"—

"We old men sometimes have a trick of not living till morning. You'd better take me while you can get me."

"Well, if you put it in that way," the stranger said, and he slipped down from his saddle.

The old man called out, "Here, Abel!" and the figure of what seemed an elderly boy came lurching and paddling round the corner of the cabin, and ducked his gray head hospitably toward the stranger. "Give this horse a feed while we're taking ours."

"All right, squire. Jest helpin' Sally put the turkey-chicks to bed out o' the cold, or I'd 'a' been round at the first splashin' in the road."

"And now come in," the squire said, reaching a hand of welcome from the edge of the porch to the stranger as he mounted the steps. "Old neighbors of ours," he explained Abel and the unseen Sally. "We've known them, boy and girl, from the begining, and when their old cabin fell down in the tail-end of a tornado a few years back, we got them here in a new one behind ours, to take care of them, and let them take care of us. They don't eat with us," he added, setting open the kitchen door, and ushering the stranger into the warm glow and smell of the interior. "Mis' Braile," he said for introduction to his wife, and explained to her, "A friend that I caught on the wing. I don't know that I *did* get your name?"

"Mandeville—T. J. Mandeville; I'm from Cambridge."

"Thomas Jefferson, I suppose. Cambridge, Ohio—back here?"

"Massachusetts."

"Well, you didn't sound like Ohio. I always like to make sure. Well, you must pull up. Mother, have you got anything fit to eat, this evening?"

"You might try and see," Mrs. Braile responded in what seemed their habitual banter.

"Well, don't brag," the squire returned, and between them they welcomed the stranger to a meal that he said he had not tasted the like of in all his Western travel.

It seemed that their guest did not smoke, and the squire alone lighted his pipe. Then he joked his wife. "Mother, will you let us stay by the fire here—it's a little chilly out doors, and those young frogs do take the heart of you with their peeping—if we don't mind your bothering round? Mr. Mandeville wants to hear all about our Leatherwood God."

"He'll hear more about him than he wants to if he listens to all you tell, Matthew," Mrs. Braile retorted.

"Oh, no; oh, no," the stranger protested, and the squire laughed.

"You wanted to know," he said, well after the beginning of their talk, "whether there were many of the Little Flock left.

Well, some; and to answer your other question, they're as strong in the faith as ever. The dead died in the faith; the living that were young in it in the late eighteen-twenties are old in it now in the first of the fifties. It's rather curious," the squire said, with a long sigh of satisfaction in the anomaly, "but after the arrest of Dylks, and his trial and acquittal before this court," the squire smiled, "when he came out of the tall timber, and had his scalp mended, and got into a whole suit of Saint Peter's clothes, he didn't find the Little Flock fallen off a great deal. They were a good deal scared, and so was he. That was the worst of the lookout for Dylks; his habit of being afraid; it was about the best thing, too; kept him from playing the *very* devil. There's no telling how far he might have gone if he hadn't been afraid: I mean, gone in personal mischief."

"Yes," the stranger assented. "And his failure in all his miracles had no effect on his followers?"

The squire laughed, with a rattling of loose teeth on his pipe-stem. "Why, he didn't fail according to the Little Flock; it was only the unbelievers that disbelieved in the miracles. Even those that went with him Over the Mountains to see the New Jerusalem come down, got to having seen it as time went on, though some had their doubts when they first came back. Before they died, they'd all seen him go up in a chariot of fire with two black horses and no driver. Nobody but those two purblind ignorant boys that tried to keep him from drowning, when he fell into the river, could be got to say that the heavenly city didn't come down and suck him up. Why, seven or eight years after he left there was a preacher who was one of his followers came back here, and preached in the Dylks Temple—the old Temple burned down, long ago and was never rebuilt—preached the divinity of Dylks, and said there was no true religion that didn't recognize him as God. As for Christianity, he said it was just a hotch-potch of Judaism and heathenism. *He* saw the Good Old Man go right up into heaven, and said he was going to come back to earth before long and set up his kingdom here. He's never done it, and that slick preacher never came back, either, after the first. He was very well dressed and looked as if he had been living on the fat of the land, somewhere, among the faithful Over the Mountains, I reckon. Knew where the fried chickens roosted. Excuse me, mother. She's heard that joke before," he explained to their guest.

"I've heard it too often to mind it," Mrs. Braile mocked back.

"Well, it seems to be new to our friend here."

Mr. Mandeville was laughing, but he controlled himself to ask, "And had the fellow no progressive doctrine, no steps of belief, no logical formulation of his claims? He couldn't have been merely a dunderheaded, impudent charlatan, who expected to convince by the miracles he didn't do?"

"Oh, no; oh, no. I didn't mean to imply that," the squire explained. "He was a cunning rascal in his way, and he had the sort of brain that has served the purpose of the imposter in all ages. He had a plan of belief, as you may call it, which he must have thought out before he came here, if he hadn't begged, borrowed or stolen it from somebody else. At first he called himself a humble teacher of Christianity, but it wasn't a great while before he pretended to be Jesus Christ who died on Calvary. That didn't satisfy him long, though. When he had convinced some that he was Christ, he began to teach that the Christ who was crucified, though he was a *real* Messiah, was not a *perfect* Messiah, because he had died and been buried, and death had had power over him just as it has over any mortal. But the real Messiah would never taste death, and he was that Messiah. Dylks would never taste death, and as the real Messiah, he would be one with God, and in fact he was the one and only God. These were the steps, and the way to belief in the godhead was clear to the meanest understanding. The meaner the understanding the clearer," the squire summed up, with another tattoo on his pipe stem. "You see," he resumed after a moment, "life is hard in a new country, and anybody that promises salvation on easy terms has got a strong hold at the very start. People will accept anything from him. Somewhere, tucked away in us, is the longing to know whether we'll live again, and the hope that we'll live happy. I've got fun out of that fact in a community where I've had the reputation of an infidel for fifty years; but all along I've felt it in myself. We want to be good, and we want to be safe, even if we are not good; and the first fellow that comes along and tells us to have faith in him, and he'll make it all right, why we have faith in him. That's all."

"Well, then," the stranger said, holding him to the logic of the facts, as he leaned toward him from his side of the fireplace, and fixed him with an eager eye, "I can't see why he didn't establish his superstition in universal acceptance, as say, Mahomet did."

"I'm glad you came to that," the squire blandly submitted. "For one thing, and the main thing, because he was a coward. He had plenty of audacity but mighty little courage, and his courage gave out just when he needed it the most. And perhaps he hadn't perfect faith in himself; he was a fool, but he wasn't a crazy fool. Then again, my idea is that the scale was too small, or the scene, or the field, or whatever you call it. The backwoods, as Leatherwood was then, was not the right starting point for a world-wide imposture. Then again, as I said, Dylks was timid. He was not ready to shed blood for his lie, neither other people's nor his own; and when it came to fighting for his doctrine, he was afraid; he wanted to run. And in fact, he did run, first and last. No liar ever had such a hold on them that believed his lie; they'd have followed him any lengths; but he hadn't the heart to lead them. When Redfield and I got hold of him, after he had tasted the *fear* of death, there that week in the tall timber, he was willing to promise anything we said. And he kept his promise; he wouldn't if he could have helped it, but he knew Jim Redfield would hold him to it, if he squeezed his life out doing it."

The stranger was silent, but not apparently convinced, and meanwhile he took up another point of interest in the story which he heard from the squire. "And whatever became of his wife, and her 'true' husband?"

"Oh, they lived on together. Not very long, though. They

died within a week of each other, didn't they, mother?"

"Just a week," Mrs. Braile said, animated by the human touch in the discussion. "They lived mighty happy together, and it was as good a death as a body could want to die. It was that summer when the fever mowed the people down so. They took their little girl with them," she sighed from a source of hidden sorrow. "They all went together."

Braile took his pipe out and gulped before he could answer the stranger's next question. "And the boy? Dylks's son, is he living?"

"Oh yes." At the pleasant thought of the boy, the squire began to smile. "He and Hingston's son took over the mill from Hingston, after he got too old for it, and carried it on together. Hingston wasn't one that hung on to the faith in Dylks, but he never made any fuss about giving it up. Just staid away from the Temple that the Little Flock built for themselves."

"And is young Dylks still carrying on the milling business?"

"Who? Joey? Oh, yes. He married Benny Hingston's sister. Benny's wife died, and he lives with them."

"And there ain't a better man in the whole of Leatherwood than Joey Billin's, as we always call him," Mrs. Braile put in. "He was the best boy anywhere, and he's the best man."

"Well, it's likely to come out that way, sometimes," the squire said with tender irony.

"And you can't say," Mrs. Braile continued with a certain note of indignation as for unjust neglect of the pair, "but what James Redfield and Jane has got along very well together."

"Oh, yes, they've got along," the Squire assented. "He's got along with her, and she's got along with the children—plenty of them. I reckon she's what *he* wanted, and they're what *she* did."

The stranger looked a little puzzled.

"That instinct of maternity," the Squire explained. "You may have noticed it in women—some of them."

"Oh! Oh, yes," Mr. Mandeville assented. He did not seem greatly interested.

"She's always been just crazy about 'em," Mrs. Braile explained. "Beginnin' with Nancy Billin's's little girl. Well!"

"Yes," the Squire amplified. "It was the best thing, or at least the strongest thing in Jane. I don't say anything against it, mother," he said tenderly to his wife. "Jane was a good girl, especially after she got over her faith in Dylks, and she's a good woman. At least, Jim thinks so."

Mrs. Braile contented herself as she could with his ironical concession.

The stranger looked at his watch; he jumped to his feet. "Nine o'clock! Mrs. Braile, I'm ashamed. But you must blame your husband, partly. Good night, ma'am; good— Why, look here, Squire Braile!" he arrested himself in offering his hand. "How about the obscurity of the scene where Joe Smith founded his superstition, which bids fair to live right along with the other false religions? Was Leatherwood, Ohio, a narrower stage than Manchester, New York? And in point of time the two cults were only four years apart."

"Well, that's a thing that's occurred to me since we've been talking. Suppose we look into it tomorrow? Come round to breakfast—about six o'clock. One point, though: Joe Smith only claimed to be a prophet, and Dylks claimed to be a god. That made it harder, maybe for his superstition."

THE END

Notes to the Text

2.3 Judge Taneyhill: Richard H. Taneyhill (1822–1898) was not a judge. Howells perhaps had in mind Judge Roger Brooke Taney, whom he mentions in his 1850 Columbus diary.

3.4–8 The stream . . . . together: this description, generally taken from Henry Howe, *Historical Collections of Ohio* (Columbus, 1889), I, 732, also appears in Howells' own *Stories of Ohio* (1897), pages 197–198.

3.11 lastingly famed in the annals of the region: cf. Richard H. Taneyhill, "The Leatherwood God," *Ohio Valley Historical Series: Miscellanies*, *No. 7* (Cincinnati, 1871), pages 7–8.

8.5–6 just then there come a kind of a snort: see the description of Dylks in Taneyhill, pages 12–14.

14.4–5 snatchun' the brands: cf. Zechariah, III, 2.

21.6–7 The words, quoted in Taneyhill but not there identified (page 16), are the opening lines of a hymn by Isaac Watts, frequently used in Methodist services (see *Hymns for the Use of the Methodist Episcopal Church*, Revised Edition [Cincinnati, 1849], page 85). Squire Braile paraphrases a different part of this hymn later; see the Note to 115.22–23, below.

21.34 under her father's roof: cf. Luke, VII, 6.

22.10 Elijah: cf. I Kings, XVII, 6.

23.7   brethren agreeing together in unity: cf. Psalm CXXXI, 1; also Taneyhill, page 10, and the Note to 62.7, below.

26.31–32   I work my work: cf. John, IX, 4.

27.20   I am not come . . .: cf. Matthew, IX, 13.

28.27   blessed be the name of the Lord: cf. Job, I, 21.

29.30   that was dead, is alive: cf. Luke, XV, 24.

32.27   God be merciful to me a sinner: cf. Luke, XVIII, 13.

34.21–22   where there was no shadow of turning: an echo of James, I, 17, where the constancy is God's. Howells echoed the same Biblical passage in *The Story of a Play* (1893), page 218, and in *Mrs. Farrell* (1921), page 185.

34.31–32   Your path is dark . . .: cf. the Biblical terminology in Psalm CXIX, 105.

39.10   the principal people: the two major figures described in this chapter are based on the historical Michael Brill and Robert McCormick (Taneyhill, pages 17–18).

41.26   I send him my Peace . . . .: an ironic allusion to Luke, X, 6, where the words are part of Jesus' instructions to his disciples.

48.6   the scorner's seat: an allusion to Psalm I, 1; see also the Note to 75.7, below.

48.13   the old Sadducee's scrutiny: Howells refers to the Leatherwood parties by the names of Jewish religious parties of New Testament times. The Scribes and Pharisees as leading parties represented new but predominating religious views; the Sadducees were conservatives (not skeptics, like Braile) who denied the new belief in the resurrection of the body.

49.15–16 'I can endure . . .': Taneyhill (page 19) reported these words of Dylks', which echo I Corinthians, III, 2.

49.28 locusts and wild honey: an allusion to Matthew, III, 4.

50.1–2 deceive the very elec': an ironic echo of Matthew, XXIV, 24, in which Jesus warns against false Christs and false prophets.

50.24 they had just got acrost the Leatherwood . . .: the account which follows was taken, with slight changes, from Taneyhill, pages 21–25. Howells made his source's written transmission into an unreliable oral transmission at this point.

52.9 'I bind the Devil for a thousand years': derived from Taneyhill, page 24, these words are based on Revelation, XX, 2.

52.31–33 set strife . . . a sword: the divisions among households and familes are mentioned in Taneyhill, page 25. The Biblical echo, Howells' own, is from one of Jesus' claims for the impact of His teaching, Matthew, X, 34–37.

53.14–15 They who put their faith in me shall never taste death: the words, found in Taneyhill, page 26, are based on Matthew, XVI, 28.

53.19 Dylks came down from the pulpit . . .: this whole report of the seizure of the Temple is a paraphrase of Taneyhill, pages 26–27.

54.33–34 What reason did they give for the faith that wasn't in them?: an ironic reversal of the language of I Peter, III, 15.

55.34–35 the devil . . . stayed with Dylks: a recollection of the Swedenborgian notion that devils accompany evil men in earthly life; see Howells' *A Boy's Town* (1890), pages 12–14.

56.36   the Good Old Man: derived from "old man," a name reported in Taneyhill, page 29.

57.5   the Little Flock: the name and its source (Luke, XII, 32) are both mentioned in Taneyhill, page 34.

57.7   the Herd of the Lost: the name appears in Taneyhill, page 39.

57.30   purple and fine linen: the phrase comes from the Biblical parable of Dives and Lazarus, Luke, XVI, 19.

60.23   like a thief in the night: an ironical echo of several New Testament passages referring to the Second Coming of Christ as being like the coming of a thief in its suddenness; e.g. I Thessalonians, V, 2, II Peter, III, 10, and Revelation, III, 3, and XVI, 15.

60.26   self conceit: an echo of the Biblical term found frequently in Proverbs (XXVI, 5, 12, 16; XXVIII, 11) and in Romans (XI, 25, and XII, 16).

60.27   an angel of light: an allusion to Satan as described in II Corinthians, XI, 14.

62.7   dwelt together in unity: an echo of Psalm CXXXI, 1; see the Note to 23.7, above.

62.8–9   We loved one another: based on John, XIII, 34.

62.19   he should never see corruption: the language, reported in Taneyhill, page 30, is derived from Psalm XVI, 10, and Acts, II, 27, and XIII, 35.

64.23–24   Him crucified: an echo of I Corinthians, II, 2, frequent among literalistic Protestant groups.

66.5   "Give me to drink": Howells has Dylks quote John, IV, 7, in the first of a series of burlesque parallels with Jesus' conversation with a Samaritan woman who had been married several times.

67.25–26   "I am that I am": an echo of the words ascribed to God in Exodus, III, 14.

68.31–32   Male and female created He them in His image: an echo of the words used in Genesis, I, 27, Matthew, XIX, 4, and Mark, X, 6.

70.6–7   Samuel hewing Agag in pieces: an allusion to I Samuel, XV, 33.

70.7–8   David setting Uriah in the forefront of the battle: an allusion to II Samuel, XI, 15.

71.3   It's been step by step with me . . .: an echo of Taneyhill's report of "Dylks' Successive Claims," pages 47–49.

75.7   the seat of the scorner: an allusion to Psalm I, 1; see also the Note to 48.6, above.

78.9   Word made flesh: John, I, 14.

82.1–2   She carried the bolt . . .: based on Taneyhill's account of Mrs. Pulley's secret conveyance of the cloth to Michael Brill's cabin (pages 27–28).

83.25   a dance before the Lord: an echo of II Samuel, VI, 14.

88.5–6   the Lion of Judah's mouth: the Messianic term is reported in Taneyhill, page 29, and derives from Revelation, V, 5.

88.9   a turn-coat of many colors: a grotesque use of the words describing Joseph's coat, Genesis, XXXVII, 3.

88.21   "Let your women keep silence in the churches": cf. I Corinthians, XIV, 34.

94.18   "If you will bring me a single hair . . .": cf. Taneyhill's account of Mary Gifford, page 33; the phrasing derives from I Samuel, XIV, 45.

99.28   goats: an allusion to Christ's division of men into good sheep and evil goats at the Last Judgment (Matthew, XXV, 31–46).

103.5   "Thou sayest": a blasphemous echo of Luke, XXIII, 3.

105.13   "The Lord will put forth His might": cf. Ephesians, VI, 10.

105.14   the arm of flesh: cf. II Chronicles, XXXII, 8, and Jeremiah, XVII, 5.

109.8   showed forth the glory . . .: an allusion to Psalm XIX, 1–2.

114.17–18   I have nowhere to lay my head: an echo of Jesus' words (Luke, IX, 58).

115.22–23   'down from the shining courts above in joyful haste': Squire Braile is paraphrasing the first two lines of the third stanza of Dylks' hymn (see Note to 21.6–7, above), which originally were—

> Down from the shining seats above,
> With joyful haste he fled . . .

118.30–31   all the mentally lame, halt and blind: an ironic echo of Matthew, XV, 30, and Luke, VII, 22.

119.2–3   the ignorant are sure to want a sign . . . along without it: cf. the seekers after signs in Matthew, XII, 38–39.

124.10   'Jehovah, Jove or Lord': Alexander Pope, "The Universal Prayer," l. 4.

128.20–21   'Many are called but few are chosen': Matthew, XXII, 14.

128.21–22   heaven and earth . . . not pass away: Matthew, XXIV, 34–35.

128.25   stone the prophets: cf. Matthew, XXIII, 37.

129.8–10   With the eyes of faith . . . wise of this world: cf. Matthew, XI, 25.

129.10–14   But now I go from you . . . the wonder of it: an echo of Isaiah, LII, 7.

129.19–34   " 'Its light . . . . delight.' ": a close quotation from Taneyhill, page 45.

129.32–33   like ear hath not heard: Howells has substituted this phrase, which echoes I Corinthians, II, 9, for Taneyhill's "ineffably sweet."

130.8–9   "But what shall we eat . . . be clothed": an ironic flaunting of Matthew, VI, 25.

138.4   Ancient of Days: cf. Daniel, VII, 9, 13, and 22.

141.18   clay in the hands of the potter: Jeremiah, XVIII, 6.

146.24   there was the Good Old Man in the water . . .: some of the details of this scene of parting are derived from Taneyhill, page 46, but the drowning of Dylks is Howells' invention.

155.27–28   seven or eight years after he left there was a preacher . . .: this account is based on Taneyhill's report of the "Return of Rev. Davis," page 52.

TEXTUAL APPARATUS

Textual Commentary

Seven forms of *The Leatherwood God* are of potential relevance to the establishment of the text of the present edition. The three earliest are a heavily revised holograph manuscript (including twenty leaves of typescript) of the first nine chapters of the novel; a typescript prepared from the complete original manuscript, revised by Howells and corrected by a Century Company editor; and a set of carbon copies of the first sixty-four pages of that typescript. Descriptions of the physical characteristics of these three items are presented in A Note on the Manuscript and Typescripts, pages 186–190. The other four versions of the text are the forms published during Howells' lifetime. The novel first appeared in the *Century Magazine*, in eight installments from April through November 1916 (volumes 91–93). The first book edition, that of the Century Company in New York (BAL 9840), is dated 1916 on the title page; a letter from Howells to his sister Aurelia dated 28 October 1916 announced the publication of the book on that date.[1] It was deposited at the Library of Congress on 2 November 1916. The English edition of Herbert Jenkins, Limited, London, was deposited at the British Museum on 29 November 1916, though the book is dated 1917; the edition was probably issued between 30 October and 3 November 1916, since Curtis Brown, Howells' London agent, reported on Friday, 3 November, that the book was out in London that week. Finally, the edition of Louis Conard of Paris appeared in 1918 as volume 88 of the Conard Standard Collection of British and American Authors.[2]

---

1. MS at Harvard, as are all other manuscript letters cited. Permission to cite letters by Howells has been granted by William White Howells for the heirs of the Howells Estate, and for the Harvard materials by the Harvard College Library. Republication of these materials requires the same permissions.

2. The book was also issued in 1916 by William Briggs of Toronto, using sheets from the Century Company edition. Sometime before 1920, Herbert Jenkins also issued the novel as #34 in the firm's two-shilling "Splendid Library" series, evidently using old sheets or reprinting from the plates made for the Jenkins 1916 edition. No copy of the "Splendid Library" issue has been located; it is noted in the *Reference Catalogue of Current Literature* (1920).

Multiple collations of copies of each of the book editions have disclosed no internal textual variants.[3] Nor is there physical evidence of distinct impressions in any of them, though a letter to Howells from Douglas Z. Doty, editor of the *Century Magazine*, dated 9 January 1917 indicates that two impressions of the Century Company edition, one of 7,500 copies and one of 2,500, had been printed in 1916, and that the company had no immediate plans for reprinting. Except for a Century Company royalty statement dated 31 March 1917 and the firm's agreement of 15 June 1916 with the Jenkins firm negotiated by Curtis Brown, no other publishing records relevant to *The Leatherwood God* are known to exist.

Though there is little secondary evidence about the development and relationships of the various forms of the text, there are elaborate patterns of textual variation among them which indicate a complex internal textual history. The relatively full documentation of the early stages of composition—the surviving portion of manuscript and the typescripts—as well as the differences between them and the published forms and among the published forms themselves suggest that the preparation and revision of *The Leatherwood God* were complicated processes. For reasons to be enumerated below, the genealogy of the text cannot finally be resolved to a single satisfactory outline, and the description developed here is therefore to be taken as the most coherent explanation consistent with the evidence available, though it is not a completely verifiable one.

The relationships of the earliest stages seem clear enough. The typescript and carbon were prepared from Howells' own manuscript, and Howells revised the face copy of the typescript extensively before submitting it to the Century Company. Because the manuscript is

---

3. The following copies of the printed texts were collated in the preparation of the present text: copies of the *Century Magazine* in the Indiana University Library and the Public Library of Pontiac, Michigan; copies of the Century first edition, BAL 9840, in the Howells Edition Center (HE9840.1.1), in the Public Library of Cincinnati and Hamilton County, Ohio (Fiction, Browsing, cop. 34), and the Public Library of Pontiac, Michigan, in the Lilly Library (PS2025.L35) and the University of Illinois libraries (Urbana: 813.H83lea, Chicago Circle: P2.3.H84) and in the collections of Donald Pizer and James Stronks; copies of the Briggs issue of the Century edition in McGill University (YF.H833l) and the University of British Columbia (PS2024.L3 1916, cop. 1) libraries; copies of the Jenkins edition in the Bodleian Library (25611.e.5183), the British Library (NN.3914) and the collection of Michael Millgate; and copies of the Conard edition in the Harvard University (AC85.H916ld) and Yale University (Za H847.916ld) libraries.

closest to Howells' hand and because it represents a coherent rather than a merely tentative form of the text, it has been adopted as copy-text for that section of the present edition for which it exists (chapters I–IX, pages 3–65). Though there are problematic readings in the finished manuscript—repetitions of words and marks of punctuation, nonsense words, misspellings—it is nonetheless Howells' own work, uninfluenced by the typing errors and copy-editing which plague the later versions.[4] The face copy of the typescript, revised by Howells and then editorially styled and corrected, has been selected as copy-text for the remainder of the body of the novel.[5] In the absence of manuscript, this typescript is closest to Howells' hand by virtue of both means of transmission and proximity in time. Though a comparison of pertinent sections of the typescript with the extant manuscript indicates that the typist took a great deal of freedom with the accidentals of the text and sometimes misread substantives as well, the typescript is certainly superior to the other eligible forms of the text, all of which followed it in time and were derived from it either

---

4. All false starts, duplicated words and marks of punctuation, and erroneous spellings and marks of punctuation are recorded in the Emendations list, as are the historical sources of correction of these errors. Such corrections are made on the authority of the present edition, and the citation of other texts is provided for the purpose of historical record, not because the texts or corrections are themselves authoritative.

The Emendations list would have contained a great many more corrective readings had not some conventions been adopted for interpreting the manuscript copy-text. Very few people write with the consistency and visual clarity of a printed page, and certainly Howells did not. But it is necessary to read his manuscript as if he did form his letters and marks of punctuation consistently, in order to avoid a mire of petty or unresolvable questions. It is sometimes impossible, for example, to distinguish between Howells' "in" and "on" or between his miniscule *a* and *u*; it is also sometimes difficult to interpret the kind and sequence of punctuation, such as the quotation mark and dash for interrupted speech—often in the manuscript the quotation mark appears to be placed squarely over the dash. Where such ambiguities cannot be solved by close examination of the manuscript, they have been settled by appeal to the evidence of the texts derived from the manuscript, by giving Howells the benefit of the doubt in matters of correct spelling and diction, and by following what appear to be his usual practices in conventions of spelling and punctuation.

5. Howells made some apparently provisional changes on the carbon copy of the typescript. The incompleteness of this stage of his work makes their relevance to the development of the full and final text of *The Leatherwood God* questionable. The editorial decision has been to disregard these readings as lying outside the clear line of Howells' attention to and revision of the whole of his text. These revisions are discussed and listed in A Note on the Manuscript and Typescripts, pp. 189–190 and 196, and are not recorded in the formal Emendations and Rejected Substantives sections of the apparatus.

directly or indirectly. A further editorial question with regard to this typescript is whether Howells' revisions on it should be considered part of the theoretical copy-text. The decision, based on both abstract and concrete considerations, was to use the typescript as revised. Despite the clearest evidence that the typescript before Howells' revision contained a good many errors in both substantives and accidentals, no possibility exists for reconstructing from it the major portion of the missing manuscript readings. In the first nine chapters of the book, where manuscript and typescript can be compared, there appears only one consistent pattern among the changes made by the typist—from Howells' quotation mark-dash to the typescript dash-quotation mark to conclude interrupted or suspended speech—which would enable the editors to reinstate manuscript readings. No other differences form identifiable patterns.[6] To accept the unrevised typescript as copy-text and then to record all the revisions Howells made on this typescript as emendations would offer useful information for those who wish to study the genesis of the text, but it would have no effect on the readings of the present edition. All of Howells' revisions would have to be accepted, given the impossibility of discriminating among those which correct the erroneous typescript to Howells' manuscript readings, those which correct Howells' manuscript errors faithfully transcribed, and those which are merely refinements of satisfactory manuscript readings reproduced in the typescript. In effect, giving all the evidence of the unrevised typescript and of Howells' revisions on it where the typescript is copy-text would result in a vast amount of unuseable textual information. The revised face copy of the typescript, then, is copy-text for chapters X through XXIII (pages 66–159).[7] But the editorial markings on this typescript—apparently

---

6. In addition to the corrections of accidentals and the distortions of substantives and dialect forms noted in the Emendations and Rejected Substantives lists for the sections in which both manuscript and typescript exist, the typescript inconsistently altered the form of Howells' compounds from hyphenated to unhyphenated and vice versa, added to or deleted Howells' commas, and altered capitalization. The typescript also replaced Howells' *wont* and *aint* with their apostrophized equivalents, but since Howells inconsistently employed both forms of the words in his manuscript, such evidence cannot be used to interpret those sections of the typescript where no manuscript is extant.

7. The readings of the unrevised typescript are recorded, however, for those sections for which manuscript also exists, since Howells' original intentions for the text in these sections are known and can be compared with the typist's treatment of it and Howells' further revisions upon it.

the results of copy-editing in the Century Company office after Howells had completed his revision—are not considered part of the copy-
text and are listed separately in A Note on the Manuscript and Typescripts (pages 190–196). Finally, the copy-text for the "Publisher's
Note" printed at the beginning of the novel is the form of that note
in the Century Company edition. The note does not appear in the
extant manuscript or typescripts and is not printed in either of the
other two book editions, though the information it contains was more
briefly given in a footnote to chapter V of the May installment in the
Century Magazine (see Rejected Substantives at 52.14).[8]

   The physical relationships of manuscript and typescripts and the
relative textual authority of these materials in the establishment of
the present text are thus fairly straightforward. Greater complications
arise, however, from the information concerning transmission and revision of the text after Howells completed his work on the typescript
face copy. Galley numbers and line breaks marked on the typescript
coincide with line ends in the Century book edition, evidence that the
first setting from this printer's copy typescript was that for the book
edition rather than for the *Century Magazine* serialization. There is no
physical evidence that the typescript was used in typesetting more
than this one time, and practical considerations would have encouraged the use of galleys or proofs of the first setting rather than the
heavily marked typescript for further settings. These observations
suggest that some form of the book-edition galleys or proofs served as
printer's copy for the magazine text—prepared by the same company—and thus in one way or another for the Jenkins and Conard
editions, either through copies of book galleys or proofs or less directly

---

8. A version of this "Publisher's Note" also appeared in the New York *Times
Book Review* on 28 May 1916, p. 224, where it is referred to as an "author's note,"
with the explanation that "there have been so many inquiries as to the source and
veridical nature of 'The Leatherwood God' that the author has been impelled to
publish the following explanation." The *Times* text of the note differs from the book
text in the following details (the location of the material in the present text is followed
by the reading of the present text, a bracket, and the *Times Book Review* reading):

line 2	largely] *om.*
lines 3–4	*Ohio Valley Series*, Robert Clarke Co.,
	Cincinnati] Ohio Valley Series
line 7	actual] real
line 10	imposter] impostor
line 11	at] of
line 12	Otherwise] The rest of

through some form of the magazine typesetting. Lacking evidence that pre-publication materials from the magazine and book editions or letters and formal publishing records might provide, these questions must be dealt with solely on the basis of the patterns of textual variation.

The relationship of at least one form of the text to the others can be defined immediately: the Conard edition, published in 1918, at least one full year after the others, was certainly prepared from a copy of the Jenkins edition, either printed book or late proof stage. The pattern of its differences from either of the American texts parallels that of the Jenkins almost exactly, and all substantive variants from the Jenkins edition are apparently compositorial lapses—dropped words and phrases or typographical errors—and not the results of authorial revision or conscious editorial clarification.[9] The *Century Magazine* text and the Jenkins edition, however, seem to be based independently on some form of the pre-publication typesetting of the Century book edition. The clearest basic explanation of their patterns of similarities and differences from the revised typescript on the one hand and the published Century edition on the other is that the magazine text was set from an early set of book galleys or proofs revised by Howells and that the Jenkins text was prepared from a later and further revised set. Howells exercised no control over the Jenkins text after the release of the later set of Century book galleys or proofs to that firm, neither correcting nor revising the Jenkins typesetting before publication. He did take the opportunity, however, to make revisions on magazine proofs independent of his work on the book as well as to prepare further revisions on the book proofs themselves after these proofs were released to the magazine and to Jenkins. Thus the maga-

---

9. The Conard and Jenkins editions agree substantively with each other against all other forms of the text at the following points, which can be located in the Rejected Substantives list: 14.31, 19.18, 29.28, 30.28, 33.26, 37.26, 49.29, 50.24, 55.26, 57.10, 61.24, 61.34, 76.5, 79.20, 80.24, 82.1, 83.14–15, 85.15, 85.31, 90.32, 96.34, 97.20, 98.1, 99.19, 101.6, 103.28, 107.2, 110.13, 110.21, 112.3–5, 117.4, 126.20, 127.7, 132.14, 133.5, 138.35, 139.19, 140.24, 141.28, 143.33, 144.8, 150.18, 154.13, 155.2, 155.19, 156.29, 158.4, 159.2 and 159.15. In addition, the Conard edition is itself substantively different from all other texts, including the Jenkins, at these points: 6.3, 10.3–4, 10.4, 15.34, 18.7, 26.3, 35.31, 36.19, 37.8 (twice), 43.26–27, 46.14, 53.36, 55.32, 60.33, 74.2, 77.17, 84.23, 88.29, 89.32–33, 114.7, 114.8, 124.19, 127.16, 127.33, 128.29, 128.34–35, 130.13 (thrice), 135.20, 137.30, 139.20, 142.10, 142.30 (twice), 144.5, 144.15 and 154.18. The Conard edition, despite its great variance in accidentals from the Jenkins text, does follow with some fidelity the latter text's preference for English rather than American forms in spelling and punctuation.

zine and Jenkins edition contain many but not all of the book galley revisions made for the Century edition, the magazine contains further independent revisions not present in any other text, and the Century book edition contains revisions which appear nowhere else.

This description is consistent not only with the basic patterns of variants among the texts but also with the very scanty historical information available about the chronology of their preparation. The April issue of the *Century Magazine*, which contained the first installment of *The Leatherwood God* (chapters I–IV), was ready for distribution by 20 March 1916 at the latest,[10] and Howells' copy probably had to be in the Century office some two months before; on the other hand, the Century Company did not sign an agreement with Herbert Jenkins for publication of the English edition until 15 June, and the proofs were probably sent to Jenkins after this date. It may be assumed also that if Howells had not transmitted a complete text of his novel to the magazine by mid-January he had turned over the first portions by then and the remainder a short time later, since the magazine editors would have wanted to see the length of the full text before making detailed serialization plans for it over the coming months.[11] Certainly all book typesetting had been completed by the time Century book proofs went to Jenkins.

This postulate of the transmission of the text after first typesetting and of separate stages of revision in both Century book edition and *Century Magazine* explains the predominant characteristics of textual variation among these forms—the greater correspondence of the magazine text than of the Century and Jenkins editions with the sub-

---

10. The date is corroborated by a letter of 30 March 1916 from Douglas Z. Doty in the *Century Magazine* office to Howells in which Doty thanks Howells for his note of 21 March praising the illustrations and the general presentation of the first magazine installment.

11. The following list provides a convenient summary of the correspondence of the magazine installments to the book sections:

Magazine Date	Magazine Chapters	Book Chapters
April 1916	I–IV	I–IV
May 1916	V–VIII	V–VIII
June 1916	IX–X	IX–X
July 1916	XI–XII	XI–XII
August 1916	XIII–XIV	XIII–XIV
September 1916	XV	XV–XVI
October 1916	XVI–XVIII	XVII–XIX
November 1916	XIX–XXII	XX–XXIII

stantive readings of Howells' revised typescript, the greater relative agreement of Century and Jenkins texts with each other than with the other forms, and the apparently independent authoritative readings of both magazine and Century book. More specifically, this outline comprehends three complicated and pervasive patterns of variation: first, the agreement of the magazine text with Howells' revised typescript against the Century and Jenkins editions; second, the independent variation of both magazine and Century edition from the agreement of typescript and Jenkins edition; and, third, the independent variation of the book editions on the one hand and the magazine on the other against the typescript.

The first pattern of variation occurs, for example, at 3.4–5 in the present text:[12] the typescript and magazine read "bush, which grew," the book editions "bush growing"; on the assumption that the type set for the Century book edition reproduced the typescript reading accurately, the reading which appeared in the proofs sent to the *Century Magazine* was also "bush, which grew" and was accurately set and printed in the magazine. At this same point Howells revised the Century book proofs some time afterward to read "bush growing," and this later reading, either in a duplicate set of book galleys or proofs revised in his own hand or in typeset form, went to Jenkins. The second pattern, in which the Jenkins edition agrees in its reading with the typescript but the Century book edition and the magazine vary independently of each other from that reading, occurs at three points in the present text: 76.5, 112.3–5 and 154.13. In the first of these three, the typescript and Jenkins edition read "her; then he sank at her side." In contrast, the Century book edition reads "her before he sank at her side," and the magazine text omits the final phrase and reads only "her." Here again the pattern of variation can be explained in terms of the postulated sequence of derivation of the texts: the book proofs which went to the magazine and those which went to Jenkins repro-

---

12. This pattern also occurs at the points listed below in the present text. Those entries noted as occurring in the Emendations list represent editorial decisions to accept the identical readings of the Century and Jenkins book texts as authoritative; those which appear in the Rejected Substantives list represent identical readings in those two texts which have not been accepted because they seem erroneous or editorial in origin, rather than authoritative.

Emendations: 3.25, 25.10, 37.36, 39.13, 39.14, 39.17, 40.36, 79.21, 122, 126, 132, 136, 140, 146, 152, 158.21, 159.14, 159.23.

Rejected Substantives: 8.6, 10.32, 14.4, 52.36, 66.3, 67.3, 71.26, 73.23, 96.17.

duced the typescript reading, and after this distribution of materials Howells revised independently in the magazine proofs and in the later Century book proofs. The third pattern occurs, among other instances, at 95.20:[13] here the typescript reads "in," the magazine "with," and the two book editions "amid." Given the three variant readings, which could have originated at different points in time and on different forms of the text, it is possible to explain the variation in terms of the basic chronology of texts and yet not satisfactorily resolve it, because this chronology permits three equally viable alternatives. One is that the typescript reading was accurately set in type for the book edition, that this original setting was part of the text which went to the magazine and was altered there, and that after this point in time the same reading was revised in the book galleys or proofs before a set of them was sent to Jenkins. A second alternative is that the original typescript reading was changed in the earliest galleys, that this reading was retained in the magazine, and that the book proofs were changed later. And a third, much like the second, is that the original typescript reading was revised in the earliest book galleys and remained thus throughout further work on the book proofs, but that this reading was changed in the magazine proofs independently.

The postulate of the physical relationships of the different versions of the text, therefore, explains the sources of the most complicated patterns of variation among them, and comprehends as well the three basic patterns of revision—in which all later texts agree against the typescript by virtue of revision of book proofs before sets of these went to magazine and Jenkins, in which the magazine alone differs from the typescript and book texts as the result of later independent revision on magazine proofs, and in which the Century book edition differs in a more limited number of cases from typescript and from the other printed forms because of later revision of the Century edition after some form of it had been sent to the *Century Magazine* and to Jenkins.[14] But there remains yet another especially problematic pat-

---

13. The same pattern of variation also occurs at the following points (recorded in Emendations)—in all cases the readings of the book editions have been accepted over those of the serial: 3.5, 3.26, 6.3, 6.6, 24.6, 50.21, 98.8–9, 104.6, 115, 158.24–159.11, 158.28, 158.30 (twice) and 158.35.

14. For the editorial policy adopted for treatment of the independent revisions of magazine and book editions, including those points where the two forms vary independently of each other from their revised-typescript source, see below, p. 181.

There are ten instances in the present text of independent revision in the Century

tern which must be reconciled with this outline—that in which the typescript and Jenkins editions agree against identical magazine and American edition readings. When such variation appears to be the result of authorial intervention (as it does at 82.1, 98.1 and 143.33 in the present edition; see Emendations) rather than of error, any number of explanations might be given, including the possibility that a second set of Century book proofs with some later revisions was also sent to the magazine so that Howells' further revisions on them could be incorporated into that other text. A more likely possibility, and one which accords with the general sense of Howells' attention to the development of his text, is that these readings are the result of a condition like that of the second pattern of variation discussed above, in which independent revision takes place on magazine proofs and book proofs—but in this case the independent revisions are identical.

The fact of independent revision on distinct lines of textual transmission, whether the results are identical or not, raises a question crucial to the presentation of a single coherent text of *The Leatherwood God*. If the theoretical purpose of this edition is to attempt as fully as possible the synthesis of the form of his novel which Howells would have approved, the matter of independent revision offers the possibility that there are in fact at least two separate literary entities with the title *The Leatherwood God*, the one begun in manuscript, revised in typescript and book proofs and culminating in the Century book edition, and the other begun in manuscript, revised in typescript and early book proofs, but further revised in separate magazine proofs and resulting in the version printed in the *Century Magazine*.

But the facts of Howells' career and of the relative coherence of the two "final" forms of the text make unlikely any concept of his conscious intention that there be two distinct versions of the novel

---

book edition, that is, of revision apparently made in the book proofs after copies of these had been transmitted to the *Century Magazine* and Herbert Jenkins, Limited: 29.28, 49.29, 79.20, 90.32, 99.19, 110.13, 110.21, 117.4, 127.7, 150.18. And there are seventy-nine instances in which independent revisions, apparently authorial, of the magazine text have been identified: 6.7, 10.2, 23.19, 30.6, 30.28, 33.17, 39.18, 43.11, 48.12, 49.30, 51.27, 52.14, 52.15, 54.19, 56.27, 56.28, 57.12, 61.13, 61.32, 64.36, 66.11 (twice), 69.20, 70.10, 72.6, 73.24, 75.4, 76.11, 78.24, 79.31–32, 80.2, 80.8 (twice), 81.1, 89.29, 92.5–6, 93.6, 93.12, 93.14, 94.8, 94.16, 96.5, 96.8, 98.6, 99.10, 99.19, 100.11 (twice), 100.25, 100.26, 101.36, 102.21, 105.5, 105.22, 105.32, 107.1, 107.15, 107.20, 107.23, 109.23, 110.20, 110.24, 110.24–25, 111.23, 114.24, 114.29, 121.13, 122.19, 122.21 (twice), 128.2, 134.1, 136.22, 138.4, 142.25, 143.35, 146.21–22, 147.34 and 158.1.

written for different audiences and with slightly different purposes. Howells was, after all, seventy-nine years old when *The Leatherwood God* was published, conscious of the waning of his novelistic powers, and yet producing what publications he could by reworking old projects set aside thirty and forty years before, anthologizing short pieces already published, and consciously using and re-using as fact or fiction autobiographical material supplied to him by his memory and such artifacts as old diaries and notes and family letters. While he was at work on *The Leatherwood God*, for example, he was also completing *Years of My Youth*, the first part of a proposed three-part autobiography. The history of that venture, as detailed in the Introduction to the book in this same edition,[15] is one of frustration of memory, of weakness of creative energy and, most importantly, of struggle for informing idea. Thus, too, with *The Leatherwood God*. The independent—sometimes identical but usually different—revisions for magazine and book suggest not consciously variant intentions but separate attentions. Howells seems to have revised each set of proofs out of a momentary concern for specific elements of the text, and not from the sense of any unified whole. Still, if these separate revisions do not constitute independent work toward separately coherent entities, they are stages of Howells' intention for his text, and both sets of independent revisions have been accepted as completely as possible in the present edition, on the grounds that though they derive from a fragmented sense of the material they nevertheless tend to represent more of the individual elements of Howells' total attention than the exclusive emphasis on either line of transmission could produce.

The present edition of *The Leatherwood God*, therefore, cannot be offered as the form which the editors believe represents Howells' "final intention." As textual critics use that phrase, "final" also signifies "best," "most coherent," and the identity of the terms results from the belief that generally an author's work on a literary text attempts and achieves increasing perfection of it. It is not at all clear that Howells ever achieved his "best" intention for this book, either through his independent sets of revisions or through some imagined combination of them. The kinds of correction and revision he was exercising seem related not so much to a sense of absolute unity as to a concern for

---

15. *Years of My Youth and Three Essays* (Bloomington and London: Indiana University Press, 1975), pp. xi–xxvii.

style and accuracy. But in fact this condition holds for much of the work of Howells and of other authors. And if there can be less certainty here than in many literary instances of the realization of a "best" and "most coherent" intention, there can at least be the satisfaction in the synthesis of the form of the work which represents most completely the author's realized intention.

Into the two major copy-text portions of *The Leatherwood God*—the extant manuscript for the first nine chapters and Howells' revised typescript for the remainder—are therefore introduced two basic kinds of emendations: those revisions and completions of the text which were introduced by Howells himself (insofar as the present editors have been able to distinguish these from mere editorial sophistication and compositorial error) and whatever non-authorial corrections have seemed necessary to accuracy and readability. Howells' revisions of his copy-texts include the full-scale revision of the face copy of the typescript prepared from his manuscript and those local revisions made in the pre-publication typeset phases of the Century book edition and the *Century Magazine*. But even when revisions are most clearly Howells' own—those in his own handwriting in the typescript, for example—there intrude questions of the possibility of the introduction of these authorial revisions under the influence of a distortion of the original version. The typescript prepared from his manuscript, for example, contains a number of errors, some of which Howells corrected to their original forms, some of which he did not recognize at all when he revised, and still others which he revised to new readings. Those which he restored to the original text when he recognized error (he did not characteristically proofread copy against its source, but instead read the form of the work before him for sense and consistency) create no problem for textual decision, and those which he did not recognize at all have been restored to their original forms in the present edition on the grounds that Howells' apparent failure to identify them cannot be taken as his sanction of them. But where the typist's error has led Howells to create new readings, the question of his conscious intention again intrudes. Though the new reading is clear evidence of his attention to the text, it is also obviously based on material not his own; whereas the original reading was unambiguously his, the later reading cannot be so easily classified. Since his work on *The Leatherwood God* after manuscript involved further refinement as well as correction of whatever version of the material he happened to have before him, he had no way of distinguishing his own mistakes from those of others. Even where the present editors have been able to make such distinctions for him (as, for example, by comparing the extant portion of the manuscript with the type-script prepared from it to identify the typist's misreadings of Howells' original), they cannot easily determine the extent to which revision was dictated by Howells' sense of the need for further refinement, error aside, and the extent to which it was dictated by the simpler urge to remove error. When such problems occur in the present text the general editorial policy has been to restore the original readings, since they are most fully Howells' own; whenever a specific situation indicates that refinement rather than correction was Howells' pri-mary motive, however, the revised reading has been accepted.[16]

The policy with respect to Howells' revisions in the Century book edition and magazine texts has been to accept all independent re-visions which are apparently Howells' own—and when they are not based on non-authorial error—with the notion that they at least rep-resent his last intention at those specific points of revision. In every instance consideration has been given to the possibility of distortion of Howells' text as a factor in his revision. And in those instances where Howells revised the same point in his text differently in book and magazine, the book reading has been accepted as the "final" reading because it is at least theoretically the latest reading; for the greater part of his work on the pre-publication materials of *The Leatherwood God* Howells had apparent control over the book text after magazine installments had already been printed. And even in the final portions of the text, where magazine and book were being printed almost si-multaneously, the patterns of the readings themselves indicate that the book readings elaborated further on readings already introduced into the magazine. Whenever specific exceptions to this chronological

16. At the following points in the text, all noted in the Emendations list, Howells' revisions of the typescript, though based on the erroneous transcription of his manu-script, have been accepted on the editorial judgment that they represent completions and further refinements of his work rather than simply corrections of recognized or felt error: 3.11, 7.19, 10.17, 15.20, 19.12, 20.19, 22.4, 22.14, 22.26, 26.15–16, 28.20, 39.20–21, 43.25, 46.18, 48.6–7, 51.2, 54.31 and 54.32. But at the other points listed below, Howells' revisions of typescript error have been rejected as dictated only by his sense of the necessity of rectifying recognized or felt error, and thus are recorded in Rejected Substantives: 13.5, 13.25, 18.12, 19.27, 19.32, 20.7–8, 23.26, 23.32, 23.36, 26.1, 30.30–31, 39.5, 53.24 and 60.26.

principle have been made because of other considerations, the situation is clarified in the Textual Notes.

In addition to accepting into the copy-texts the revisions which were made by Howells himself, the present edition also introduces necessary corrections of these copy-texts. Many of these corrections were first made in the preparation of the original publications—some by the typist who worked from Howells' manuscript, some by the Century Company editor who checked over the typescript and also introduced stylistic sophistications and even some substantive changes,[17] and some presumably by the compositors, proofreaders and house editors of the various published texts. Such sources of course have no authority relative to Howells' intentions for his text, but when they make corrections which seem necessary, these corrections have been introduced on editorial authority, with the first form of the text which contains a specific correction cited as a matter of historical fact. Some necessary corrections have not been made in any form of the text before the present edition, and these can be distinguished in the Emendations list by the symbol HE, which indicates the origin as well as the authority of the reading with the present editors. This edition has not accepted substantive or accidental differences from the copy-text in other texts when the likelihood exists of their having originated in such non-authorial sources as compositorial error, misinterpretation of copy, stylistic sophistication and mere grammatical preference. Among such apparently non-authorial elements are the more frequent paragraphing of the magazine text, the preferences in spelling of the different texts for such forms as "farther" for Howells' "further" or "shrunk" for "shrank," and the attempts at consistency in the treatment of Howells' dialect usages.

This last matter, particularly the question of the rendering of *-ing* as *-in'* or *-un'*, has been especially difficult to resolve because of the evidence of participation by Howells himself in some stages of the refinement of dialect forms. There was clearly some evolution of his usage in manuscript and in his revisions of the typescript, but many inconsistencies remained after his work on these forms as well as in the printed texts prepared from them—even though the latter also indicate further attempts at consistency. It is in the printed forms

---

17. Again, refer to A Note on the Manuscript and Typescripts, pp. 189 and 190–196, for a full discussion of the editorial markings on Howells' revised typescript.

that the extent of Howells' participation in the revision of dialect is most in doubt. The forms -*ing*, -*in*' and -*un*' appear in close proximity in the copy-texts, and the regularization of them in the printed texts is just as chaotic. The typescript evidences many alterations by Howells of manuscript -*in*' to -*un*', and the Century editor working over the typescript made a good many more such revisions. Some -*in*' forms which remained after Howells' work on the typescript are further revised to -*un*' in the printed texts, and some standard English forms are there rendered in dialect as well. In the face of such confusing evidence, no secure decision can be made about Howells' part in revisions whose only evidence lies in the printed texts. Therefore, the present edition has foregone regularization and retained the last clearly authoritative reading, that of either the manuscript or the revised typescript. The result is certainly inconsistent and may well miss some revision of dialect made by Howells himself; but that danger has to be weighed against the impossibility of developing an acceptable rationale in the erratic evidence of the printed texts. This same policy has been applied to those cases where other dialect forms are altered (for example, *How'd it* and *How d't*, '*u'd* and '*uld*) and where dialect is replaced by standard English. But all of the rejected dialect variants in the printed texts are recorded in Rejected Substantives.

Preparation of this edition has involved decisions not only about the sources of specific readings in Howells' own intentions, the necessity for individual corrections and the possibility of non-authorial revision, but also about certain specific classes of normalizations. Two such classes in particular have warranted special consideration: the consistent revision of Howells' use of the quotation mark and dash to indicate uncompleted speech, and Howells' own inconsistent apostrophization of the verbal contractions *won't* and *ain't*. Where Howells' invariable quotation mark-dash pattern appears in the extant manuscript, the typescript form prepared from that text is inconsistently changed to dash-quotation mark. Because of the complete consistency of Howells' usage in manuscript, the editors have on their own authority reinstated the postulated manuscript form where the revised typescript is copy-text in the absence of manuscript.[18] On the

---

18. At the following points in the present edition, the typescript copy-text dash-quotation mark has been changed on editorial authority to quotation mark-dash to make these instances consistent with Howells' manuscript usage: 68.26, 69.30,

other hand, Howells was certainly not consistent in his preference for *won't* or *wont, ain't* or *aint*, although the extant manuscript indicates the predominance of the latter forms. The typist working from Howells' manuscript generally apostrophized them, but with some exceptions; where the typist missed such revisions, they were supplied by the Century editor who worked over the typescript. Since to maintain this inconsistency would only distract from the more significant elements of the text for the modern reader, the present edition normalizes to the apostrophized form, acknowledging that such is not Howells' own consistent usage. Wherever this pattern of normalization is at variance with the copy-texts, the fact of normalization and its historical source are noted in the Textual Note to the Emendations entry at 5.24 (thus all apostrophized forms of these two verbal contractions which appear in the text but are not listed in that Note are to be assumed to appear in the copy-texts).

All the revisions made in the copy-texts are reported either in the Emendations list or in comprehensive Textual Notes keyed to this list. No silent emendations, regularizations or normalizations have been attempted. The present text, however, has not reproduced what have been considered merely visual appurtenances of the copy-texts: type style, styling of chapter openings, spacing of indentations, and format for the use of italic punctuation.[19] Nor have the chapter synopses which appeared at the beginnings of the May through September *Century Magazine* installments or the references to the September through November installments as parts 7, 8 and 9 been recorded — on the grounds that these are irrelevant to the text itself and most certainly not introduced by Howells.

70.13, 70.26, 70.30, 72.16, 72.33, 73.33, 73.36, 77.24, 77.32, 78.12, 81.11, 81.16, 106.8, 112.17, 113.32, 115.25, 119.18, 123.8, 123.20, 134.21, 134.26, 140.27, 146.16, 147.8 and 147.16. All other occurrences of the quotation mark-dash punctuation in the present text should be assumed to duplicate the form of the copy-texts at those points.

19. We have normalized the use of italic punctuation after italic letters. Only question marks and exclamation points are set in italics after italicized letters in our text, and all others in roman. This policy differs from that of the copy-texts only at the following points: roman exclamation points in copy-texts italicized in this text at 8.7, 35.32, 71.5, 86.11, 91.25, 103.7 and 116.5; roman question marks in copy-text italicized in this text at 50.4, 98.9, 115.13, 116.29 and 149.6; italic semicolon set in roman in this text at 61.35; and italic comma set in roman in this text at 72.34. All other marks of punctuation should be assumed to follow the forms of the copy-texts.

Finally, the complicated chronology of the sources of the relevant forms of *The Leatherwood God* has necessitated adoption of certain conventions in the sections of the apparatus which follow. The Emendations and Rejected Substantives lists are organized according to a somewhat synthetic chronology which does not precisely indicate the true relationships of the texts in point of time: for example, the lists do not acknowledge that the Jenkins text, though published after the Century book edition, actually had its origin in an earlier pre-publication form of the Century text. For convenience, the lists are organized so as to present the readings of the texts in the following order, which is based primarily on the order of completion or publication: manuscript, unrevised typescript (but only for that portion of the text where manuscript is extant), revised typescript, editorially revised typescript (but only when editorial revisions have been accepted as necessary or when they involve substantive or dialect differences), magazine, Century book edition, Jenkins edition, and Conard edition. Further, the Emendations list contains the full substantive record of the readings of all texts from copy-text to the point of the reading accepted in this edition, in the order of this synthetic chronology; Rejected Substantives records all readings after that point of emendation when such readings are at variance with the accepted reading, and also all rejected readings after copy-text. The effect of this format must always be interpreted in light of the sequence of texts discussed in this commentary; for example, when a Century book reading is accepted into the copy-text, and the Jenkins book reading is at variance with it, the Jenkins book reading, whose actual source may lie at some earlier point in time, will nonetheless appear in Rejected Substantives, where it is interpreted as having come later. We hope the straightforwardness of the presentation of evidence will offset the inconvenience these conventions must inevitably cause. In addition, we have adopted a special format for dealing with revisions which occur within longer, anterior revisions; this format is described in the headnote to Emendations.

D.J.N.

A Note on the Manuscript and Typescripts

Three extant forms of *The Leatherwood God* antedate its setting in type. These are (1) a predominantly holograph version of one hundred and ninety-five leaves (twenty of the leaves typed by Howells himself) measuring, with minor variations, 5½ in. x 8½ in. (torn or cut halves of 8½ in. x 11 in. typing paper), owned by the American Academy of Arts and Letters; (2) a ribbon-copy typescript of the complete text, consisting of two hundred and eighteen leaves measuring 8½ in. x 10½ in., used as printer's copy by the Century Company, and now in the possession of Professor William White Howells; and (3) a carbon copy of the first sixty-four leaves of this typescript, owned by the American Academy of Arts and Letters.

The manuscript comprises a complete text of chapters I through IX of the novel, and bears four basic paginations. The first, coinciding with chapter I, consists of forty-seven leaves numbered [1], 2, 2=2, 3, 3, 5–39 (39 is the numbered verso of 38), 40, 40–46. The second pagination coincides with chapters II through VII of the present text; this section was originally made up of chapters II through VI, but Howells introduced the division at what finally became chapter IV in revising the typescript (see Emendations at 27.32–28.1), and in fact added the division for chapter VI itself late in the preparation of the manuscript-typescript materials. The ninety leaves in this second section are numbered 21–24, 21–29 (renumbered 25–33), 32–33 (renumbered 34–35), 36–54, 56–57 (renumbered 55–56), 57–66, 66 (renumbered 67), 68–110. The third pagination coincides with chapter VIII in the present text (originally chapter VI in the manuscript; revised by Howells in the full printer's copy typescript—see Emendations at 48), and is numbered 65–100 over thirty-six leaves. Chapter IX of the present text (originally chapter VIII in the manuscript; revised in printer's copy typescript to IX—see Emendations at 59), consisting of twenty-two leaves, bears the pagination 101–110 (renumbered 80–89), 90–92, 111–113 (renumbered 93–95), 14–15 (renumbered 96–97), 95–98 (renumbered 98–101).

The bulk of this manuscript version of *The Leatherwood God* is written on an unwatermarked white linen paper, and though five other kinds of paper are represented only one of these casts light on the history of composition. In chapter I, leaves [1] through 21, 40 and 40 [*bis*] through 46 are on paper watermarked "Buckeye Bond," of which Howells had received a shipment late in 1900.[1] Further, pages 2=2 through 21 of this same group of leaves are typed, in a distinctive face which does not appear in Howells' manuscripts or letters until mid-1900; on the brown paper in which the extant manuscript material was once wrapped appeared the note in Howells' hand, "My typing of beginning before 1900."[2] The dating of the paper and the peculiar typeface suggest that his phrase means the typed material in the manuscript was a copy made in 1900 or later of some other form of the text which Howells had prepared before that time (in this regard, see the Introduction, pages xi–xvii).

Each of the four non-consecutive pagination series in the manuscript begins with a number corresponding to the page containing the same material in the full ribbon-copy typescript, where pagination is regular and consecutive. This coincidence suggests that, at least for chapters II and following, Howells was making fresh long-hand copy of earlier material for the typist who prepared the full typescript, and that he was doing such recopying and revising in installments, completing preparation of each portion as he received the completed typescript of the previous one. The existence of the typescript portions of chapter I may mean either that Howells retyped all of an extensive pre-1900 draft and then recopied portions of that typescript again in readying certain sections for the typist, or that the extant typescript section is the only portion of the earlier work which was retyped and that the rest of the extant manuscript is a reworking of whatever material this typescript was also based upon. The fact that the last of the typed pages contains only three typed lines and continues immediately in Howells' autograph suggests the latter alternative.

The second extant pre-publication form, the ribbon-copy typescript of two hundred and eighteen leaves, was prepared from the full manuscript of *The Leatherwood God* whose extant portions have just been described. It constitutes a text of the entire novel, and was

---

1. WDH to Aurelia Howells, 18 November 1900. MS at Harvard.
2. The wrapper is no longer with the other materials at the American Academy of Arts and Letters. It is described by John K. Reeves, "The Literary Manuscripts of W. D. Howells: A Descriptive Finding List," *Bulletin of the New York Public Library*, LXII (1958), 353.

used as setting copy for the Century Company book edition; it contains Howells' own revisions, frequent editorial markings (see below, page 189 and pages 190–196, for details, as well as the Textual Commentary, pages 171–173), spindle holes, inky fingerprints, and brackets and numberings marking division of the text into fifty-six book galleys. The original typed numbering of the text was apparently 1–278; pages 142–169 and 208–240 must have been discarded sometime after the typing was completed, and the remaining pages following page 141 were renumbered 142–218 with a rubber stamp.[3] Pages 1–64 coincide with the first two pagination sequences of the extant manuscript, and are typed on paper watermarked "W. S & B. REGENT LINEN"; pages 65–79 correspond to the third pagination sequence and are watermarked "BERKSHIRE PARCHMENT LINEN U.S.A."; pages 80–89 correspond to the fourth sequence and are watermarked "BERKSHIRE BOND." The remaining leaves (90–218) are all on paper watermarked "BERKSHIRE LINEN U.S.A."; pages 126–141 are on laid paper, unlike the rest of the Berkshire Linen and the other papers used the typescript, which are wove. The changes in paper, like the pagination sequences in the manuscript, apparently mark the units in which the novel was typed and returned to Howells for revision.

The typescript bears evidence of at least four and perhaps five stages of revision, two of them not by Howells. The first stage of revision, done by the typist, is in pencil and consists of a limited number of corrections and apparent mistranscriptions from the manuscript (these also appear on coincident portions of the extant typescript carbon). The second stage, by Howells, is also in pencil and is minimal except for the section coinciding with chapter XII in the present edition (pages 111–125 in the typescript). Many of these authorial revisions were later either erased, thereby restoring the original typed text, or confirmed by being written over in black ink as part of the second stage of Howells' revision. These ink revisions are extensive and touch every aspect of the novel except its over-all structure; the

---

3. The original pages 142–169 of the typescript would have fallen after the paragraph ending at 104.36 in the present text, the point at which the division for chapter XVI—later deleted in magazine and book editions—began in the revised typescript. The original pages 208–240 fell between the present chapters XVIII and XIX. Since the manuscript from which these missing leaves were typed is also missing, there is no way to reconstruct their contents.

great majority of the changes between the manuscript and the printed texts were introduced at this time. There is evidence of another stage of revision by Howells, in pencil, in chapters VIII and IX of the present text. The most interesting of these is the final determination of the name "Jim Redfield," written in pencil over the typed "Jim Foreacre" and the two intermediate ink revisions, "Jim Wildacre" and "Jake Woodacre" (at 54.28 in the present text). Other instances of this late stage of revision include the "To pray, I reckon" at 46.27, added in pencil and certainly written after the inked deletion of the same idea in Nancy's speech in the previous line, and the positioning of the phrase "in their doubt" at 48.6–7.

No clear pattern of revision is evident in either the extant manuscript or the typescript which indicates that Howells was engaged in a consistent and orderly process. No attempt has been made in the present text to offer a full record of the resultant internal alterations in these texts; thus cancellations, self-editings, interlinings, careted insertions and so on which are authorial in origin have been accepted as pre-copy-text alterations, and thus integral parts of the copy-text and not listed in the apparatus to the present edition. This policy has been adopted not because such internal evidence is not significant but because the mechanics of transcription have not been adequately developed to meet the needs of the scholar who wishes to base his research on such detailed examination; he must work with the typescript itself or with a well-prepared photo-facsimile. The present edition can offer only a summary of the evidence and the results of close study of the questions of interpretation of the text.

In addition to Howells' corrections and revisions of the typescript, the extant leaves contain evidence of further work on the material, apparently by an editor in the Century Company office. This editorial intervention, in red ink except for eight non-authorial marks in blue which delete earlier red editorial corrections (see below, page 195), consists of the regularization of accidentals (punctuation, spelling, and dialect forms), clarification of some details of Howells' handwriting and the supplying of necessary words and punctuation. A record of the significant details of this stage of revision is given in a section at the end of this Note on the Manuscript and Typescripts (pages 190–196).

The third extant pre-publication form of the novel is a set of carbon copies of the first sixty-four pages of the typescript, on the same paper (watermarked "W. S & B. REGENT LINEN") as the ribbon copy. Besides a limited number of changes in punctuation either in pencil on the leaves or made in pencil or pen through the carbon paper to match alterations by the typist on the ribbon copy—presumably to correct mistranscriptions of the manuscript source—there are a few authorial revisions entered directly onto the carbon copies. All are listed in a separate section at the end of this Note (see below, page 196). Three of these (at 7.19, 10.32 and 11.5) are revisions not also made on the typescript original, but introduced into some later stage of preparation of the book and incorporated into the form that was finally published. Three others (10.29, 13.33–34 and 19.16) represent carbon-copy revisions of material not revised elsewhere. All the rest are revisions of words or phrases that are revised to the same or a different reading either in the ribbon copy of the typescript or at some later pre-publication phase. Of all these revisions, only the three unique to the carbon copy deserve consideration as possible emendations of the text. But the general sparsity of revision in the carbon and the lack of conclusive evidence concerning Howells' intentions for this material both suggest the provisionality of this material. The case is parallel to Howells' alternate erasures of and ink confirmations of his early pencilled revisions of the ribbon copy. The present text therefore does not adopt any of these readings and records them nowhere but in the appended list.

D.J.N.

I. EDITORIAL ALTERATIONS OF THE TYPESCRIPT

The following lists record all editorial markings in the typescript which affect the contents of the text itself. Thus they do not include the many instances of clarification of Howells' handwriting by the overwriting or repetition of marks of punctuation and letters or the rewriting of words in the vicinity of the originals, the clarification of the location of added or heavily revised material when such clarification is correct, the use of *stet* marks to verify Howells' reinstatement of previously deleted material or the use of carets to distinguish conjunctive marks of punctuation. Nor do they include such strictly typographical marks as the styling of chapter openings, the setting of long and short dashes, the indentation of quotations or the specifica-

tion of type style and page depth. They do include all changes in substantives by the addition or deletion of words, all changes in punctuation, spelling and hyphenation, all changes in capitalization, all
erroneous clarifications and all general instructions about the styling
of forms. All of the editorial alterations recorded on these lists are in
red ink on the typescript, with the exception of the material described
under the heading "Compositorial or editorial re-revisions," page 195.

The lists record the location of each reading in the present edition.
The primary reading cited is that of the typescript *before* editorial
correction; this citation may differ from the reading of the present
edition at the point in question if the editorial correction of that reading has been accepted, if the reading has been regularized for reasons
noted in the Textual Commentary or a Textual Note, or—in the first
nine chapters—if the manuscript copy-text extant for that section of
the text has a variant reading which takes precedence over the corresponding typescript material. An asterisk indicates that the editorial
correction restores the typescript to Howells' manuscript form; thus
entries without asterisks denote editorial readings not sanctioned by
Howells' original or not represented by corresponding extant manuscript material which would make comparison possible. All editorial
corrections which have been accepted as necessary for the sense of
the text of the present edition are recorded at proper points in Emendations, and those which are substantive in nature and which have
not been accepted are recorded in Rejected Substantives. The editorial material is here arranged in categories by kinds of revisions
rather than by sequential tabulation in order to minimize the amount
of repetitive description and to allow the interested reader to make
judgments about the extent and importance of the different details
of editorial styling.

Substantive changes (typescript reading precedes the slash in each entry,
editor's revision follows): *13.36 on/in *14.4 white/while 19.18
fiercely/purely [followed by editorial question mark] 28.12 and
scamper/scamper 39.23 after until/until *44.26 in/on 63.27 Dylks's/
Dylkss' 86.19 they they/they 93.22 anothers'/another's 144.23 had/
and had

Changes of dialect -*in*' endings to -*un*': 10.23 chinkin' 10.23 daubin'
10.30 prayin' 13.30 goin's 13.30 camp-meetin' 14.5 burnin'
15.7 tryin' 49.11 goin' 49.25 teachin' 49.34 doin's 50.1 doin's
50.6 sayin' 50.19 preachin' 50.32 outpourin' 50.33 accordin'

50.34 mornin'   50.34 prayin'   50.35 singin'   50.35 readin'   50.35
mornin'   51.7 prayin'   51.7 singin'   51.7 readin'   51.7 mornin'
51.15 havin'   51.16 swearin'

Miscellaneous changes in dialect forms (typescript reading precedes the
slash in each entry, editor's revision follows): 13.22 something/somepin
*14.17 some'pin/somepin   14.19 anything/anythun   14.31
anything/anythun   50.18 anything/anythun'   55.30 Billun's/Billuns's
113.36 unfittin'est/unfittinest   139.1 ag'in/agin   139.11 ag'in/agin
141.4 ag'in/agin   147.11 'o'/o'

Changes in spelling (typescript reading precedes the slash in each entry,
editor's revision follows): 6.24 gutteral/guttural   12.35 gayety/gaiety
15.13 staid/stayed   *19.27 gutteral/guttural   26.15 offence/offense
34.26 goodbye/good-by   35.23 Goodbye/Good-by   44.29 moulded/
molded   73.32 courace/courage   74.2 goodbye/good-by   76.22
catechising/catechizing   87.29 stedfast/steadfast   88.10 chastising/
chastizing   93.9 pretence/pretense   94.30 hight/height   94.30 pretence/
pretense   103.29 reenactment/reënactment   119.33 punchion/puncheon
126.24 sacriligious/sacrilegious   126.25 practiced/practised   131.3
acknowledgement/acknowledgment   147.13 practiced/practised
153.18 offence/offense

Revision of *-re* endings to *-er*: 3.13 centre   3.23 centres   30.28 centre
86.33 fibre

Deletion of one of the double consonants in the following words:
18.23 worshippers   53.1 worshippers   53.11–12 worshipped   55.10
worshipped   68.13 worshipping   79.11 counselled   90.12 worshipped
96.32 worshippers   97.2 worshippers   98.6 women-worshippers
126.22 grovelling   150.28 travellers   152.2 travelling   152.28 travelling

Insertion of a comma after the following words: 3.5 pliable   4.2
Methodist   6.10 said   8.25 sad-lookun'   9.25 field   10.31 well
13.36 wide   25.9 log-cabin   26.18 present   39.2 intention   39.23
daughters   39.24 women   40.9 and   40.9 joke   40.28 infidel
42.13 Well   43.17 called   49.22 Abel   51.7 singin'   53.13 Son   54.20
yes   55.18 said   58.1 woman   72.1 stood   72.5 looking   72.5 too
73.23 hearth   89.1 Dylks   94.7–8 congregation   94.33 repeating
102.10 within   102.20 for   105.25 Now   112.7 coals   112.17 oh
115.7 bandage   116.1 But   116.30 this   119.36 cooking   121.9 her
127.2 continuance   129.2 halt   129.15 Oh   132.5 Oh   132.20 Oh
142.11 hair   144.2 bed   144.3 latch   147.17 Oh   149.16 Oh   149.28
said   156.17–18 borrowed   157.10 as   157.19 then   157.23 And

Deletion of comma after the following words: *40.7 creatures   40.28
law   43.19 bars   44.17 wall   46.9 heels   *53.25 force   *55.19

another   *57.34 said   59.7 experience   59.23 had   67.35 tells
81.28 wrought   87.9 expectant   87.17 mothers   87.21 Dylks   94.8
congregation   114.21 believe   127.36 so   133.4 Joey   144.23 labors
144.25 Joey   147.13 crick   149.17 Joey   150.9 Joey   152.12 cabin
155.21 down

Revision of quotation mark-dash punctuation indicating interrupted or
suspended speech to dash-quotation mark at the following points:
20.29   27.7   31.28   58.2   61.35   115.15   115.20   116.1   116.9
116.11   116.28   116.30   116.32   117.7   118.11   119.6   119.32
123.27   125.5   140.15   145.6   149.19   151.21   153.23   153.24

Revision of double quotation marks to single quotation marks before
and/or after the following words: 7.35 Let   7.36 pray   8.5 What
8.5 for   8.7 Salvation   15.1 Salvation   49.11 die   49.12 I've
49.13 shell

Marking of verbal contractions to be spaced between body of word and
apostrophe or body of word and negative (e.g. *he'll—he 'll, didn't—
did n't*): 12.23 squire'll   13.16 soon's   13.25 couldn't   15.20 Who's
34.13 father'd   34.14 I've   34.28 doesn't   34.35 I'm   35.4 There's
35.11 It'll   35.15 You'll   35.17 there'll   35.19 there'll   35.21 I'm
35.24 I'm   35.24 I'll   35.32 I'm   36.10 didn't   36.12 didn't
36.12 that's   36.12 didn't   36.16 I'll   36.21 wouldn't   36.22 dasn't
36.23 Whyn't   36.23 Didn't   36.25 he's   36.36 He's   37.1 There's
37.4 there's   37.6 we'll   37.11 we'd   37.12 you'd   37.20 I'd
37.23 We'll   37.32 She's   38.1 He'd   42.5 He's   42.14 didn't
42.14 hadn't   42.15 I'd   42.16 I'd   42.22 you'd   43.4 I'll   43.6
needn't   43.13 I'll   43.16 I've   43.23 it's   43.29 Didn't   43.30
didn't   44.12 she's   44.23 I'll   44.23 father'll   44.23 he's   44.25
(twice) I'll   44.33 it's   44.34 I'll   44.35 There'll   44.36 it'd
44.36 mustn't   44.37 cow'd   44.37 wasn't   45.1 he'll   45.4 I'll
45.10 Laban's   45.12 I'm   45.20 It's   45.22 you'd   42.24 It's
45.36 ha'n't   46.20 father'll   46.21 I'm   55.25 fur's

Insertion of dash after the following words and punctuation: 13.32 you?"
46.1 back,"   46.2 interval,   69.33 No,"   103.21 Redfield,"
149.17 dear,"   153.18 'light,"

Miscellaneous changes in accidentals (typescript reading precedes the
slash in each entry, editor's revision follows): 9.29 said,/said;   10.30
it,/it;   *29.4 gone,/gone;   *29.9 "No,"/"No."   *30.8 said. "Don't/
said, "don't   37.16 on,/on: 37.22 cheerily,/cheerily.   39.9 doubted,/
doubted;   40.30–31 *Common Sense*/"Common Sense"   40.31 *The Age of
Reason*/"The Age of Reason"   42.5 sent,/sent;   42.22 me./me,
49.12 off,'/off';   50.31 'em'./'em.'   51.14 'Look/"Look   60.14
you—/you   64.29 David!/David!"   70.23 wont/won't   70.36 aint/

ain't   89.14 Leatherwood;/Leatherwood: 103.21 man,/man—
111.9 But/"But   113.14 Oh!/Oh!"   116.10 whispered,/whispered—
119.12 Heigh!"/Heigh?"   119.28 said,/said.   120.36 in./in."
121.11 you,/you;   123.35 time./time,   123.36 wont/won't   124.19
hesitated,/hesitated.   124.35 wait,/ wait—   125.36 wont/won't
129.20–34 'The . . . . delight/The . . . . delight [single quotation mark
placed by Howells at the beginning of each typed line of this quotation
deleted; see Textual Note to 129.20 for a full list of deletions]
132.6 off,/off.   133.6 aint/ain't   133.9 aint/ain't   133.26 aint/ain't
134.7 wont/won't   139.18 aint/ain't   139.19 aint/ain't   141.21 aint/
ain't   141.25 wont/won't   144.5 crying,/crying.   144.9 wont/won't
145.11 believe—/believe   147.16 this—"/this,"—   147.17 He/"He
147.21 more.—/more.   148.5 why/'Why   148.6 together?/together?'
148.12 mother;/mother!   149.18 him,/him—   149.31 spoke—/spoke:
157.18 it,/it.

Revision of hyphenated or end-line hyphenated compounds to double-
word forms: 23.21–22 law-books   *25.1 log-/cabin   25.6–7 woodspastures   25.8 meadow-lands   *25.9 log-cabin   *27.21 good-night
28.6 spring-house   *29.11 woods-pasture   31.18 woods-pasture   31.25
corn-/field   39.13 quarter-section   39.14 mill-privilege   136.18–19
light-heartedly   136.20 cross-roads   147.5 night-time   152.7 log-cabin

Revision of hyphenated or end-line hyphenated compounds to single-
word forms: *9.15 broad-/cloth   *20.33 fellow-ship   *23.12 broad-/
cloth   *27.28 day-break   *28.6 door-step   *31.34 door-/way   52.27
clay-bank's   66.1 door-step   67.11 butter-milk   88.9 turn-coat
104.23 out-distanced   106.1 with-/out   119.32 poor-/house
121.1 re-opened   138.28 a'-/ready   144.22 night-gown

Revision of multiple-word forms or single-word compounds to
hyphenated compounds: 5.13–14 claybank   5.27 claybank   6.5
claybank   6.14 claybank   6.26 claybank   *34.3 tonight   34.7
tomorrow   34.26 goodbye   35.23 Goodbye   35.25 goodby   42.5
tonight   42.14 tonight   42.15 today   60.26 self conceit   71.11 tonight
72.12 tonight   74.2 goodbye   78.30 everyday   83.23 tonight
87.8–9 deep drawn   89.10 bottomland   94.6   tonight   99.11 well
known   99.28 tonight   123.13 good for nothing   128.16 every day
130.31 tonight   131.8 tonight   135.2 Tonight   140.10 tonight
142.18 tonight   156.32 pipe stem   159.20 tomorrow

Miscellaneous revisions of other compounds or possible compounds
(typescript reading precedes the slash in each entry, editor's revision
follows): 5.5 double log-cabin/double-log cabin   *25.8 cornfields/corn
fields   *25.18 anyone/ any one   *27.7 anyone/ any one   28.5
cornfield/corn field   *29.8 anyone/any one   33.16 Cross Roads/

Crossroads   44.27 cornfield/cornfield [revised to two words and then restored]   104.29 race horse/racehorse   124.25 any way/anyway   125.3 trap door/trapdoor   129.27 jet-/black/jet-black   148.30 day light/daylight   154.27 out doors/outdoors

Revision of capitalized forms to lower-case: 3.23 Republic   27.18 Temple   *30.8 Don't   41.7 World   41.26 Peace   42.7 Salvation   43.33 Peace   51.20 What   52.6 Savior   *56.15 Some   56.15 Believers   67.6 Western   76.9 If   97.20 What   123.35 You'll   133.23 Well   147.16 The

Revision of lower-case forms to capitalized forms: north 3.19   east 3.19   south 3.19   mid-Western 3.20   squire 12.10 12.23 12.30 13.33 13.35 14.1 14.9 15.18 48.17 48.23 63.13 101.31 102.4 102.10 102.15 102.20 104.5 104.16 104.18 104.27 105.23 106.28 115.16 115.21 116.29 117.7 117.25 117.36 118.6 119.7 120.2 120.20 120.25 120.27 121.9 122.6 122.10 122.21 123.1 123.16 124.12 124.17 124.30 125.31 137.20 137.21 138.2 138.5 138.21 138.23 139.12 139.18 153.18 153.34 154.1 154.22 154.33 155.4 155.17 156.13 156.31 157.12 158.23   he 16.34 77.36 state *29.21   pop 36.23   uncle 36.29   mom 37.32 134.22 134.36 his 40.7   scripture 41.29   father 43.21 143.36   sin 77.6   mother 80.17 80.31 81.6 81.10 81.17 125.32 127.31 132.5 (twice) 133.3 133.28 134.8 134.25 134.31 143.30 143.36 144.5 144.8 144.14 144.17 144.18 145.1 145.2 145.10 145.11 146.12 147.7 147.20 147.32 148.12 148.26 149.9 149.20 149.32 150.17 150.22 150.33 156.4 158.1   mill 93.1   spirit 94.28 cross-roads 136.20 [both words]   why 148.5   the [the squire] 155.7

Erroneous clarifications of Howells' text:

4.3–4   the stringency of their several creeds had so far relaxed] *Howells' interlined* had so far relaxed   *marked to be placed before the stringency; in right margin the words* "reduced & Q [uer] y it"—*possibly meaning that* relaxed *was to be set as* "reduced" *but questioned in the proofs of the text which would go to Howells.*

70.35   David] *editor's question mark over this word, and* "Jane ?" *written in the margin.*

Special typographical instructions marked, involving no actual alteration of the matter of the text:

46.21   I'm] *editor's instruction in margin:* "Space all the contracted words."

48.16   claybank] *close-up marks over and under this word; marks repeated in the margin with editor's note,* "one word—will make it so in front part."

Compositorial or editorial re-revisions of red-ink material, all done in blue pencil (original typescript reading appears first, then the red-ink revision, then the blue-pencil re-revision): 42.9 floppin'/floppun'/

floppin'   42.10 workin'/workun'/workin'   42.11 needin'/needun'/
needin'   42.13 Goin'/Goun'/Goin'   42.13 wonderin'/wonderun'/
wonderin'   42.16 come,/come;/come,   42.17 talkin'/talkun'/talkin'
42.20 perfessin'/perfessun'/perfessin'

II. AUTHORIAL REVISIONS OF
THE TYPESCRIPT CARBON

	Present Text	*Original TS Carbon*	*Authorial Revision of TS Carbon*
7.19	the	those	the
7.20	Mought been	Might been	Might'a' been
9.21	escaped	escaped, involuntarily gay	escaped, involuntarily gay,
10.17	back	back, noiselessly	back noiselessly
10.29	the	the	these
10.32	hunderd	hundred	hunderd
11.5	an	one	an
13.33–34	squire tilted against the wall in his chair, and smoking behind his wife	squire tilted against the wall in his chair, smoking behind his wife.	squire who had gone back to the porch, and sat tilted against the wall in his chair, smoking.
15.15	David Gillespie	Major Parr	ole man Gillespie
15.24–25	girl! I bet she'll know all about it.	girl! . . . it. They say she took on more'n anybody.	girl!
15.26	Say, say, Jane,"	Say, say,"	Say! say!"
15.28–29	her; then in apparent haste she moved	her. Then the girl's apparent hurry caused her to move	her. Then she began to move
19.16	in	in	in together

Textual Notes

3.11   Howells' revision to "region" in the typescript seems not to have been dictated by the erroneous transcription of his manuscript reading there, since he first corrected "Old West" to the original "older West" before going on to introduce the final reading.

4.1–2   The Century editor added a comma after "Methodist" in revising Howells' revised typescript. The present edition retains the original manuscript punctuation while accepting Howells' transposition of words, apparently made in an early stage of book proofs.

5.3   The readings of the magazine and the book editions here and at 5.13 in Rejected Substantives seem to have resulted from the failure of the Century compositor to interpret Howells' complicated deletions and transpositions in this section of the typescript. The typescript version is therefore retained in preference to the alternative substantive readings of the published texts.

5.22   In revising the typescript Howells changed many *-ing* and *-in'* forms to *-un'*, and in many cases the Century editor who worked over this typescript continued the process of dialect revision. The present edition, however, retains only those *-in'* and *-un'* forms which are demonstrably authorial (see the Textual Commentary, pages 182–183). In addition to the reading at 5.22, Howells' revisions to *-un'* in the typescript—which are recorded only here and are not repeated in further entries in the Emendations list itself—occurred at 6.9, 6.17, 6.23, 6.29(twice), 6.30(thrice), 6.31, 6.32, 7.2, 7.10, 7.11(twice), 7.14, 7.15, 7.23(twice), 7.23–24, 7.29, 7.33, 7.34(twice), 8.4, 8.12, 8.14, 8.15, 8.21, 8.25, 8.30, 10.21, 10.24, 12.16, 12.18 (thrice), 12.19, 12.21, 12.33, 14.4, 15.5, 43.9, 52.26,

55.20, 56.8(twice), 56.9, 56.15, 56.16, 88.3, 88.5, 88.28 (twice), 101.26 and 139.6.

5.24   In accordance with the editorial decision to normalize the forms of *won't* and *ain't* in the present text, unapostrophized manuscript and revised typescript copy-text forms have been changed here and at all later points in the text where these forms occur. The following lists record the locations of all other such changes and cite the texts in which they first appeared: *won't*: 10.14(TS), 12.1(TS), 14.8(TS), 26.12(TS), 26.13(TS), 27.5(TS), 27.6(TS), 35.30(HE), 36.30(TS), 69.17(S), 70.23(*ETS*), 123.36(*ETS*), 125.36(*ETS*), 134.7(*ETS*), 141.25(*ETS*), 144.9(*ETS*);

ain't: 36.15(TS), 42.4(TS), 42.21(TS), 70.36(*ETS*), 133.6(*ETS*), 133.9(*ETS*), 133.26(*ETS*), 139.18(*ETS*), 139.19(*ETS*), 141.21(*ETS*).

6.7   This reading represents the first instance of a reading unique to the serial among all the forms of the text; here and in similar cases the present edition adopts the serial reading (see the Textual Commentary, page 181). In accordance with the technical conventions adopted for presentation of the textual evidence in the lists for this text (see the Textual Commentary, page 185), the readings of the published book texts, though their real origin precedes the magazine reading cited here, appear in Rejected Substantives.

7.6   The duplicated and contradictory punctuation of the revised typescript is the result of Howells' incomplete revision. He had originally changed the manuscript reading in typescript to "now,; and" before going on to delete the newly introduced "and". The semicolon which Howells did not delete has been retained in preference to the comma which he added, since that punctuation would have been acceptable only had the connective "and" remained.

8.31   Here and at 81.34 the hyphenated form "linsey-woolsey" supplied in the magazine text is accepted to make the form consistent with the otherwise prevalent usage of the copy-texts. Further, at 78.31 and 81.34 the typescript spelling "woolsy" is replaced by the prevalent usage of the manuscript, "woolsey."

9.23   Here and at 20.9 the hyphenated form "camp-meeting" supplied in the typescript is accepted to make the form consistent with the otherwise prevalent usage of the copy-texts.

13.25   The word "now" was added to the manuscript at some late stage of Howells' working over it, and is difficult to read in its position between two regular manuscript lines. The typist misread the word as "not," and Howells, without striking it, reinstated "now" when he revised. The present edition rejects "not" on the assumption that Howells did not consciously approve it as an addition to his text.

19.12   Howells' revision of the typescript has been accepted— though it occurs in the presence of the typist's erroneous transcription of the manuscript—because that error did not apparently influence his sense of the passage; he had corrected "in" to "on" before going on to change "dips" to "candles."

20.19   The typist omitted the whole sentence in which this revision occurs, probably because it appears on the verso of the manuscript page. Howells apparently located the original sentence in his manuscript and recopied it with the one alteration recorded here, which is adopted as a conscious authorial revision.

22.4   The extent of Howells' revisions here and at 22.14 in Emendations is so great that their basis in the typist's erroneous transcription rather than in Howells' desire for compression seems unlikely.

22.19   The typist had recorded Howells' manuscript "Abel" as
"Abe" here, at 22.26 and 23.18 and in a passage deleted
in Howells' revision of the typescript at 22.26. In the first
instance Howells had originally revised the typescript to
"Abel" and then restored "Abe" again, presumably to
make the form consistent with the later erroneous readings. Despite his conscious rejection of his own manuscript
form here, the present edition retains it as being consistent
with his original and most coherent intention and rejects
his revision as only an effort to maintain the false consistency introduced by the typist. In other sections of the text
Braile always refers to Reverdy as "Abel."

23.36   The typist could not read Howells' manuscript here, and
left a blank in which Howells supplied a new word,
apparently without rechecking the original.

26.15–16   Howells' revision of the typescript is accepted despite its
basis in error because Howells had restored the original
manuscript reading before introducing the new words.

26.18–19   The typist omitted Howells' manuscript comma after the
second "anything," but this cannot be taken as having
any apparent influence on his substantive revision of the
typescript.

28.20   The present edition rejects the introduction of the new
paragraph in the typescript while accepting the authorial
revision in this typescript at the same point (see Emendations at 28.20).

31.33   There is no textual authority for this revision, but it is the
least arbitrary way to correct editorially a grammatically
incomplete sentence that went unnoticed in all the early
forms of the text.

52.31   The typist clarified Howells' manuscript passage by in-
serting "and" after "husband," thereby establishing a
balanced pairing of nouns. The present edition rejects

this alteration as a needless sophistication—since the manuscript material can be read as a noun series—but does supply a comma to clarify the manuscript reading.

53.28   The capitalized form "Temple" supplied by the typist has been adopted to make this manuscript occurrence of the word agree with the otherwise prevalent usage of the copy-texts.

54.5   The present edition revises to the form "woods pasture" for purposes of agreement with the otherwise prevalent usage of the copy-texts.

62.28   The typist's expansion of Howells' manuscript abbreviation is adopted here to make the form coincide with Howells' own expansion of the same form to "Saint" in the manuscript at 62.22 in the present text.

69.31   The present edition accepts the apparently authorial substantive revision made here in the magazine text, but retains the capitalized form which is consistent with Howells' usage in other instances of such epithets.

74.2   The present edition regularizes the revised typescript copy-text to accord with the two-word form "good bye" used consistently in the manuscript copy-text sections (see 34.26 and 35.23 in the present text).

101.36   Actually, "them" is the reading of the magazine, not of the revised typescript (see the preceding Rejected Substantives entry at 101.36). But the point of difference in this entry is the variation in paragraphing: the typescript form is retained over the introduction of a new paragraph in the magazine, a change which was editorial rather than authorial in nature, given the extensive re-paragraphing in the magazine alone among the published texts.

102.18   The original typescript reading here was "crowd which"; Howells had originally revised this to "crowd; it," but then deleted "it" and kept "which." The present edition deletes the semicolon and thus restores the original un-revised typescript reading, despite Howells' own revision of the punctuation.

129.20   Howells placed a single quotation mark at the beginning of each line of the typescript rendering of Dylks' reading from Scripture, apparently to draw attention to its origin. The present text accepts the Century editor's deletion of these marks, which occur here and before the following words in the quotation: be(129.21), stars(129.22), [sil-]ver(129.23), [rich-]er(129.24), gardens(129.25), fruits(129.26), The(129.26), [jet-]black(129.27), increasing(129.28), with(129.29), [differ-]ent(129.30), the courts(129.31), [resi-]dences(129.32), swelling (129.33).

154.13   Here and at 154.29, 156.8 and 158.35, the Century book edition and magazine vary independently and self-consistently from the revised typescript and the foreign book editions in the form of the stranger's name. The book-edition reading has been accepted in all four places as the more common name as well as presumably the more "final" revision by Howells (see the Textual Commentary, page 181).

Emendations

The following list records all changes in substantives and accidentals introduced into the several copy-texts for the different portions of *The Leatherwood God* (see the Textual Commentary, pages 171–173, for a description of them). The reading of the present edition appears to the left of the bracket; the authority for that reading, followed by a semicolon, the reading of the copy-text and subsequent texts agreeing with it, as well as the variant substantive readings of texts after copy-text and before the reading accepted into the present text, appear to the right of the bracket. This list does not record non-authorial revisions of accidentals in texts between copy-text and the reading of the present edition or apparently non-authorial accidentals at points where substantive readings have been accepted. Readings of texts subsequent to the source of the adopted reading may be presumed to agree with the adopted reading unless recorded in Rejected Substantives. Texts are listed in the synthetic chronological order described in the Textual Commentary, page 185.

Within an entry, the curved dash ∼ represents the same word that appears before the bracket and is used in recording punctuation and paragraphing variants. The abbreviation HE indicates emendation made for the first time in the present edition. If a corrected form adopted here has appeared in an earlier state of the text, that text is cited for historical interest, even though it may have no textual authority. *Om.* means that the reading to the left of the bracket does not appear in the text to the right of the semicolon. The italicized form *ETS* indicates a reading introduced into the author's revised typescript of *The Leatherwood God* by a Century Company editor (see the list appended to A Note on the Manuscript and Typescripts, pages 190–196, for a full list of these non-authorial, editorial markings). An asterisk indicates that the reading is discussed in the Textual Notes.

Because of the number and complexity of texts and stages of authorial revision involved in the history of *The Leatherwood God*, one further convention has been adopted. The symbol † placed before an entry indicates that the reading at that point is part of a longer emendation, recorded in a preceding entry, which includes the section of the present text in which this specific emendation occurs.

The following texts are referred to:

AMS   195 leaves of manuscript
TS   Printer's copy typescript of 218 leaves before Howells' revisions
HTS   The same printer's copy typescript as revised by Howells
S   *Century Magazine*, XCI–XCIII (April-November 1916)
A   The Century Company, 1916: First Edition
B   Herbert Jenkins, Limited, 1917
C   Louis Conard, 1918

3.1   third decade] HTS; earliest decades AMS, TS
3.2   of] S; of the AMS, TS–HTS
3.3   tobacco] HTS; tobacco which flourished AMS, TS
3.3   fertile] S; fertile AMS, TS; *om.* HTS
3.4   bottomlands] HTS; bottomlands of the stream AMS, TS
3.4   had] HTS; had got AMS, TS
3.4–5   bush growing] A; bush, thickly growing AMS, TS; bush, which grew HTS, S
3.5   which with its] A; whose AMS, TS; and with its HTS; and which with its S
3.5   pliable] HTS; supple AMS, TS
3.5   served] S; served AMS, TS; supplied HTS
3.6   many] HTS; many of the rude AMS, TS
3.6   They] TS; they AMS
3.9   then] S; once more AMS, TS–HTS
3.9   man] HTS; anomalous being, at once a wonder and scandal AMS, TS
*3.11   region] HTS; older West AMS; old West TS
3.13   At the time he appeared] HTS; The constantly prospering settlement had increased in the comfortable log-cabins and substantial frame-houses, that dotted the farms. The mills dropped along the course of the creek ground the harvests of the nearer and farther neighborhood, and AMS, TS

3.15–18	It . . . brick.] HTS; *om.* AMS, TS
†3.17	but] S; *om.* HTS
†3.17	older] S; bright HTS
3.18–19	The population,] TS; The population, / The population, AMS
3.20	Middle Western] S; Western AMS, TS; midwestern HTS
3.21	their] HTS; the AMS, TS
3.22	on] S; upon AMS, TS–HTS
3.24	civic] S; *om.* AMS, TS–HTS
3.24	East;] S; East; they rested in the security of their practical democracy; and in the comfort to which poverty and wealth were both unknown they concerned themselves with none of AMS, TS; East; they rested in the security of their practical democracy; and where poverty and wealth were both unknown they concerned themselves with none of HTS
3.25	problems] S; enterprises AMS, TS; interests HTS
3.25	vex] A; trouble AMS, TS–HTS, S
3.26	were unknown to them] S; *om.* AMS, TS–HTS
3.26	their chief interest and the] A; the prime interest of their lives, and it was of this that they thought and talked. The AMS, TS; the chief interest of their lives, and it was of this that they mainly thought and spoke. The HTS; their chief interest, and the S
*4.1–2	Presbyterian, Methodist, Lutheran] HE; Lutheran, Presbyterian, Methodist AMS, TS–HTS; Presbyterian, Methodist, Lutheran, S, A–C
4.3–4	in the general prosperity the stringency of their several creeds had so far relaxed] HTS; the friendly material experiences had so far mellowed the severity of their several creeds AMS, TS
4.5	toleration.] HTS; toleration, and a common intelligence far beyond that of other pioneer communities. AMS, TS
4.7	they] HTS; they all AMS, TS
4.9	dwelling,] TS; ~ AMS

5.1	of] HTS; *om.* AMS, TS
5.2	early] HTS; early morning AMS, TS
5.3	in the day] HTS; into everything AMS, TS
5.5	log] HTS; *om.* AMS, TS
5.5	shared] HTS; took his share of AMS, TS
5.6	exhilaration] TS; exhileration AMS
5.6	comfortably] HTS; *om.* AMS, TS
5.8	on] HTS; *om.* AMS, TS
5.8	odors] S; allied appetizing odors AMS, TS; allied odors HTS
5.8	from her cooking] HTS; *om.* AMS, TS
5.8	dense] HTS; *om.* AMS, TS
5.9	that stirred] HTS; stirring illimitably to the vision AMS, TS
5.13	of] HTS; rather of AMS, TS
5.14	rode up] HTS; came in sight in the space AMS, TS
5.14	in the space where] HTS; *om.* AMS, TS
5.15	ranks of the] HTS; *om.* AMS, TS
5.16	a grist] HTS; an evenly divided grist AMS, TS
5.16–17	corn . . . other] HTS; grain weighting either end AMS, TS
5.17	the mill] HTS; mill AMS, TS
5.18	but he yielded apparently] S; being apparently unnoticed by Braile he yielded AMS, TS; but apparently he yielded HTS
5.19	come] HTS; insisted AMS, TS
5.20	slightest] S; lightest AMS, TS–HTS
5.21	he] TS; he he AMS
*5.22	mornun'] HTS; morning AMS, TS
*5.24	Won't] TS; Wont AMS
5.27	an] HTS; her AMS, TS
5.27	repose] HTS; lethargy AMS, TS
5.27–6.1	pushed her] HTS; rode her up AMS, TS
6.1–2	Brother Hingston's] HTS; Herald's AMS, TS
6.3	anyway] A; *om.* AMS, TS–HTS; anyway, S
6.4	left] S; left, anyway AMS, TS–HTS
6.6	putty] A; pretty AMS, TS–HTS; poortty S
*6.7	overslep'."] S; overslep'," he parleyed. AMS, TS–HTS

6.7–8	Then, as Braile remained silent, he went on] S; Then he continued, AMS, TS; Then, as Braile kept silent, he went on HTS
6.8	hearn] HTS; heard AMS, TS
6.15	were a line of mocking] HTS; emitted a mocking gleam AMS, TS
6.16	feathers] TS; feathes AMS
6.17	the other said] HTS; said the man on the claybank AMS, TS
6.18	the old] TS; the the old AMS
6.18	indifference.] TS; ~ AMS
6.23	Grove] S; Sove AMS, TS–HTS
6.24	guttural] *ETS*; gutteral AMS, TS–HTS
6.30	rippun'] HTS; rippin AMS; rippin' TS
6.33	drug] HTS; dragged AMS, TS
6.33	*my*] HTS; my AMS, TS
7.1	"Well,] TS; " ~," AMS
7.1	hain't] HTS; ha'n't AMS, TS
*7.6	now;] S; this time; AMS, TS; now,; HTS
7.6	he] TS; he to AMS
7.11	prayun'] HTS; the prayin' AMS, TS
7.14	Grove] S; Sove AMS, TS–HTS
7.18	Braile asked] HTS; asked Braile, AMS, TS
7.19	the riotous outlaws] HTS; the outlaws AMS; those outlaws TS
7.19	name.] TS; ~ AMS
7.20	Mought] S; Might AMS, TS–HTS
7.22	fellers] HTS; fellows AMS, TS
7.27	anywheres] HTS; anywhere AMS, TS
7.29	his] HTS; the AMS, TS
7.30	stageun's] HTS; stagin's AMS, TS
7.35–36	'Let us pray!'] *ETS*; " ~ ~ ~!" AMS, TS–HTS
7.36	stageun's] HTS; stagin's AMS, TS
8.3	tight] HTS; right AMS, TS
8.5	'What shall we pray for?'] *ETS*; " ~ ~ ~ ~ ~?" AMS, TS–HTS
8.7	'Salvation!'] *ETS*; " ~:" AMS, TS–HTS
8.20	there] TS; there there AMS
8.22	Grove's] S; Sove's AMS, TS–HTS

8.23	hengun'] HTS; henging AMS; hanging TS
8.24–25	pale like] HTS; pale AMS, TS
8.25	sad-lookun'] HTS; sad-lookin' like AMS, TS
8.26	putty] HTS; pretty AMS, TS
*8.31	linsey-woolsey] S; linsey woolsey AMS, TS–HTS
8.33	on] HTS; *om.* AMS, TS
8.36	Braile limbered] S; Old Michael Braile unlimbered AMS, TS; Braile unlimbered HTS
8.36	splint-bottom] HTS; splint-bottomed AMS, TS
9.3	and tilted it back] HTS; *om.* AMS, TS
9.6	If he] HTS; He AMS, TS
9.7	incident] HTS; scene AMS, TS
9.8	with his own sense of] HTS; in AMS, TS
9.8	it] HTS; but it AMS, TS
9.8–9	could not have been] S; was not AMS, TS; was perhaps not HTS
9.9	hope of impressing] S; belief that he should impress AMS, TS–HTS
9.10	it] S; of the incident AMS, TS; of it HTS
9.10	might have been] HTS; was AMS, TS
9.12	had] HTS; had laid AMS, TS
9.14	Reverdy] HTS; as Reverdy AMS, TS
9.16–17	held up] S; upheld AMS, TS–HTS
9.19	braided himself] HTS; himself braided AMS, TS
9.19	had] HTS; *om.* AMS, TS
9.21	escaped] HTS; escaped, involuntarily gay AMS, TS
9.22	fur-colored] HTS; yellow AMS, TS
9.22	bare feet] TS; barefeet AMS
*9.23	camp-meeting] TS; campmeeting AMS
9.24	richly] HTS; handsomely AMS, TS
9.27	his mare's] HTS; the claybank's AMS, TS
9.28	She] HTS; The claybank AMS, TS
9.29	Braile said, "you] HTS; said Braile, "You AMS, TS
9.30	breakfast, now] HTS; breakfast AMS, TS
9.32	on] HTS; remote from either with AMS, TS
9.35	o'] HTS; of AMS, TS
9.36	anyway] HTS; anyhow AMS, TS
10.1	Braile said again] HTS; said Braile AMS, TS

10.2	within, which had risen above their voices,] S; which had risen above their voices within AMS, TS–HTS
10.5	on] HTS; upon AMS, TS
10.15	reckon] HTS; know AMS, TS
10.16	Braile." Reverdy] HTS; Braile," said Reverdy. He AMS, TS
10.17	back] HTS; bank, noiselessly AMS; back, noiselessly TS
10.18	smooth] HTS; rein-worn AMS, TS
10.19–20	porch. "My] HTS; ~. ¶ "~ AMS, TS
10.22	shanty] HTS; shack AMS, TS
10.23	the mud and moss of] HTS; *om.* AMS, TS
10.24	lettun'] HTS; lettin AMS; lettin' TS
10.25	she's] HTS; she keeps AMS, TS
10.26	cabin] HTS; house AMS, TS
10.27–28	Braile, or a frame house, even.] HTS; Braile. AMS, TS
10.28	this] HTS; the AMS, TS
10.29	just] S; do AMS, TS–HTS
10.30	prayin'] TS; prayin AMS
11.1	presence] HTS; presence in the fact AMS, TS
11.4	Braile, who . . . him,] S; Braile who . . . him had AMS, TS–HTS
11.5	an] S; one AMS, TS–HTS
11.6	brows;] HTS; ~, AMS, TS
11.6	he] HTS; had AMS, TS
11.7	now,] HTS; *om.* AMS, TS
11.7	began] TS; begun AMS
11.10	with plaintive severity] HTS; plaintively, yet severely AMS, TS
11.15	Abel] HTS; Mr. Reverdys AMS; Mr. Reverdy TS
11.19	adulations] TS; adululations AMS
11.27	last] HTS; at AMS, TS
11.29	a] HTS; an AMS, TS
11.33	it was,] HTS; ~ ~ AMS, TS
11.35	Leatherwood] HTS; the settlement AMS, TS
12.9	thing."] HTS; thing," and AMS, TS
12.12	silently] HTS; quietly to the end AMS, TS

12.22	at] HTS; catching AMS, TS
12.32	havin'] TS; havin AMS
12.33	gittun'] HTS; gittin AMS; gittin' TS
13.7	showed] S; showed plainly AMS, TS–HTS
13.14	required] HTS; demanded AMS, TS
13.16	breakfas'] TS; breakfas AMS
13.24	hungry,] TS; ~ ; AMS
13.26	on] TS; in AMS
13.27–28	Mrs. Reverdy snickered, and she] HTS; and Mrs. Reverdy AMS, TS
13.29	a] HTS; an AMS, TS
13.30–31	If I've heard it from one I've heard it from a dozen.] HTS; *om.* AMS, TS
13.31	Abel's tol'] HTS; Abel tole AMS, TS
13.36	soundless] HTS; wide, soundless AMS, TS
14.4	Grove] S; Sove AMS, TS–HTS
14.6	tol'] HTS; tole AMS, TS
14.6	like] S; *om.* AMS, TS–HTS
14.13	Braile,] TS; ~ AMS
14.16	mouth,] HTS; ~ : AMS, TS
14.20	him;] S; him, and which AMS, TS–HTS
14.21	it] S; *om.* AMS, TS–HTS
14.22	comun'] HTS; comin AMS; comin' TS
14.23	tol'] HTS; tole AMS, TS
14.33	a] HTS; an AMS, TS
14.34	stood] HTS; sot AMS, TS
14.35	a] HTS; an AMS, TS
14.35	somepin] HTS; something AMS, TS
14.36	still!] HTS; ~ . AMS, TS
15.1	'Salvation,'] *ETS*; "Salvation" that he broke out with, AMS, TS; "Salvation," HTS
15.4	nothun'] HTS; nothing AMS, TS
15.5	no] HTS; any AMS, TS
15.6	Grove] S; Sove AMS, TS–HTS
15.15	David Gillespie] HTS; Major Parr AMS, TS
15.17	him."] TS; him."/-tion to what he said." AMS
15.20	the pike crossing] HTS; cross-roads AMS; the cross-roads TS
15.22	Mrs.] HTS; But Mrs. AMS, TS

15.25	it.] HTS; it. They say she took on more'n anybody. AMS, TS
15.25	her,] HTS; ~ AMS, TS
15.26	Jane,] HTS; *om.* AMS, TS
15.28	her. The] HTS; her, and the AMS, TS
15.28	stopped] HTS; stopped and waited AMS, TS
15.28–29	her; then in apparent haste she moved] HTS; her. Then the girl's apparent hurry caused her to move AMS, TS
15.30	itself] TS; itself itself AMS
15.32	patient] HTS; perhaps impatient AMS, TS
15.33	Abel!] TS; ~ ? AMS
15.34	with] HTS; from AMS, TS
16.2	soon." He] HTS; soon," he AMS, TS
16.3	shoulder,] TS; ~," AMS
16.7	said] HTS; added AMS, TS
16.12	their folly] HTS; *om.* AMS, TS
16.13	kinds] TS; kind AMS
16.20	he'd stayed] HTS; he'd staid AMS, TS
16.24	little—with the bead on—] HTS; ~ ~ ~ ~ ~, AMS, TS
16.28	required] HTS; required them AMS, TS
16.33	heaven] TS; heavin AMS
16.33	minute] HTS; moment AMS, TS
17.10	called.] TS; ~, AMS
17.16	at] HTS; at the AMS, TS
17.19	with you to the next] HTS; to that AMS, TS
17.19	Temple] HTS; Temple tonight AMS, TS
18.5	parried] HTS; known how to parry AMS, TS
18.8	went] HTS; went home AMS, TS
18.14	end. A] HTS; ~. ¶ ~ AMS, TS
18.16	behind] HTS; back of AMS, TS
18.23	their] HTS; their rich AMS, TS
18.26	for] HTS; with AMS, TS
19.2–3	spacious log-built house] HTS; double log cabin AMS, TS
19.6	congregation. The] HTS; ~. ¶ ~ AMS, TS
19.7	by] HTS; by the noise of AMS, TS
19.7	breathing,] TS; ~ AMS

19.9   coaxed] HTS; cooed AMS, TS
*19.12   candles on] HTS; dips on AMS; dips in TS
19.14   the] HTS; the dense AMS, TS
19.16   consciously expecting] HTS; unconsciously waiting
                for AMS, TS
19.17   with] HTS; with old AMS, TS
19.17–20   girl. She was . . . . dreamy. ¶ The stranger] HTS;
                girl. ¶ He AMS, TS
†19.19   in] S; from HTS
19.21–22   Temple] HTS; Temple in common for their worship
                AMS, TS
19.23   guest,] HTS; ~ AMS, TS
19.23   girl] TS; ~, AMS
19.23   vague] S; dreamy AMS, TS–HTS
19.24   been given a seat at the front, perhaps] HTS; a seat
                with the women, AMS, TS
19.25   perhaps in confusion] HTS; and perhaps from
                surprize, AMS, TS
19.26   presence.] TS; ~ AMS
19.26   keen] HTS; om. AMS, TS
19.27   eyebrows] TS; eye brows AMS
19.33   glances] TS; glance AMS
19.35–36   a Methodist who preached, but somehow to-night]
                HTS; the Reverend Henry Parr who was to preach;
                he was a Methodist, but perhaps because of his
                Presbyterian birth and breeding, AMS, TS
20.2   than] S; om. AMS, TS–HTS
20.2   hold] HTS; depth AMS, TS
20.3   perplexed] HTS; confused AMS, TS
20.10   air,] HTS; air, as if dispersing it, AMS, TS
20.12   what] TS; what what AMS
20.15   gone] HTS; got AMS, TS
20.15   again;] S; again; but AMS, TS–HTS
20.16   quite] HTS; om. AMS, TS
*20.19   lingered] HTS; come back AMS; om. TS
20.20–21   neighborhood and] HTS; creek, AMS, TS
20.25   them] HTS; them AMS, TS
20.26   talkin'] HTS; talking AMS, TS

20.30	Dylks—] HTS; ~, AMS, TS
21.3–4	supplication. He] TS; supplication, he AMS
21.4	Lord's] TS; Lords AMS
21.4	Prayer;] HTS; ~, AMS, TS
21.4	then] HTS; and then AMS, TS
21.4	said] HTS; cried AMS, TS
21.4–5	sing," and line] HTS; sing." ¶ Line AMS, TS
21.8	expounded] HTS; explained AMS, TS
21.8	stanza,] HTS; stanza both AMS, TS
21.9	before] HTS; and then AMS, TS
21.9	He] HTS; Then he AMS, TS
21.9–10	out a . . . text] S; out as a sort of text a passage of scripture AMS, TS–HTS
21.10	it; he] HTS; it. He AMS, TS
21.12	rather than] TS; than rather AMS
21.15	was the] HTS; was AMS, TS
21.16	dreadful,] TS; ~ AMS
21.18	the man's] S; his resounding and compelling AMS, TS; the man's compelling HTS
21.24	snort,] HTS; ~ AMS, TS
21.24	then] HTS; *om.* AMS, TS
21.25	Salvation!] HTS; ~. AMS, TS
21.32	hard and cold,] HTS; *om.* AMS, TS
*22.4	and he] S; and when he could free himself from the crowd, he AMS; and when he could pull himself away from the crow, he TS; and when he could pull himself from the crowd he HTS
22.4	went] HTS; walked AMS, TS
22.13	in this] TS; in this in this AMS
22.14	partake] HTS; share her interest in the night's events, or even AMS; share her interest in the night's events, or TS
22.15	David] HTS; old AMS, TS
22.17	and that he] HTS; or AMS, TS
22.22	Jefferson,] S; ~ AMS, TS–HTS
22.26	Leatherwood.] HTS; Leatherwood, and he isn't half as modest as Abel. AMS; Leatherwood, and he is n't half as modest as Abe. TS

22.28	Gillespie's."] HTS; Gillespie's." ¶ "Yes; I'm sorry to agree with you," Mrs. Braile said at this. ¶ "About Peter Hingston or the fried chicken?" AMS, TS
22.31	works] HTS; works and Christian charity AMS, TS
22.32	they've] TS; theyve AMS
22.33	settlement] HTS; town AMS, TS
23.7	unity] HTS; worship AMS, TS
23.19	come, Martha, you] S; come, come, Martha! You AMS, TS–HTS
23.23	trying] HTS; passing sentence on AMS, TS
23.26	allow, Martha,] S; allow AMS, TS–HTS
23.28–29	owned. "But] HTS; owned reluctantly. But AMS, TS
23.32	towns would] HTS; towns 'd AMS, TS
23.33	religion] HTS; Christianity AMS, TS
23.33	him."] HTS; him. But if ever he's up to mischief, — AMS, TS
24.6	me was like our] A; me AMS, TS–HTS; me was so much like our S
24.8	were. "I] HTS; ~. ¶ "~ AMS, TS
24.8	from the first] HTS; *om.* AMS, TS
25.2	Brailes] TS; Braile's AMS
25.2	was] HTS; was far out AMS, TS
25.5	grew] HTS; used to grow AMS, TS
25.5	lake] HTS; great lakes AMS, TS
25.6	openly] HTS; amply AMS, TS
25.7	of] HTS; common in AMS, TS
25.9	farther] HTS; *om.* AMS, TS
25.10	defined by its] HTS; the marking its bulk with the AMS; marking its bulk with the TS
25.10	fresh] A; freshly AMS, TS–HTS, S
25.10	dark] HTS; night AMS, TS
25.13	vanished] HTS; obeyed, vanishing AMS, TS
25.13	through,] HTS; ~ AMS, TS
25.17	morning] HTS; afternoon AMS, TS
25.25	It wasn't] HTS; Not AMS, TS
26.7	been] HTS; lived AMS, TS
26.8	present] HTS; *om.* AMS, TS

26.11	Nothing—first.] HTS; Nothing. I have no wish for revenge—first. AMS, TS
*26.15–16	now see] HTS; look AMS; back TS
*26.18–19	anything] HTS; anything, or *not* say anything, AMS, TS
26.23	Gillespie] HTS; "Man! Man!" Gillespie AMS, TS
26.28	No, no! Keep] HTS; Ha! No, keep AMS, TS
26.29	poor."] HTS; poor. You can't buy me off." Then AMS, TS
27.4	down,] HTS; ∼ AMS, TS
27.11	teasing.] TS; ∼ AMS
27.13–14	and frame houses] HTS; *om.* AMS, TS
27.14	of Leatherwood] HTS; *om.* AMS, TS
27.26–27	an ox lying in the field or a horse] HTS; a horse lying in the field or AMS, TS
27.27	broke] TS; ∼, AMS
27.32–28.1	ready./ IV ¶ The] HTS; ready. ¶ Before that the AMS, TS
28.1	a] HTS; a fearful AMS, TS
28.2	stole] HTS; and stole AMS, TS
28.2	steps] HTS; ∼; AMS, TS
28.2	checked] HTS; ∼, AMS, TS
28.2	limp] HTS; long, limp AMS, TS
28.3–4	rotting logs. But she] HTS; logs of the fallen trees, but AMS, TS
28.4–5	and safely gained the border of] HTS; gained the last shadow of a pawpaw thicket bordering AMS, TS
28.10	in the] HTS; in its AMS, TS
28.10	dark] S; dark inside AMS, TS–HTS
28.11	of] TS; on AMS
28.12	scamper] *ETS*; whisk and scamper AMS, TS; and scamper HTS
28.13	whisking] HTS; flitting AMS, TS
28.15	consciousness] HTS; consciousness through the dense trouble that involved her AMS, TS
28.16	recognizably] HTS; *om.* AMS, TS
28.16–17	sister, but her eyes and hair were black. She] HTS; sister and she AMS, TS

28.20	kept.] HTS; kept; it must be delicately told, but so quickly. AMS; kept; it must be delicately, but so quickly, told. TS
28.23	heart] HTS; mind, AMS, TS
28.23	physically dragged her down] S; were a physical weight AMS, TS; physically pulled her down HTS
28.24	crocks; she] HTS; crocks. She AMS, TS
28.25	step;] HTS; step and she knew AMS, TS
28.25	moment] S; moment AMS, TS; moment more HTS
28.28	Maybe He's] HTS; I believe He must be AMS, TS
29.3	gone;] HTS; ∼, AMS, TS
29.14	slept] HTS; slept a wink AMS, TS
29.22	*got*] HTS; got AMS, TS
29.28	Me?] A; I! AMS, TS; I? HTS, S
30.6	Oh] S; Oh, yes AMS, TS–HTS
30.8	Woman!] HTS; ∼, AMS, TS
30.8–9	the dead] HTS; them AMS, TS
30.11	boy,] HTS; ∼ AMS, TS
30.15	casuistry,] HTS; ∼ AMS, TS
30.28	large communities] S; civilized countries AMS, TS; great communities HTS
30.31	back,] TS; ∼," AMS
30.34	on] HTS; up on AMS, TS
31.3	know!] HTS; ∼. AMS, TS
31.5	long.] HTS; ∼? AMS, TS
31.8	money] HTS; money in the lawsuit AMS, TS
31.17	turned] HTS; turned disconsolatedly AMS, TS
31.21	grooves in] HTS; the grooves of AMS, TS
31.22	asleep,] HTS; ∼ AMS, TS
31.29	and] HTS; that pierced her breast like a knife. ¶ She AMS, TS
31.30	simple] HTS; dear AMS, TS
*31.33	sundown] HE; sundown, when AMS, TS–HTS, S, A–C
31.34	of a man] HTS; *om.* AMS, TS
31.35	if the baby were awake] HTS; if should the baby was awake AMS; should the baby be awake TS
32	V] HTS; IV AMS, TS
32.1	The] TS; The and AMS

32.3	the self-forgetfulness] HTS; this selfforgetfulness AMS, TS
32.7	and] HTS; and still putting the last touches to her preparation AMS, TS
32.17	quiet] HTS; equability AMS, TS
32.20	Nancy?] TS; ~. AMS
32.21	soul?] HTS; ~! AMS, TS
33.2	Yesterday morning or day before—] HTS; This morning, AMS, TS
33.3	first."] TS; ~" AMS
33.17	he asked.] S; *om.* AMS, TS–HTS
33.22	*he*] HTS; Joseph AMS, TS
33.27	"We] HTS; "Not any more than it ever was. We AMS, TS
33.30	times] HTS; times times today AMS; times today TS
33.32	We've] HTS; We AMS, TS
34.3	to-night,] TS; to-night AMS
34.7–8	It seems as if my] HTS; My AMS, TS
34.8	was] HTS; is AMS, TS
34.8	now.] HTS; now; I can't think. AMS, TS
34.9	minute] HTS; spell AMS, TS
34.11	said,] TS; ~. AMS
34.18	of] HTS; of their AMS, TS
35.7	mind."] TS; ~. AMS
35.31	*me. I*] HTS; me. I AMS, TS
35.32	*I'm not a*] S; I'm not a AMS, TS–HTS
35.32	*man!*] HTS; *man.* AMS, TS
36.5	what] HTS; *om.* AMS, TS
36.5	singing.] HTS; singing—
	"Plunged in a gulf of dark despair,
	We wretched sinners lay." AMS, TS
36.17	to] HTS; *om.* AMS, TS
36.21	wouldn't] TS; wouldnt AMS
36.28	I] HTS; And I AMS, TS
37.14	strange man] HTS; stranger AMS, TS
37.17	Over-the-Mountains] HTS; Over the Mountains AMS, TS
37.22	cheerily,] HTS; ~. AMS, TS

37.23   woon't] HTS; won't AMS, TS
37.32   me] HTS; us AMS, TS
37.36   soft] A; soft mud AMS, TS–HTS, S
38.2   long] TS; ~, AMS
39   VI] HTS; V AMS, TS
39.2   intention,] *ETS*; ~ AMS, TS–HTS
39.4   there] HTS; *om.* AMS, TS
39.6   gave,] HTS; ~ AMS, TS
39.9   doubted;] *ETS*; ~, AMS, TS–HTS
39.11   and] HTS; and honored for AMS, TS
39.13   Hingston's] A; Hingston was the owner of a AMS,
                 TS–HTS, S
39.14   bottom] A; bottom it AMS, TS–HTS, S
39.15   and his] TS; his AMS
39.15   brick] HTS; frame-built AMS, TS
39.16   behind the mill was the largest and finest] HTS;
                 that topped the rising ground above them was the
                 most dignified AMS, TS
39.17   patriarchal;] A; patriarchal; but he ruled less by
                 will than by good-will in his family AMS, TS–HTS,
                 S
39.18   the neighborhood] S; in the neighborhood which
                 AMS, TS–HTS
39.20–21   for the storage . . . for their barns] S; when the yield
                 was too great for storage of their wheat and corn
                 in the deep bins of his mill AMS; when the yield
                 was too great for storage of their wheat and corn in
                 the deep bins of his mills TS; for the of their wheat
                 and corn in the deep bins of his mill for storage
                 when the yield was too great for their barns HTS
39.23   growing] HTS; *om.* AMS, TS
39.23   until] *ETS*; after AMS, TS; after until HTS
39.24   will] HTS; law AMS, TS
40.2   a wistful kindness] HTS; an entreating wistfulness
                 AMS, TS
40.8   always] HTS; wholly AMS, TS
40.8   Himself.] HTS; Himself. It was on this point that
                 Matthew Brill and he agreed, and with the slow
                 movement of his intelligence he was never without

the hope that the old infidel would yet perceive that their common premise implied a common conclusion. AMS; It was on this point that Matthew Braile and he agreed, and with the slow movement of his intelligence he was never without the hope that the old infidel would yet perceive that their common premise implied a common conclusion. TS

40.10	event in] S; event with AMS, TS–HTS
40.17	Brethren.] TS; ~ AMS
40.21–23	friends: Enraghty . . . kind and calm.] HTS; friends. Enraghty's farm bordered Hingstons, and they were familiarly in and out of each other's houses. AMS, TS
40.36	talk] A; walk AMS, TS–HTS, S
41.9	fields] TS; fields and AMS
41.13	sacrilegious] TS; sacreligious AMS
41.18	personally] HTS; *om.* AMS, TS
41.18	each] HTS; each personally to AMS, TS
42	VII] HTS; VI AMS, TS
42.5	*sent*] HTS; sent AMS, TS
42.9	*I*] HTS; I AMS, TS
42.10	Power] HTS; Salvation AMS, TS
42.13	wonderin'] TS; wonderin AMS
42.14	be'n] HTS; been AMS, TS
42.16	come;] HTS; ~, AMS, TS
42.20	them two] HTS; they AMS, TS
42.21	clos't] HTS; close AMS, TS
42.22	me, though] HTS; me. AMS, TS
42.23	dast to] HTS; *om.* AMS, TS
42.26	top rail of the bar to] HTS; bars of AMS, TS
43.11	*squeal*] HTS; squeal AMS, TS
43.11	As they went on, Sally kept] S; Sally had been AMS, TS–HTS
43.12	loud,] HTS; ~ AMS, TS
43.15	"No] TS; '~ AMS
43.15	said. "Good] HTS; said, "good AMS, TS
43.18	her] HTS; her cabin AMS, TS
43.22	coldly] HTS; coldly, after her nature AMS, TS
43.23	it's] TS; its AMS

43.25   evening's] HTS; evenings AMS; evening TS
43.34   unto] HTS; to AMS, TS
43.34   me.'] TS; ~. AMS
44.2   answer] HTS; tone AMS, TS
44.2   there] HTS; *om.* AMS, TS
44.10   be quiet] HTS; quietly AMS, TS
44.14   "The baby? Oh,] HTS; "Oh, the baby! AMS, TS
44.18   in] HTS; on AMS, TS
44.19   into] TS; onto AMS
44.20   morning air] HTS; air had changed, and AMS, TS
44.30   its] S; its little AMS, TS–HTS
44.34   get] HTS; get us AMS, TS
44.37   *our*] S; *om.* poor AMS; our poor TS; *our* poor HTS
45.4   "But] TS; ~ AMS
45.5   got] HTS; got down AMS, TS
45.5   from] HTS; *om.* AMS, TS
45.6   atilt] HTS; *om.* AMS, TS
45.21   warm] HTS; ~, AMS, TS
45.32   cooed,] HTS; ~ AMS, TS
46.1   back,] TS; ~ AMS
46.5   notice."] TS; ~. AMS
46.16   sound] HTS; sound different, AMS, TS
46.18   with words bitter beyond] HTS; bitter words
             beyond all AMS; better words beyond all TS
46.20   minute."] TS; ~. AMS
46.21   woods."] HTS; woods. To pray." To pray for AMS;
             woods. To pray." TS
46.22   The] HTS; The little AMS, TS
46.25   Jane] HTS; Ann AMS, TS
46.26–27   woods," she said. ¶ "To pray, I reckon."] S; woods
             to pray." ¶ "I was afraid." AMS, TS; woods, she
             said." ¶ "To pray, I reckon." HTS
46.31   ended] HTS; finished AMS, TS
48   VIII] HTS; VI AMS, TS
48.6–7   some in their doubt seeking the help of his powerful]
             HTS; some seeking in doubt the help of his powerful
             AMS; some seeking in the help of his fiercer,
             powerful TS
48.8   from them all] HTS; of them AMS, TS

48.8	same] HTS; same grim AMS, TS
48.12	entirely] S; *om.* AMS, TS–HTS
48.13	old] HTS; tough old AMS, TS
48.20	sprinkled,] HTS; ~ AMS, TS
48.21	Squire] HTS; disciple of Tom Paine AMS, TS
49.1	No. But] HTS; *om.* AMS, TS
49.4	wusn't] HTS; wasn't AMS, TS
49.7	nights,] TS; ~ ; AMS
49.7	which] HTS; and AMS, TS
49.9	o'] HTS; *om.* AMS, TS
49.9	no,] HTS; well AMS, TS
49.9	Jim Redfield] HTS; Jake Powers AMS, TS
49.11	die.'] *ETS*; ~." AMS, TS–HTS
49.11	lifts] HTS; lifts up AMS, TS
49.12	Jim] HTS; Jake AMS, TS
49.12	'I've] *ETS*; "I've AMS, TS–HTS
49.13	*crack*] HTS; crack AMS, TS
49.13	your] HTS; your durn AMS, TS
49.13	shell,'] *ETS*; ~," AMS, TS–HTS
49.14	Jim] HTS; Jake AMS, TS
49.17	"I'm] HTS; 'I'm AMS, TS
49.29	in] A; on AMS, TS–HTS, S
49.30	I got] HTS; I recollect I got AMS, TS
49.30	comb, I remember] S; comb AMS, TS–HTS
49.33	Hingston] HTS; Herald AMS, TS
50.2	elec'] HTS; elect AMS, TS
50.3	Hingston] HTS; Herald AMS, TS
50.5	Squire!] HTS; Squire. You make fun of everything. AMS, TS
50.6	deceived! That's] S; deceived; that's AMS, TS–HTS
50.7	Brother Enraghty] HTS; Enraghty AMS, TS
50.7–8	Brother Hingston] HTS; Herald AMS, TS
50.16	preachin'] HTS; preaching AMS, TS
50.21	putty] A; pretty AMS, TS–HTS; poortty S
50.24	acrost] HTS; across AMS, TS
50.32	outpourin'] TS; outpourin AMS
50.35	singin'] TS; singin AMS
50.35	hymes] HTS; hymns AMS, TS

51.2	tell] HTS; till AMS; will TS
51.5	on!"] TS; ~!' AMS
51.6	sir, so] HTS; sir," Reverdy went on, so AMS, TS
51.9	at] HTS; *om.* AMS, TS
51.11	Apostle.' "] S; ~." AMS, TS–HTS
51.19	with a reluctance] HTS; with reluctance, AMS, TS
51.22	git] HTS; get AMS, TS
51.23	ag'in] HTS; again AMS, TS
51.23	kep'] HTS; kept AMS, TS
51.23	still,] HTS; ~ AMS, TS
51.25	air;] HTS; ~, AMS, TS
51.27	come] S; came AMS, TS–HTS
51.27	holler] HTS; hollow AMS, TS
51.29	'Fear . . . done,'] TS; "~ . . . ~," AMS
51.31	and stuck] HTS; stuck AMS, TS
51.32	it;] HTS; ~, AMS, TS
51.32	he] HTS; *om.* AMS, TS
51.33	bubblin'] TS; bubbling AMS
51.33	kittles] HTS; kettles AMS, TS
51.34	prayed,] HTS; ~ AMS, TS
52.2	follered] HTS; followed AMS, TS
52.4	winder] HTS; window AMS, TS
52.9	'I . . . years,'] TS; "~ . . . ~," AMS
52.10	said,] TS; ~ AMS
52.13	sayin'] TS; sayin AMS
52.14	no] S; any AMS, TS–HTS
52.14	more;] HTS; more, but AMS, TS
52.15	slowly] S; *om.* AMS, TS–HTS
52.22	know *I*] HTS; know I AMS, TS
52.22	*any*thing] HTS; anything AMS, TS
*52.31	husband,] HE; husband AMS; husband and TS–HTS, S, A–C
52.35	fell] TS; fall AMS
53.2	Temple] HTS; temple AMS, TS
53.3	common,] HE; ~ AMS; ~. TS–HTS, S, A–C
53.4	prophet] HTS; strange prophet AMS, TS
53.6	should come] HTS; come AMS; came TS
53.9	Dylks proclaimed] HTS; *om.* AMS, TS
53.10	Temple] HTS; Temple Dylks proclaimed AMS, TS

53.16	going] HTS; about AMS, TS
53.21	it] HTS; *om.* AMS, TS
53.23	idolatry] HTS; wild idolatry AMS, TS
53.23	girls,] HTS; ~ AMS, TS
53.25	keep] HTS; save AMS, TS
*53.28	Temple] TS; temple AMS
53.28	their] HTS; *om.* AMS, TS
53.29	tumult] HTS; ~, AMS, TS
53.29	dismay,] HTS; ~ AMS, TS
53.36	hence,] HTS; ~ AMS, TS
54.2	told] HTS; declared to AMS, TS
*54.5	woods pasture] HE; wood's pasture AMS, TS– HTS; woods-pasture S, A–C
54.9	'nuther] HTS; nuther AMS, TS
54.10	'lowed] S; knowd AMS, TS; knowed HTS
54.11	this] HTS; this and promising AMS, TS
54.13	unsparing] HTS; unsparingly circumstantial AMS, TS
54.15	don't] TS; dont AMS
54.19	he say it] HTS; he say so AMS, TS
54.19	himself,] S; himself, and AMS, TS–HTS
54.21	logic] HTS; reasoning AMS, TS
54.25	then] HTS; *om.* AMS, TS
54.26	more] HTS; *om.* AMS, TS
54.28	Redfield] HTS; Foreacre AMS, TS
54.31	count."] HTS; ~"— AMS; ~."— TS
54.32	Why,] HTS; ~ AMS, TS
54.32	the Hounds] HTS; *they* AMS; they TS
54.33	Redfield] HTS; Foreacre AMS, TS
54.36	fellows] HTS; fellow AMS, TS
55.1	they] HTS; he AMS, TS
55.1	a sound that] HTS; the sound AMS, TS
55.3	quite with] HTS; with all of AMS, TS
55.7	always] HTS; *om.* AMS, TS
55.8	Redfield] HTS; Foreacre AMS, TS
55.14	himself] HTS; himself best AMS, TS
55.24	goin'] TS; goin AMS
55.30	ha'] HTS; 'a' AMS, TS
55.30	Billun's] HTS; Reed's AMS, TS

55.30	ha'] HTS; 'a' AMS, TS
55.32	Hingston] HTS; Herald AMS, TS
55.34	devil,] HTS; ~ AMS, TS
56.2	Gillespie!'—] TS; ~!"— AMS
56.3	'It's . . . Hugh,'] TS; "~ . . . ~," AMS
56.4	lookin'] HTS; lookin' and bewildered AMS, TS
56.11	sayin'."] S; sayin'. AMS, TS–HTS
56.12	back?] TS; ~. AMS
56.13	heared] HTS; hear AMS, TS
56.27	Dylks," he said.] S; Dylks." AMS, TS–HTS
56.28	*Mr.*] S; Mr. AMS, TS–HTS
56.34–57.11	road. Then she . . . . calling back.] HTS; road AMS, TS
57.12	with . . . her going] S; watched her going with a sardonic smile AMS, TS–HTS
57.13	quite] HTS; *om.* AMS, TS
57.14	serious] HTS; serious and earnest AMS, TS
57.18	the] HTS; *om.* AMS, TS
57.21	used to be] HTS; was AMS, TS
58.3	lettin'] HTS; letting AMS, TS
58.7	fool?] TS; ~. AMS
59	IX] HTS; VIII AMS, TS
59.2	of his] HTS; of the AMS, TS
59.5	adoring] HTS; worshipping AMS, TS
59.10	possible] HTS; possible and credible AMS, TS
59.11	him,] TS; ~ AMS
59.13	who] HTS; that AMS, TS
59.14	whom] HTS; that AMS, TS
59.17	girl] HTS; wayward girl AMS, TS
59.25	glance] HTS; hopeless glance AMS, TS
59.26	she said] S; said AMS, TS–HTS
60.1	had] TS; was had AMS
60.8–9	at the Temple.] HTS; there. He told me. AMS, TS
60.11	*me*] HTS; me AMS, TS
60.18	she's] HTS; she AMS, TS
60.21	all of a sudden] HTS; suddenly AMS, TS
60.23	came on] HTS; came to AMS, TS
60.24	over me] HTS; *om.* AMS, TS
60.31	night?] TS; ~. AMS

61.3	go,] HTS; ~ AMS, TS
61.13	*he*] S; he AMS, TS–HTS
61.14	*chance*] HTS; chance AMS, TS
61.15	interest,] HTS; ~. AMS, TS
61.17	on,] HTS; ~ AMS, TS
61.18	like] HTS; as AMS, TS
61.26	me.] HTS; me. After the plow has gone over you, I reckon you don't mind the harrow much. AMS, TS
61.29	now;] HTS; ~, AMS, TS
61.32	of—] S; of it: AMS, TS–HTS
61.35	*him*;] HTS; him, AMS, TS
61.35	to kill"—] HTS; to"— AMS, TS
62.5	*He*] HTS; He AMS, TS
62.10	parting,] TS; ~ AMS
62.13	crying] HTS; *om.* AMS, TS
62.13	mother] HTS; mother crying AMS, TS
62.16	sealed?] HTS; ~ ! AMS, TS
62.18	heard] HTS; hearn AMS, TS
62.21	reached] TS; *om.* AMS
62.22	in] HTS; through AMS, TS
62.26	It'll] TS; I'll AMS
62.27	couldn't] HTS; wouldn't AMS, TS
*62.28	Saint] TS; St AMS
62.30	up] HTS; all AMS, TS
62.32	'em] HTS; *om.* AMS, TS
62.32–33	fool Davis who'd] HTS; fool, who's AMS, TS
62.35	could] HTS; *om.* AMS, TS
63.2	Some times I'm] HTS; I'm some times AMS, TS
63.24	Then,] HTS; ~ AMS, TS
63.27	feet,] HTS; ~ AMS, TS
63.31	*me*] HTS; me AMS, TS
64.1	for to-night] HTS; Sunday week AMS, TS
64.11	There] S; They AMS, TS–HTS
64.17	there] HTS; in that AMS, TS
64.17–18	conscience,] HTS; conscience, it's because AMS, TS
64.19	place] S; ~, AMS, TS–HTS
64.20	Mr.] HTS; that AMS, TS

64.36	almost pitifully,] S; pitifully AMS, TS–HTS
65.3	good."] TS; ~. AMS
65.4	from] HTS; _om._ AMS, TS
65.7	swiftly] TS; ~, AMS
65.7	lips] HTS; lips as if AMS, TS
65.12	baby,] HTS; baby on the floor AMS, TS
65.13	from the floor] HTS; _om._ AMS, TS
66	X] HTS; XI TS
66.11	hast well said] S; sayest well HTS
66.11	he] S; for him HTS
68.6	it] S; It HTS
68.15	gets] S; that goes on HTS
69.15	good-for-nothing] S; good-for nothing HTS
69.20	your] S; you're HTS
*69.31	All-powerful] HE; All-mighty HTS; all-powerful S; All-mighty A–C
70.10	proved] S; put HTS
71.11	Brother] S; brother HTS
71.22	despair] S; dispair HTS
71.28	a] S; the HTS
72.1	he strode] S; passed HTS
72.6	where] S; _om._ HTS
72.6	from] S; to HTS
72.34	Laban?"] S; ~ ? HTS
73.5	Nancy,"] S; ~." HTS
73.24	joyful,] S; joyous HTS
73.32	courage] _ETS_; courace HTS
*74.2	good bye] HE; goodbye HTS, C; good-by A, S; good-bye B
75.4	the figure of another] S; another figure of a HTS
76.5	her.] S; her; then he sank at her side. HTS
76.9	if] _ETS_; If HTS
76.11	sank beside her] S; sank HTS
76.17	me."] S; me." ¶ "Do you believe in the Son of God?" ¶ "I believe in the Son of Man. That's what _He_ did, mostly." HTS
77.26	she'd] S; she's HTS
77.36	He] _ETS_; he HTS
78.16	out of] S; in HTS

78.24	or] S; *om.* HTS
79.20	to] A; to the HTS, S
79.21	in the backwoods phrase] A; after the backwoods use HTS, S
79.31–32	the children] S; children HTS
80.2	intervals] S; intervals, but sometimes in close groups HTS
80.8	which] S; which it HTS
80.8	been] S; *om.* HTS
81.1	she asked.] S; *om.* HTS
81.3	he'd] S; he's HTS
81.11	discouragedly,] S; ∼. HTS
82.1	She] S; She now HTS
85.2	Hingston'll] B; Hingston 'll HTS, S, A
85.33	or] S; or they HTS
86.19	they] *ETS*; they they HTS
87.9	expectant] *ETS*; ∼, HTS
87.10	feet] S; ∼, HTS
88.15–16	crowd, . . . believer."] S; ∼. . . . ∼," HTS
89.4	Matthew] S; Michael HTS
89.22	Matthew] S; Michael HTS
89.29	tie] S; life HTS
90.32	raiment] A; garment HTS, S
91.5	who] S; *om.* HTS
91.28	whom] S; which HTS
91.32	angry,] S; ∼ HTS
92.5–6	than of] S; than HTS
92.10	hallowed] S; made HTS
92.10	stuff,] S; stuff sacred, HTS
93.6	raiment had been] S; raiment HTS
93.12	home, weeping,] S; weeping home, HTS
93.14	desecrated] S; dishonored HTS
93.22	another's] *ETS*; anothers' HTS
94.5	Good] S; *om.* HTS
94.8	disbelieved] S; denied HTS
94.16	I'd] S; I would HTS
94.30	height] *ETS*; hight HTS
95.20	amid] A; in HTS; with S
96.5	retorted] S; answered HTS

96.8   pushed] S; surged HTS
96.20   mischief.] S; ~, HTS
96.27   there!] S; ~,! HTS
97.20   what] *ETS*; What HTS
97.24   Well] S; Why HTS
97.32   impostor] S; imposter HTS
97.35   who] S; ~, HTS
97.36   with] S; with a HTS
98.1   threw] S; flung HTS
98.4   it] S; *om.* HTS
98.6   outraged] S; descrated HTS
98.7   lock] S; bleeding lock HTS
98.8–9   horror. ¶ "Don't] A; horror. "Why? Don't HTS;
                horror. "Why, don't S
99   XIV] S; XV HTS
99.10   god] S; idol HTS
99.19   with] S; and HTS
99.19   melancholy] A; piercing HTS, S
100.11   each] S; either HTS
100.11   Dylks] S; him HTS
100.25   about him] S; *om.* HTS
100.26   blood] S; blood, about him HTS
101.36   among them] S; in their midst HTS
102.2   and] S; and and HTS
*102.18   crowd] HE; ~; HTS, A–C; ~, S
102.21   Then he said] S; Then HTS
104.6   slowly] A; fumblingly HTS; stiffly S
104.12   Braile] S; he HTS
104.17   suspicions] S; suspicion HTS
104.36–105.1   Flock. ¶ The] S; Flock/XVI/ ¶ The HTS
105.5   breathlessly] S; breathless HTS
105.14   flesh] S; flash HTS
105.22   declared] S; answered HTS
105.32   they've] S; they're HTS
107   XV] S; *om.* HTS
107.1   woods] S; forest HTS
107.11   dispossessed] S; dispossesed HTS
107.12   hazelnuts] S; hazlenuts HTS
107.15   Few men or boys] S; Few, of men or boys, HTS

107.16	dry land] S; dryland HTS
107.20	ridge] S; path HTS
107.23	here] S; there HTS
109.23	people,] S; people; he would HTS
110.2	drunk] S; drank HTS
110.13	stooped] A; crouched HTS, S
110.20	the other,] S; another HTS
110.21	he crept slowly by,] A; slowly he crept by HTS, S
110.24	into] S; in HTS
110.24–25	cabin of peeled logs] S; log cabin HTS
111.9	"But] *ETS*; ~ HTS
111.23	again] S; back HTS
111.34	reckon,"] S; ~", HTS
112.3–5	had come . . . away to silence.] A; was bending over it with a rope of her hair in her hand, which she coiled into the knot at the nape of her neck, while she chirped and cooed to the little one. HTS; was bending over it with a rope of her hair in her hand, which she coiled at the nape of her neck while she chirped and cooed to the little one. S
112.22	wasn't] S; was not HTS
113.14	Oh!"] *ETS*; ~ ! HTS
113.16	soft] S; *om.* HTS
113.16	pledget] S; pletchet HTS
114.24	back there again] S; back HTS
114.29	had] S; *om.* HTS
115	XVI] A; XV HTS; *om.* S
115.1	chair] S; clair HTS
115.9	this] S; it HTS
116.17	Dylks's] S; Dylk's HTS
117.4	The] A; Not the HTS, S
117.35	could] S; should HTS
118.17	impostors] S; imposters HTS
119.33	puncheon] *ETS*; punchion HTS
120.36	in."] *ETS*; ~ . HTS
121.11	you;] *ETS*; ~ , HTS
121.13	me after] S; *om.* HTS
121.14	boy— And] S; boy; and HTS
122	XVII] A; XVI HTS, S

122.9	scruff] S; scurff HTS
122.19	him] S; that fellow HTS
122.21	"Suppose] S; "Well, suppose HTS
122.21	see] S; try HTS
123.2	comfortably] S; comfortebly HTS
124.19	hesitated.] *ETS*; ~, HTS
124.36	first.] S; ~, HTS
126	XVIII] A; XVII HTS, S
126.12	assembly] S; asembly HTS
126.24	sacrilegious] *ETS*; sacriligious HTS
127.7	showed] A; looked a HTS, S
127.11	but] S; *om.* HTS
128.2	But] S; But I reckon HTS
128.16	ordinarily] S; ordinarally HTS
*129.20	The] *ETS*; '~ HTS
130.9	journey?] S; ~. HTS
131.13	you to] S; you, HTS
132	XIX] A; XVIII HTS, S
132.5	mother!"] S; ~! HTS
132.15	threshold] S; threshhold HTS
134.1	from] S; from his HTS
134.8	too?"] S; ~? HTS
134.23	didn't] A; did n't HTS, S
136	XX] A; XIX HTS, S
136.22	would] S; should HTS
137.2	Matthew] S; Michael HTS
137.27	me 'n'] S; me' n' HTS
138.4	it] S; his going HTS
139.10	afeared] S; afread HTS
140	XXI] A; XX HTS, S
140.1	long-haired] S; long, lank HTS
141.2	that] S; that lock of HTS
141.20	hickory] S; hickory wood HTS
141.22	in] S; in case of HTS
142.25	No] S; No, no HTS
143.33	as that night when Dylks called her, that] S; *om.* HTS
143.35	Laban!"] S; ~ "." " HTS
143.35	said] S; came again HTS

144.12	crick] S; creek HTS
144.23	and had] *ETS*; had HTS
145.11	*I* believe] S; I believe HTS
146	XXII] A; XXI HTS, S
146.21–22	the other one] S; him HTS
147.11	o'] *ETS*; 'o' HTS
147.13	me 'n'] S; me' 'n' HTS
147.17	"He] *ETS*; ~ HTS
147.19	somewheres] S; somewhere's HTS
147.21	more.] *ETS*; ~.— HTS
147.34	before, Joey dear] S; before HTS
150.18	come] A; came HTS, S
152	XXIII] A; XXII HTS, S
152.4	and with] S; and HTS
153.31	his] S; its HTS
154.1	said,] S; said, but HTS
154.3	ours,"] S; ~", HTS
*154.13	Mandeville—T.J. Mandeville] A; Ammidown—T.J. Ammidown HTS; Manderville—T.J. Manderville S
154.27	the] S; your HTS
157.18	it.] *ETS*; ~, HTS
157.19	then,] *ETS*; ~ HTS
158.1	didn't] S; about. Didn't HTS
158.21	Billin's] A; Billings HTS, S
158.24–159.11	irony. ¶ "And you . . . . could with his ironical concession. ¶ The stranger looked at his watch; he jumped to his feet. "Nine o'clock] A; irony. ¶ The stranger looked at his watch; he jumped to his feet. "Nine o'clock HTS; irony. ¶ The stranger looked at his watch; he jumped to his feet. ¶ "And you . . . . could with this. ¶ "Nine o'clock S
†158.28	assented] A; asserted S
†158.30	*he*] A; he S
†158.30	*she*] A; she S
†158.35–159.3	assented. He . . . . amplified. "It] A; assented. ¶ "It S
159.14	obscurity of the] A; obscure HTS, S
159.23	for his superstition] A; *om.* HTS, S

Rejected Substantives

The following list records all substantive variants subsequent to the reading accepted at each point in the present edition which have been rejected as non-authorial. The reading of the present edition appears to the left of the bracket; the source of that reading, followed by a semicolon, the subsequent variant reading or readings and their sources appear to the right of the bracket. The reading of any unlisted text, antecedent or subsequent, other than copy-text, which is extant for that portion of the present text (see the Textual Commentary, pages 171–173, for a description of the copy-texts) may be presumed to agree with the reading to the left of the bracket unless recorded in Emendations. Texts are listed here in the synthetic chronological order described in the Textual Commentary, page 185. If the authority for the present reading is other than the copy-text for that section, the copy-text reading is recorded in Emendations. The curved dash ∼ represents the same word that appears before the bracket and is used in recording punctuation and paragraphing variants. *Om.* means that the reading to the left of the bracket does not appear in the text cited to the right of the semicolon. The italicized form *ETS* indicates a reading introduced into the author's revised typescript of *The Leatherwood God* by a Century Company editor (see A Note on the Manuscript and Typescripts, pages 190–196, for a full list of these nonauthorial, editorial markings). An asterisk indicates that the reading is discussed in the Textual Notes.

The following texts are referred to:

AMS   195 leaves of manuscript
TS   Printer's copy typescript of 218 leaves before
       Howells' revisions
HTS   The same printer's copy typescript as revised by
       Howells
S   *Century Magazine*, XCI–XCIII
       (April–November 1916)

A The Century Company, 1916: First Edition
B Herbert Jenkins, Limited, 1917
C Louis Conard, 1918

4.3–4	in the general prosperity the stringency of their several creeds had so far relaxed] HTS; the general prosperity had so far relaxed the stringency of their several creeds *ETS*, S, A–C
4.6	ceremonials] AMS; ceremonies TS–HTS, S, A–C
5.3	infused a] AMS; infused TS–HTS, S, A–C
*5.3	in] HTS; into S, A–C
5.13	of] HTS; of rather S, A–C
5.19	without. "Whoa] AMS; ~. ¶ "~ S
5.24	back, "Won't] TS; ~: ¶ "~ S
6.3	meal] AMS; metal C
6.7	overslep'."] S; overslep'," he parleyed. A–C
6.8	wonderin'] AMS; wonderun' S
6.9	doin's] AMS; doun's S, A–C
6.10	smoke, "You're] AMS; ~: ¶ "~ S
6.19	ask, "Who] AMS; ~: ¶ "~ S
6.22	phrase, "There] AMS; ~: ¶ "~ S
6.24	Hoonch] AMS; Hoonck A
6.28	goin'] AMS; goun' S, A–C
7.5	Hoonck] AMS; Hoonch TS–HTS, S, A–C
7.9	not. "There] AMS; ~. ¶ "~ S
7.10	diff'ent] AMS; diff'rent S, A–C
7.30	stageun's] HTS; stagun's S
7.36	stageun's] HTS; stagun's S
8.6	come] AMS; came A–C
8.17–18	quietly, "And] AMS; ~: ¶ "~ S
8.21	of a] AMS; of S, A–C
8.23	hengun'] HTS; hengun A–C
8.25	some] AMS; same TS
8.26	putty] HTS; poortty S
9.3	ask, "Goin'] AMS; ~: ¶ "~ S
9.25	much] AMS; well TS–HTS, S, A–C
10.2	within, which had risen above their voices,] S; which had risen above their voices within A–C
10.3–4	over the puncheon floor] AMS; *om.* C

10.4	knives and] AMS; *om.* C
10.11	saying, "The] AMS; ~: ¶ "~ S
10.23	chinkin'] AMS; chinkun' S, A–C
10.23	daubin'] AMS; daubun' S, A–C
10.25	worse'n] AMS; wuss'n TS–HTS, S, A–C
10.30	prayin'] TS; prayun' S
10.30	on] AMS; in TS–HTS, A–C; un S
10.31	as't] AMS; ast S
10.32	hunderd] AMS; hundred TS, A–C
11.11–12	responsively, "Not] AMS; ~: ¶ "~ S
11.12	as] AMS; so TS–HTS, S, A–C
11.19	opinion, "I] AMS; ~: ¶ "~ S
11.23	anger. "This] AMS; ~. ¶ "~ S
11.26	again. "Well] AMS; ~. ¶ "~ S
11.27	log-rollin'] AMS; log-rollun' S
11.29	a] AMS; a' S
12.5	him. "You] AMS; ~. ¶ "~ S
12.12	asked, "And] AMS; ~: ¶ "~ S
12.15	become] AMS; became TS–HTS
12.20	don'] AMS; don't S, A–C
12.20	*me*] AMS; me TS–HTS, S, A–C
12.30	*me*] AMS; me TS–HTS, S, A–C
12.32	havin'] TS; havun' S
12.34	*do*] AMS; do TS–HTS, S, A–C
13.5	lax] AMS; last TS; *om.* HTS, S, A–C
13.6	control] AMS; central TS
13.22	something] AMS; somepin *ETS*; somepun' S; somepin A–C
*13.25	now,] AMS; not TS; now, not HTS, S, A–C
13.30	If] HTS; It B
13.33–34	and smoking] AMS; smoking TS–HTS, S, A–C
13.36	in] AMS; on TS–HTS
14.4	come] AMS; came TS, A–C
14.4	while] AMS; white TS–HTS
14.5	burnin'] AMS; burnun' *ETS*, S, A–C
14.17	a] AMS; a' S
14.17	somepin] AMS; some'pin TS–HTS; somepun' S
14.19	anything] AMS; anythun' *ETS*, S; anythin' A–C
14.22	jus'] AMS; jes S; jes' A–C

14.30   get] AMS; git TS–HTS, S, A–C
14.31   anything] AMS; anythun *ETS*; nawthun' S, A;
         nowthun' B–C
14.33   a] HTS; a' S
14.35   a] HTS; a' S
14.35   somepin] HTS; somepun' S
14.36   so] AMS; as TS–HTS, S, A–C
15.4   nothun'] HTS; nawthun' S; nowthun' A–C
15.7   tryin'] AMS; tryun' *ETS*, S, A–C
15.19   *some*] AMS; some TS–HTS, S, A–C
15.24   if] AMS; it TS
15.25   get] AMS; git TS–HTS, S, A–C
15.32   hospitality, "Here's] AMS; ~ : ¶ "~ S
15.34   with a full mouth] HTS; *om.* C
16.2   soon." He] HTS; soon," he S, A–C
16.2   to] AMS; ot TS
16.10   taken. "The] AMS; ~ . ¶ "~ S
16.20   wouldn't] AMS; wouldn't have TS–HTS, S, A–C
16.30   talked. "One] AMS; ~ . ¶ "~ S
16.31   come] AMS; came TS–HTS, S, A–C
17.1   *that*] AMS; that TS–HTS, S, A–C
17.16   saying, "Oh] AMS; ~ : ¶ "~ S
18.7   aside] AMS; *om.* C
18.12   that was said to have] AMS; seemed to have TS; that
         had HTS, S, A–C
18.24   drove] AMS; rode TS–HTS, S, A–C
18.27   fervent] AMS; devout TS–HTS, S, A–C
19.1   Temple where the] AMS; Temple. ¶ The TS–HTS,
         S, A–C
19.4   narrowed space] AMS; narrow path TS–HTS, S, A–C
19.12   wavering round] AMS; dancing around TS
19.13   then] AMS; the TS
19.16   in, together] AMS; in TS–HTS, S, A–C
19.18   fiercely] HTS; purely *ETS*; pearly S; gray A; purely
         B–C
19.20   stretched] AMS; stretched out TS–HTS, S, A–C
19.21   sectaries] AMS; sectarians TS–HTS, S, A–C
19.23   girl] AMS; girl who TS
19.27   guttural] AMS; guttral TS; gutteral HTS

19.30	on] AMS; in TS–HTS, A–C
19.32	hair was combed back from his forehead and fell] AMS; hair combed back from his forehead and fell TS; hair, combed back from his forehead, fell HTS, S, A–C
19.36	fervor] AMS; favor TS
20.4	some] AMS; scores TS
20.6	his] AMS; the TS–HTS, S, A–C
20.7–8	torpid . . . disappointment] AMS; tired congregation started to go out in disappointment TS; disappointed congregation rose to go out HTS, S, A–C
20.12	what they] AMS; that thing TS
20.19–20	A tall, stout . . . from the aisle.] AMS; *om.* TS
20.28–29	stranger. "Will] AMS; ~. ¶ "~ S
20.29–30	Brother"— ¶ "Call] AMS; ~"— "~ TS
20.33	the] AMS; his TS
20.35	them: "Shall] AMS; ~. ¶ "~ S
21.1	steps: "We] AMS; ~. ¶ "~ S
21.3	places] AMS; place TS
21.4	ended] AMS; ended it TS–HTS, S, A–C
21.9	led] AMS; lead TS
21.12–13	unerring; women] AMS; unerring; men TS
21.17	threatening] AMS; threating TS
21.24	gave] AMS; began TS
21.27	old] AMS; old David TS–HTS, S, A–C
22.7	said, "Is] AMS; ~: ¶ "~ S
22.14	felt] AMS; shared TS–HTS, S, A–C
*22.19	Abel] AMS; Abe TS–HTS, A–C
22.23	*really*] AMS; really TS–HTS, S, A–C
22.26	Abel] AMS; Abe TS–HTS, A–C
22.29	answer. "You] AMS; ~. ¶ "~ S
22.32	*this*] AMS; this TS–HTS, S, A–C
22.35	slaved] AMS; shaved TS
22.35	by himself] AMS; *om.* TS–HTS, S, A–C
22.35	farm's] AMS; farms are TS
23.1	the Gillespies] AMS; Gillespie TS–HTS, S, A–C
23.5	halted] AMS; patted TS
23.13	folks'] AMS; folk's TS
23.18	Abel] AMS; Abe TS–HTS, A–C
23.19	come, Martha, you] S; come, come, Martha! You A–C

23.26	the long] AMS; long TS; his long HTS, S, A–C
23.26	the black] AMS; black TS–HTS, S, A–C
23.27	the snort] AMS; his snort HTS, S, A–C
23.29	persecute] AMS; prosecute TS
23.32	much worse] AMS; much more TS; more HTS, S, A–C
*23.36	forthplanted] AMS; -planted TS; forward-planted HTS, S, A–C
24.1	whimpered] AMS; whimpered a TS–HTS, S, A–C
24.8	were. "I] HTS; ~. ¶ "~ S
25.12	catch] AMS; cathch TS
25.12	open. "Go] AMS; ~. ¶ "~ S
25.14	aloof by] AMS; aloof TS–HTS, S, A–C
25.16	guest. "Did] AMS; ~. ¶ "~ S
25.21	stood. "I] AMS; ~. ¶ "~ S
25.22	splitting] AMS; spliting TS–HTS, A
25.22	open] AMS; *om.* TS
26.1	solemnity of his] AMS; solemnity TS; solemn HTS, S, A–C
26.2	risks] AMS; costs TS–HTS, S, A–C
26.3	with an impatient hand] AMS; impatiently C
26.19	*look*] AMS; look TS
26.19	even] AMS; now TS
26.21	*had*] AMS; had TS
26.23	desperately, "Listen] AMS; ~ : ¶ "~ S
26.25	I've got some money;] AMS; *om.* TS–HTS, S, A–C
26.31	I work] AMS; I want TS
26.33	from] AMS; over TS–HTS, S, A–C
26.35	forth. "If] AMS; ~. ¶ "~ S
26.36	the] AMS; a TS–HTS, S, A–C
27.3	*did*] AMS; did TS
27.3	Devil] AMS; devil TS
27.4	*me*] AMS; me TS
27.9	advice] AMS; advise TS
27.22	morning: I] AMS; morning. TS
27.31	his] AMS; *om.* TS
28.5	Then] AMS; There TS–HTS, S, A–C
28.9	cream-covered] AMS; dream-covered TS
28.10	hut] AMS; chest TS
28.11	honeyed] AMS; honey TS

28.12	ripening] AMS; opening TS
28.18	any] AMS; a TS–HTS, S, A–C
*28.20	kept; . . . quickly. She] AMS; kept. ¶ She TS–HTS, S, A–C
28.21	knees and] AMS; knees; HTS, S, A–C
28.21	hang] AMS; hung heavy TS–HTS, S, A–C
28.24	morning's] AMS; morning TS
29.10	sat] AMS; sat still TS
29.16	the] AMS; this TS–HTS, S, A–C
29.19–20	spring. "Nancy] AMS; ∼. ¶ "∼ S
29.24	*let*] AMS; let TS–HTS, S, A–C
29.26	*are*] AMS; are TS
29.27	in] AMS; a TS
29.28	Me] A; I B–C
30.3	*Why . . . . Why*] AMS; Why . . . . Why TS
30.6	Oh] S; Oh, yes A–C
30.10	*no*] AMS; no TS
30.12	*have*] AMS; have TS
30.12	*he*] AMS; he TS
30.12	*why*] AMS; why TS
30.20	them] AMS; tham TS
30.23	erect. "And] AMS; ∼. ¶ "∼ S
30.28	large communities] S; great communities A; the great communities B–C
30.30–31	if no one . . . coming back, it] AMS; no one . . . coming back, it TS; no one . . . coming back. It HTS, S, A–C
30.31	*he*] AMS; he TS
30.31	*you*] AMS; you TS
30.32	*you*] AMS; you TS
31.11	again. "Oh] AMS; ∼. ¶ "∼ S
31.16–17	you." ¶ He] AMS; ∼." ∼ TS–HTS, S, A–C
31.22	low] AMS; *om.* TS
31.27	kisses. "Oh] AMS; ∼. ¶ "∼ S
32.4	life: "Your] AMS; ∼: ¶ "∼ S
32.4	waiting] AMS; waitin' S, A–C
32.9	face and head,] AMS; *om.* TS–HTS, S, A–C
32.19	ask, "Why] AMS; ∼: ¶ "∼ S
32.23	ask, "Joseph] AMS; ∼: ¶ "∼ S
33.3	waiting] AMS; waitin' S, A–C

33.6	walking] AMS; walkin' S, A–C
33.6	thinking] AMS; thinkin' S, A–C
33.17	he asked.] S; *om.* A–C
33.22	living] AMS; livin' S
33.22	*he*] HTS; he S, A–C
33.24	it. "I] AMS; ~. ¶ "~ S
33.25	knowing] AMS; knowin' S
33.26	Yes] AMS; Yet B–C
34.26	arms. "Laban] AMS; ~. ¶ "~ S
34.33	asked, "Does] AMS; ~: ¶ "~ S
35.10–11	tremulously: "I] AMS; ~: ¶ "~ S
35.15	shook. "You'll] AMS; ~. ¶ "~ S
35.31	*I*] HTS; I C
36.19	and he . . . in it.] AMS; *om.* C
37.7	bein'] AMS; being TS–HTS, S, A–C
37.8	again] AMS; *om.* C
37.8	he] AMS; *om.* C
37.19	gasped. "I] AMS; ~. ¶ "~ S
37.23	woon't] HTS; won't S, A–C
37.26	they] AMS; the' S; there B–C
37.29	ideal, "Oh] AMS; ~: ¶ "~ S
37.30	him. "Yes] AMS; ~. ¶ "~ S
38.1	herself, "He'd] AMS; ~: ¶ "~ S
38.1	got] AMS; get TS–HTS, S, A–C
39.5	the] AMS; *om.* TS; an HTS, S, A–C
39.13	home] AMS; *om.* TS–HTS, S, A–C
39.14	its] AMS; *om.* TS–HTS, S, A–C
39.18	the neighborhood] S; in the neighborhood which A–C
39.21–22	their use] AMS; the use TS–HTS, S, A–C
41.1	exhalation] AMS; inhalation TS
41.4	heathen. He] AMS; ~. ¶ ~ TS
42.3–4	together. "Oh] AMS; ~. ¶ "~ S
42.9	floppin'] AMS; floppun' S, A–C
42.10	workin'] AMS; workun' S, A–C
42.11	needin'] AMS; needun' S, A–C
42.13	Goin'] AMS; Goun' S, A–C
42.13	wonderin'] AMS; wonderun' S, A–C
42.17	talkin'] AMS; talking TS; talkun' S, A–C
42.20	perfessin'] AMS; perfessun' S, A–C

42.21	clos't] HTS; close't S, A–C
42.26	bar] HTS; bars S, A–C
43.1	again. "Why] AMS; ~. ¶ "~ S
43.11	*I*] AMS; I TS
43.11	As they went on, Sally kept] S; Sally had been A–C
43.24–25	Well?" ¶ If] AMS; ~ ?" ~ S
43.26–27	him, and . . . her silence.] AMS; him. He made another attempt. C
43.31	know] AMS; knew TS–HTS, A–C
43.32	said, "Father] AMS; ~ : ¶ "~ S
43.34	unto] HTS; to S
44.2	answer. "You] AMS; ~. ¶ "~ S
44.10	aside. "Go] AMS; ~. ¶ "~ S
44.26	on] AMS; in TS
44.29	moulded] AMS; molded *ETS*, S, A
44.36	It'd] AMS; It'u'd S
45.20	baby. "It's] AMS; ~. ¶ "~ TS–HTS, S, A–C
45.27	pegs] AMS; peg TS–HTS, S, A–C
45.28	surd] AMS; loud TS–HTS, S, A–C
45.36	hearth. "It's] AMS; ~. ¶ "~ S
46.3	and] AMS; but S
46.14	seemed] AMS; *om.* C
46.32	him: "What] AMS; ~ : ¶ "~ S
46.33	throat. "Nothing] AMS; ~. ¶ "~ S
46.35	*his*] AMS; his TS
48.12	entirely] S; *om.* A–C
48.18	him: "Well] AMS; ~ : ¶ "~ S
48.24–25	evasively: "You] AMS; ~ : ¶ "~ S
48.25	hain't] AMS; haint TS
48.25	go'n'] AMS; go'n TS–HTS, A–C; goun' S
49.4	wusn't] HTS; wasn't S, A–C
49.6	*last*] AMS; last TS
49.17	toothlessly. "I'm] AMS; ~. ¶ "~ S
49.25	teachin'] AMS; teachun' A
49.29	in] A; on B–C
49.30	comb, I remember] S; comb A–C
49.34	doin's] AMS; doun's S, A–C
49.34	'uld] AMS; 'u'd S
50.1	doin's] AMS; doun's S, A–C

50.5	know] AMS; knew TS
50.5	was] AMS; were S, A–C
50.10	'pointments] AMS; 'p'intments S, A–C
50.12	preached] AMS; preched TS
50.12	at] AMS; of TS
50.15	*he*] AMS; he TS–HTS, S, A–C
50.16	preachin'] HTS; preachun' A
50.18	anything] AMS; anythun *ETS*
50.19	preachin'] AMS; preachun' S, A–C
50.20	How d'it] AMS; How d' it TS–HTS; How'd it A–C
50.24	acrost] HTS; across B–C
50.26	diff'ent] AMS; diff'rent TS
50.32	with] AMS; *om.* TS
50.32	outpourin'] TS; outpourun' S, A
50.33	accordin'] AMS; accordun' S, A
50.34	mornin'] AMS; mornun' S, A–C
50.34	prayin'] AMS; prayun' S, A–C
50.35	singin'] TS; singun' S, A–C
50.35	hymes] HTS; hymns S, A–C
50.35	readin'] AMS; readun' S, A–C
50.35	mornin'] AMS; mornun' S, A–C
51.4	said, "Go] AMS; ~ : ¶ " ~ S
51.6	kep'] AMS; kept TS
51.7	prayin'] AMS; prayun' S, A–C
51.7	singin'] AMS; singun' S, A–C
51.7	readin'] AMS; readun' S, A–C
51.7	mornin'] AMS; mornun' S, A–C
51.14	tale. "Look] AMS; ~. ¶ " ~ S
51.15	just] AMS; jest S
51.15	havin'] AMS; havun' S, A
51.16	swearin'] AMS; swearun' S, A–C
51.27	come] S; came A–C
51.27	deep] AMS; dry TS
51.28	standin'] AMS; standun' S, A–C
51.30	burnin'] AMS; burnun' S, A–C
51.32	hissin'] AMS; hissen' TS; hissun' S, A–C
51.33	bubblin'] TS; bubblun' S, A–C
51.33	boilin'] AMS; boilun' S, A–C
52.7	shinin'] AMS; shinun' S, A–C

52.9	Devil] AMS; devil TS–HTS, S, A–C
52.10	perfect] AMS; *om.* TS–HTS, S, A–C
52.13	just] AMS; jest S
52.13	sayin'] TS; sayun' S, A–C
52.13	'The] AMS; 'The 'The TS
52.14	no] S; any A–C
52.14	snorted."] AMS; snorted."[1] [*footnote*] [1]The fiction throughout generally follows the historical facts, especially as they are narrated by Judge Taneyhill in a volume of the "Ohio Valley Series," Robert Clarke Co. S
52.15	slowly] S; *om.* A–C
52.16	said, "Well] AMS; ~ : ¶ " ~ S
52.17	if *you*] AMS; if you TS–HTS, S, A–C
52.19	doin's] AMS; doun's S, A–C
52.22	*any*thing] HTS; anything S, A–C
52.23	Enraghty] AMS; Enrighty TS–HTS
52.23	got] AMS; got the TS–HTS, S, A–C
52.26	he] AMS; *om.* TS
52.26	out, "Well] AMS; ~ : ¶ " ~ S
52.29	circumstance] AMS; circumstances TS
52.30	strengthened] AMS; strengthed TS–HTS
52.35	the old] AMS; his old TS
52.36	exulted] AMS; exalted TS, A–C
53.3	and they] AMS; They TS–HTS, S, A–C
53.24	Savior and beseeching] AMS; Savior and beseeched TS; Savior, and besought HTS, S, A–C
53.25	them. The] AMS; ~ . ¶ ~ TS–HTS, S, A–C
53.27	members] AMS; few members TS–HTS, S, A–C
53.31	sectaries] AMS; sectarians TS–HTS, S, A–C
53.36	hence, and then dismiss the congregation] HTS; hence C
54.1	goin'] AMS; goun' S
54.6	just] AMS; jest S
54.14	prophecy of the] AMS; prophecy of TS–HTS, S, A–C
54.19	himself,] S; himself, and A–C
54.28	ag'inst] AMS; aginst TS
54.29	Nixon] AMS; Ninon TS
54.33	Nixon] AMS; Ninon TS

55.6	you'll] AMS; yu'll TS
55.8	Nixon] AMS; Ninon TS
55.13–14	ravings?" ¶ The] AMS; ~ ?" ~ S
55.24	come with] AMS; came with TS
55.24	goin'] TS; goun' S, A–C
55.26	ha' been] AMS; been B–C
55.27	kneelin'] AMS; kneelun' A
55.27	stoopin'] AMS; stoopun' A
55.30	Billun's] HTS; Billuns's *ETS*, A; Billun's' S
55.31	skeered] AMS; akeered TS
55.32	Hingston] HTS; *om.* C
55.36	Just] AMS; Jest S
56.1	standin'] AMS; standun' A
56.4	lookin'] HTS; lookun' A
56.4	walkin'] AMS; walkun' S, A
56.11	sayin'] AMS; sayun' S, A–C
56.13	Just] AMS; Jest S
56.20	irony. "Well] AMS; ~. ¶ "~ S
56.27	Dylks," he said.] S; Dylks." A–C
56.28	*Mr.*] S; Mr. A–C
56.32–33	him. ¶ She said, "Oh] AMS; ~. ~ ~ : ¶ "~ S
57.10	definitively] HTS; definitely B–C
57.12	with . . . her going] S; watched her going with a sardonic smile A–C
58.6	indoors. "The] AMS; ~. ¶ "~ S
59.2–3	which had filled his sleep] AMS; *om.* TS–HTS, S, A–C
59.4	yet] AMS; *om.* TS–HTS, S, A–C
59.4	him] AMS; him then TS
59.26	she said] S; said A–C
60.3	it. "I] AMS; ~. ¶ "~ S
60.26	in] AMS; to TS; by HTS, S, A–C
60.32	once. "Up] AMS; ~. ¶ "~ S
60.33	fathers] AMS; father C
61.4	kneelin'] AMS; kneeling TS
61.5	childern] AMS; children TS–HTS, S, A–C
61.13	*he*] S; he A–C
61.15	interest, "Well] HTS; ~ : ¶ "~ S
61.17	goings] AMS; goin's S
61.24	up] AMS; up in B–C

61.32	of—] S; of it: A–C
61.34	liar] AMS; a liar B–C
62.10	not] AMS; only TS
62.22	going] AMS; goin' S
62.24	her. "I] AMS; ~. ¶ " ~ S
62.26	believer] AMS; believe TS
62.35	*I*] AMS; I TS–HTS, S, A–C
63.4	*are*] AMS; are TS
63.7	wants] AMS; want's TS
63.9	raising] AMS; raisin' S, A–C
63.15	he] AMS; *om.* TS
63.20	brother. "You] AMS; ~. ¶ " ~ S
63.27	Dylks's] AMS; Dylk's TS–HTS; Dylkss' *ETS*; Dylk's B
63.30–31	smoking flax like] AMS; *om.* TS–HTS, S, A–C
64.1	work. "He] AMS; work. "He's TS–HTS, A–C; work. ¶ "He's S
64.16	myself] AMS; *om.* TS–HTS, S, A–C
64.29	it's] AMS; its TS
64.29	staying] AMS; stayin' S, A–C
64.30	you're] AMS; you've S
64.32	door. "Are] AMS; ~. ¶ " ~ S
64.36	almost pitifully,] S; pitifully A–C
65.2	yet, "I'll] AMS; ~ : ¶ " ~ S
66.3	arm's length] HTS; arms' length A–C
66.4	her. "What] HTS; ~. ¶ " ~ S
66.11	hast well said] S; sayest well A–C
66.11	he] S; for him A–C
66.24	hai'n't] HTS; hain't S, A–C
67.3	sweep] HTS; swoop A–C
67.10	satisfaction. "That] HTS; ~. ¶ " ~ S
67.21	laughed. "Is] HTS; ~. ¶ " ~ S
67.28	ha'nt] HTS; hain't S; ha'n't A–C
68.8	*I am*] HTS; I am S
68.19	well. "Yes] HTS; ~. ¶ " ~ S
69.14	book-l'arning] HTS; book-learning S
69.20	your] S; you're A–C
69.30	answered, "If] HTS; ~ : ¶ " ~ S
70.10	proved] S; put A–C
70.15	forbearance. "Oh] HTS; ~. ¶ " ~ S

70.21	so. "Why] HTS; ~. ¶ "~ S
71.5	*easy*] HTS; easy S, A–C
71.26	fallen] HTS; falling A–C
72.6	where] S; *om.* A–C
72.33	say, "And] HTS; ~: ¶ "~ S
73.4	it. "I] HTS; ~. ¶ "~ S
73.7	recognition. "She] HTS; ~. ¶ "~ S
73.23	bustled] HTS; hustled A–C
73.24	joyful,] S; joyous A–C
73.25	wall] HTS; well A
73.29	mother, "Now] HTS; ~: "~ S
74.2	out of the door] HTS; *om.* C
74.3	door. "Kiss] HTS; ~. ¶ "~ S
74.4	him. "No] HTS; ~. ¶ "~ S
75.4	the figure of another] S; another figure of a A–C
75.20	kept] HTS; ~, S
76.5	her.] S; her before he sank at her side. A; her; then he sank at her side. B–C
76.11	sank beside her] S; sank A–C
76.13	began, "What] HTS; ~: ¶ "~ S
77.14	sigh. "Yes] HTS; ~. ¶ "~ S
77.17	him. "And] HTS; ~. ¶ "~ S
77.17	supposin'—supposin'—] HTS; supposin'— C
77.31	rise. "I] HTS; ~. ¶ "~ S
77.33	gesture. "Squire] HTS; ~. ¶ "~ S
78.9	Word] HTS; the Word S
78.10	Word] HTS; the Word S
78.12–13	Jimmy"— ¶ The] HTS; ~ —" ~ S
78.24	or] S; *om.* A–C
79.4–5	expectation] HTS; expectations S, A–C
79.20	to] A; to the B–C
79.31–32	the children] S; children A–C
80.2	intervals] S; intervals, but sometimes in close groups A–C
80.8	which] S; which it A–C
80.8	been] S; *om.* A–C
80.24	woods] HTS; wood B–C
81.1	she asked.] S; *om.* A–C
81.14	justly. "Yes] HTS; ~. ¶ "~ S

82.1   She] S; She now B–C
83.1   crowd] HTS; crown B
83.14–15   hymn. There] HTS; hymn. ¶ Those S; hymn. There
            A; hymn. ¶ These B–C
84.23   up] HTS; upon C
84.30   answered, "I'd] HTS; ~: ¶ "~ S
84.33   over. "Did] HTS; ~. ¶ "~ S
85.15   women'll] HTS; woman'll B–C
85.16–17   raiment." ¶ The] HTS; ~." ~ S
85.29   voice: "Neighbors] HTS; ~: ¶ "~ S
85.31   floor] HTS; *om.* B–C
87.33   suggestion, "Why] HTS; ~: ¶ "~ S
88.3   up, " 'Deed] HTS; up: ¶ " " ' Deed S
88.13   criticism. "That's] HTS; ~. ¶ "~ S
88.14   nothin'] HTS; nothun' S
88.28   wusn't] HTS; wasn't S, A–C
88.29   night, or the Good Old Man don't ever come] HTS;
            night C
89.3   sect] HTS; set S, B–C
89.29   tie] S; life A–C
89.32–33   dismounted from their saddles or wagons, and] HTS;
            om. C
90.18   saying, "Well] HTS; ~: ¶ "~ S
90.20   boasting, "I'm] HTS; ~: ¶ "~ S
90.32   raiment] A; garment B–C
91.9   harm. "Oh] HTS; ~. ¶ "~ S
91.14   up. "We] HTS; ~. ¶ "~ S
91.20–21   imploring, "Oh] HTS; ~: ¶ "~ S
92.5–6   than of] S; than A–C
92.12–13   silent. "Oh] HTS; ~. ¶ "~ S
93.6   raiment had been] S; raiment A–C
93.12   home, weeping] S; weeping home A–C
93.14   desecrated] S; dishonored A–C
94.8   disbelieved] S; denied A–C
94.14   week. "If] HTS; ~. ¶ "~ S
94.16   I'd] S; I would A–C
95.13   upon. "Enraghty's] HTS; ~. ¶ "~ S
95.22   Redfield. "I] HTS; ~. ¶ "~ S
95.23   just want] HTS; want just S

95.32	bringin'] HTS; bringing S, A–C
96.2	waited. "It's] HTS; ∼. ¶ "∼ S
96.5	retorted] S; answered A–C
96.8	pushed] S; surged A–C
96.17	*see*] HTS; see A–C
96.19	self-control. "There] HTS; self-control. ¶ "There S
96.28	You're] HTS; Your're A–C
96.34	behind them] HTS; there B–C
97.1	o'] HTS; of S, A–C
97.5	worst] HTS; worse S, A–C
97.20	what] *ETS*; what do B–C
97.24	sumpin'] HTS; sumpun' S
98.1	threw] S; flung B–C
98.3	said, "You] HTS; ∼: ¶ "∼ S
98.6	outraged] S; desecrated A–C
98.7	feet. "There's] HTS; ∼. ¶ "∼ S
98.9	*his*] HTS; his S, A–C
99.10	god] S; idol A–C
99.12	him, "Don't] HTS; ∼: ¶ "∼ S
99.15	scoffer, "Why] HTS; ∼: ¶ "∼ S
99.19	with] S; and A–C
99.19	melancholy] A; piercing B–C
99.19	call] HTS; call cry S, B–C
100.11	each] S; either A–C
100.11	Dylks] S; him A–C
100.15–16	yells. "Did] HTS; ∼. ¶ "∼ S, A–C
100.16	broke] HTS; brok' S
100.25	about him] S; *om.* A–C
100.26	blood] S; blood, about him A–C
100.33	other. "*Now*] HTS; other. ¶ "*Now* S
101.6	shrank] HTS; shrunk B–C
101.20	split-bottomed] HTS; splint-bottomed S, A–C
101.23	puzzle. "What's] HTS; ∼. ¶ "∼ S
101.33–34	right." ¶ Braile] HTS; ∼." ∼ S
101.36	among them] S; in their midst A–C
*101.36	them. "What] HTS; ∼. ¶ "∼ S
102.8	said, "All] HTS; ∼: ¶ "∼ S
102.10–11	him, "Bring] HTS; ∼: ¶ "∼ S
102.12	fur] HTS; fer S, A–C

102.21	Then he said] S; Then A–C
103.28	of] HTS; in B–C
104.2	and] HTS; or S
105.5	breathlessly] S; breathless A–C
105.16	forces. "I] HTS; ~. ¶ "~ S
105.22	declared] S; answered A–C
105.23	him. "If] HTS; ~. ¶ "~ S
105.28–29	while." ¶ The] HTS; ~." ~ S
105.32	they've] S; they're A–C
106.4	man. "Of] HTS; ~. ¶ "~ S, B–C
107.1	woods] S; forest A–C
107.2	a swamp] HTS; the swamp B–C
107.15	Few men or boys] S; Few, of men or boys, A–C
107.20	ridge] S; path A–C
107.23	here] S; there A–C
109.20	should] HTS; would S
109.23	people,] S; people; he would A–C
110.13	stooped] A; crouched B–C
110.20	the other,] S; another A–C
110.21	he crept slowly by] A; slowly he crept by B–C
110.24	into] S; in A–C
110.24–25	cabin of peeled logs] S; log cabin A–C
110.31	weakly, "Nancy] HTS; ~: ¶ "~ S
111.3	door, "Jane] HTS; ~: ¶ "~ S
111.21	stonily, "Wait] HTS; ~: ¶ "~ S
111.23	again] S; back A–C
112.3–5	had come . . . away to silence] A; was bending over it with a rope of her hair in her hand, which she coiled into the knot at the nape of her neck, while she chirped and cooed to the little one B–C
112.7	coals] HTS; ~, *ETS*, S, A–C
112.14	bread. "Is] HTS; ~. ¶ "~ S
112.24–25	unflinchingly. "I] HTS; ~. ¶ "~ S
112.32	suggested, "I] HTS; ~: ¶ "~ S
113.1	breath. "Yes] HTS; ~. ¶ "~ S
113.19	gratefully. "It's] HTS; ~. ¶ "~ S
113.24–25	feet. "I] HTS; ~. ¶ "~ S
113.30	joints. "I] HTS; ~. ¶ "~ S
114.7	scornful] HTS; *om.* C

114.8   then] HTS; *om.* C
114.10   hopelessly. "It] HTS; ~. ¶ "~ S
114.24   back there again] S; back A–C
114.26   said, "Go] HTS; ~: ¶ "~ S
114.29   had] S; *om.* A–C
114.30   said, "Well] HTS; ~: ¶ "~ S
115.12–13 mockery, "Why] HTS; ~: ¶ "~ S
116.17   Dylks's] S; Dylk's B
116.24–25 close. "Well] HTS; ~. ¶ "~ S
116.33   demanded, "Well] HTS; ~: ¶ "~ S
117.4   The] A; Not the B–C
117.7   said, "I] HTS; ~: ¶ "~ S
117.18   others] HTS; the others S
119.28   Dylks. "Why] HTS; ~. ¶ "~ S
120.14   wide. "Perhaps] HTS; ~. ¶ "~ S
120.16   gasped, "Well] HTS; ~: ¶ "~ S
121.3   away, "I] HTS; ~: ¶ "~ S
121.13   me after] S; *om.* A–C
122.2   delay. "I] HTS; ~. ¶ "~ S
122.19   him] S; that fellow A–C
122.21   Suppose] S; Well, suppose A–C
122.21   see] S; try A–C
123.10   blame] HTS; blame' S
123.21   tremulously, "Did] HTS; ~: ¶ "~ S
124.9   hesitated. "If] HTS; ~. ¶ "~ S
124.12   bed. "Then] HTS; ~. ¶ "~ S
124.15   said, "I] HTS; ~: ¶ "~ S
124.19   hesitated, "I'd] HTS; ~. ¶ "~ S
124.19   to] HTS; to've C
125.19   porch. "Well] HTS; ~. ¶ "~ S
126.20   adoration] HTS; ardouration B–C
127.7   showed] A; looked a B–C
127.16   little; her face hardened, and she] HTS; little, and C
127.28   faith] HTS; ~, S
127.31   motionless. "Well] HTS; ~. ¶ "~ S
127.33   heat] HTS; beat C
128.2   But] S; But I reckon A–C
128.29   *I*] HTS; I C
128.34–35 her, unconscious of his look] HTS; her C

129.5	out, "Where] HTS; ~ : ¶ "~ S
129.15	again. "Oh] HTS; ~ : ¶ "~ S
129.19	vision. " 'Its] HTS; ~. ¶ " '~ S
130.4	bodies. "Take] HTS; ~. ¶ "~ S
130.12	wearing: "These] HTS; ~. ¶ "~ S
130.13	rusty] HTS; *om.* C
130.13	of] HTS; in C
130.13	dollars] HTS; *om.* C
130.16	wife. "That] HTS; ~. ¶ "~ S
131.5	hers, "I] HTS; ~ : ¶ "~ S
132.14	knees] HTS; knee B–C
132.16	forehead. "How] HTS; ~. ¶ "~ S
133.5	on'y] HTS; only B–C
133.16	it. "Mother] HTS; ~. ¶ "~ S
133.31	renunciation, "I] HTS; ~ : ¶ "~ S
133.36	said, "You] HTS; ~ : ¶ "~ S
134.1	from] S; from his A–C
134.22	her, "What] HTS; ~ : ¶ "~ S
135.10	said, "If] HTS; ~ : ¶ "~ S
135.13	shoulder. "Yes] HTS; ~. ¶ "~ S
135.20	fiercely] HTS; *om.* C
135.25	sigh. "Oh] HTS; ~. ¶ "~ S
136.20	then] HTS; *om.* S
136.22	would] S; should A–C
137.6	faced, "Well] HTS; ~ : ¶ "~ S
137.8	enforce. "It] HTS; ~. ¶ "~ S
137.22	putty] HTS; poortty S
137.27	putty] HTS; poortty S
137.30	Flocks, any more] HTS; Flocks C
137.33	relented. "Sally] HTS; ~. ¶ "~ S
138.1	goin's] HTS; goun's S, A–C
138.4	it] S; his going A–C
138.5	usin'] HTS; usun' S
138.6	sayin's] HTS; sayun's S, A–C
138.23	Abel] HTS; Abe B
138.26	Sally. "Well] HTS; ~. ¶ "~ S
138.29	goin'] HTS; goun' S, A–C
138.30	expectin'] HTS; expectun' S, A–C
138.31	your'n] HTS; yourn S

138.35	o'] HTS; of B–C
139.1	gettin'] HTS; gittun' S, A–C
139.10	afeared] HTS; afread B
139.19	*me*] HTS; me B–C
139.20	to bad rubbage] HTS; *om.* C
140.24	childern] HTS; children B–C
141.22	and 'd] HTS; and 'u'd S
141.23	and 'd] HTS; and 'u'd S
141.28	hain't] HTS; ain't B–C
142.10	of] HTS; on C
142.17	add, "Hughey] HTS; ~ : ¶ " ~ S
142.23	said, "I've] HTS; ~ : ¶ " ~ S
142.25	No] S; No, no A–C
142.30	What] HTS; Why C
142.30	for] HTS; *om.* C
142.35	door. "Aunt] HTS; ~ . ¶ " ~ S
143.33	as that night when Dylks called her, that] S; *om.* B–C
143.35	back, "Laban] HTS; ~ : ¶ " ~ S
143.35	said] S; came again A–C
143.36	again, "It] HTS; ~ : ¶ " ~ S
144.5	he] HTS; she C
144.8	gettin'] HTS; getting B–C
144.15	Or] HTS; Oh C
144.32	said, "It] HTS; ~ : ¶ " ~ S
144.34	said, "But] HTS; ~ : ¶ " ~ S
145.4	most] HTS; 'most S
146.21–22	the other one] S; him A–C
147.33	voice, "He] HTS; ~ : ¶ " ~ S
147.34	before, "Joey dear] S; before A–C
148.30	Oncst] HTS; Oncet S, A–C
149.31	spoke— "Joey] HTS; ~ : ¶ " ~ S
150.18	come] A; came B–C
150.26	laughed. "You] HTS; ~ . ¶ " ~ S
150.32	door, "I] HTS; ~ : ¶ " ~ S
151.12	resentfully, "What] HTS; ~ : ¶ " ~ S
151.22	short: "David] HTS; ~ : ¶ " ~ S
152.10	either] HTS; each S
152.18	porch. "Why] HTS; ~ . ¶ " ~ S
153.29	out, "Here] HTS; ~ : ¶ " ~ S

154.13	Mandeville—T. J. Mandeville] A; Ammidown—T. J. Ammidown B–C
154.18	got] HTS; *om.* C
154.26	wife. "Mother] HTS; ~. ¶ "~ S
155.2	died] HTS; die B–C
155.17–18	pipe-stem. "Why] HTS; pipe-stem. ¶ "Why S
155.19	unbelievers] HTS; other unbelievers B–C
156.9	ask, "And] HTS; ~: ¶ "~ S
156.29	belief] HTS; believe B–C
157.14	plenty] HTS; plently A
157.34	squire. "And] HTS; ~. ¶ "~ S
158.1	didn't] S; about. Didn't A–C
158.4	a death] HTS; as death C
158.9	question. "And] HTS; ~. ¶ "~ S
159.2	Billin's's] A; Billin's B–C
159.23	superstition] A; superstitions B–C

Word-Division

List A records compounds or possible compounds hyphenated at the end of the line in the copy-text (or in other texts at points where readings have been adopted from them) and resolved as hyphenated or one word as listed below. If Howells' manuscripts of this period fairly consistently followed one practice respecting the particular compound or possible compound, the resolution was made on that basis. Otherwise his *Century* and other periodical texts were used as guides. List B is a guide to transcription of compounds or possible compounds hyphenated at the end of the line in the present text: compounds recorded here should be transcribed as given; words divided at the end of the line and not listed should be transcribed as one word.

	LIST A	142.28	indoors
3.4	bottomlands	155.3	eighteen-twenties
14.33	earthquake	155.33	hotch-potch
17.14–15	*every*thing		
23.4	to-night		LIST B
25.21	woodpile	3.7	door-latches
28.7	overhung	6.11	camp-meeting
32.13	boylike	7.23	camp-meetun's
36.17	mill-stones	21.24	heart-shaking
37.26	apple-butter	23.21	law-books
56.31	pipe-stem	25.6	woods-pastures
66.15	upright	60.18	stiff-necked
69.31	All-powerful	72.36	father-hunger
83.6	outcasts	84.21	week-day
107.5	huckleberries	96.31	entry-way
107.12	hazelnuts	112.25	goose-grease
107.20	grape-vines	119.9	linsey-woolsey
114.13	shame-facedly	136.9	hard-working
119.32	poor-house	136.18	light-heartedly
123.7	self-pity	143.22	heart-heavy
129.27	jet-black	155.17	pipe-stem

253

THIS EDITION OF

THE LEATHERWOOD GOD

has been set in English Monotype Baskerville,
printed on Warren's Olde Style by The Press of A. Colish
and bound by William Robbins and Sons.

The format is by Bert Clarke.